Cosmopolitan Learning for a Global Era

Ensuring that higher education students are fully prepared for lives as global citizens is a pressing concern in the contemporary world. This book draws on insights from cosmopolitan thought to identify how people from different backgrounds can find common ground. By applying cosmopolitan insights to higher education practice, Sarah Richardson charts how students can be given the opportunity to experience a truly international education, which emphasises deep cultural exchange rather than mere transactional contact.

Written in an engaging and accessible style, the author uses empirical evidence to show that simply studying alongside those different to themselves or even studying overseas, are inadequate in preparing students to lead the diverse societies of tomorrow. Instead, the book calls for a coherent approach to higher education that properly prepares students to lead global lives. Chapters highlight a number of key aspects of higher education practice – from curriculum to pedagogy to educator skills to assessment – and demonstrate how these can be reconsidered to give students the opportunity to gain cosmopolitan attributes during their higher education.

Cosmopolitan Learning for a Global Era will be of great interest to researchers, scholars and postgraduate students, with a particular focus on cosmopolitan thought, international education and higher education more broadly, as well as university educators and leaders across a wide range of disciplinary areas.

Sarah Richardson is Principal Research Fellow in the Tertiary Education Research Programme at the Australian Council for Educational Research, Australia. With more than 20 years' experience as an educator and researcher, she now leads multiple high-level research and consulting projects in the higher education sector in both Australia and internationally, with clients including multilateral organisations, national and regional governments, as well as non-governmental organisations and institutions.

'This is a book of enormous value to those concerned about the promise of higher education in the globalizing era. As higher education institutions become increasingly internationalized, they can no longer, the book argues, ignore the demands of cultural diversity and exchange. Sarah Richardson shows how the conceptual resources associated with the idea of cosmopolitanism can be utilized to address these demands, both in understanding the flourishing of cosmopolitan values and practices but also in steering them in pedagogically productive directions.'

Fazal Rizvi, *The University of Melbourne*

Routledge Research in Higher Education

Experiences of Immigrant Professors
Challenges, Cross-Cultural Differences, and Lessons for Success
Edited by Charles Hutchison

Integrative Learning
International research and practice
Edited by Daniel Blackshields, James Cronin, Bettie Higgs,
Shane Kilcommins, Marian McCarthy and Anthony Ryan

Developing Creativities in Higher Music Education
International Perspectives and Practices
Edited by Pamela Burnard

Academic Governance
Disciplines and Policy
Jenny M. Lewis

Refocusing the Self in Higher Education
A Phenomenological Perspective
Glen L. Sherman

**Activity Theory, Authentic Learning and Emerging
Technologies**
Towards a transformative higher education pedagogy
Edited by Vivienne Bozalek, Dick Ng'ambi, Denise Wood,
Jan Herrington, Joanne Hardman and Alan Amory

Understanding HIV and STI Prevention for College Students
Edited by Leo Wilton, Robert T. Palmer and Dina C. Maramba

From Vocational to Professional Education
Educating for social welfare
Edited by Jens-Christian Smeby and Molly Sutphen

Academic Bildung in Net-based Higher Education
Moving beyond learning
Edited by Trine Fossland, Helle Mathiasen and Mariann Solberg

University Access and Success
Capabilities, diversity and social justice
Merridy Wilson-Strydom

Reconsidering English Studies in Indian Higher Education
Suman Gupta, Richard Allen, Subarno Chattarji and Supriya Chaudhuri

Globally Networked Teaching in the Humanities
Theories and Practices
Edited by Alexandra Schultheis Moore and Sunka Simon

Higher Education Access and Choice for Latino Students
Critical Findings and Theoretical Perspectives
Edited by Patricia A. Pérez and Miguel Ceja

The Experiences of Black and Minority Ethnic Academics
A comparative study of the unequal academy
Kalwant Bhopal

Sustaining Mobile Learning
Theory, research and practice
Edited by Wan Ng and Therese Cumming

Narratives of Doctoral Studies in Science Education
Making the transition from educational practitioner to researcher
Edited by Shirley Simon, Christina Ottander and Ilka Parchmann

Cosmopolitan Learning for a Global Era
Higher education in an interconnected world
Sarah Richardson

Crossing Boundaries and Weaving Intercultural Work, Life, and Scholarship in Globalizing Universities
Edited by Adam Komisarof and Zhu Hua

Cosmopolitan Learning for a Global Era

Higher education in an interconnected world

Sarah Richardson

LONDON AND NEW YORK

First published 2016 by Routledge
2 Park Square, Milton Park, Abingdon, Oxon OX14 4RN

and by Routledge
711 Third Avenue, New York, NY 10017

Routledge is an imprint of the Taylor & Francis Group, an informa
business

© 2016 S. Richardson

The right of S. Richardson to be identified as author of this work has
been asserted by her in accordance with sections 77 and 78 of the
Copyright, Designs and Patents Act 1988.

All rights reserved. No part of this book may be reprinted or
reproduced or utilised in any form or by any electronic, mechanical,
or other means, now known or hereafter invented, including
photocopying and recording, or in any information storage or
retrieval system, without permission in writing from the publishers.

Trademark notice: Product or corporate names may be trademarks or
registered trademarks, and are used only for identification and
explanation without intent to infringe.

British Library Cataloguing in Publication Data
A catalogue record for this book is available from the British Library

Library of Congress Cataloging in Publication Data
Richardson, Sarah.
Cosmopolitan learning for a global era : higher education in an
interconnected world / Sarah Richardson.
pages cm
Includes bibliographical references and index.
1. International education. 2. Education and globalization. 3.
Cosmopolitanism. 4. Education, Higher–Aims and objectives. I. Title.
LC1090.R53 2016
370.116–dc23
2015015194

ISBN: 978-0-415-71790-8 (hbk)
ISBN: 978-1-315-87100-4 (ebk)

Typeset in Baskerville
by Cenveo Publisher Services

Contents

1	Global citizens	1
2	Transforming the academy	14
3	Cosmopolitan thought	30
4	In search of a global education	44
5	Learning to become part of the global tribe	56
6	Innovations in global learning	74
7	Cosmopolitan classrooms	91
8	Learning at a distance	107
9	Theory to practice and back again	125
	References	135
	Index	161

1 Global citizens

Setting the scene

Global. International. Intercultural. Cosmopolitan. The world we inhabit is all of these. In many ways it has always been. Humans have never lived in isolation from one another, as hundreds of years of global exchange attest. Nevertheless, the reach of these dynamics is more profound for those of us living in the twenty-first century than ever before. Our ability to respond appropriately to, and to thrive in, this context requires a paradigm shift in how we think about the world around us. In much of human history the concepts of 'like' and 'unlike' or 'same' and 'different' have been characterised as diametrically opposed. But the reality of contemporary life ensures that boundaries are increasingly blurred. This means that in/out, near/far, here/there, us/them, self/other are beginning to seem more and more alike.

For young people learning to navigate modern lives, this new reality requires a certain set of skills. To thrive in a world of blurred boundaries, young people need to gain attributes that will enable them to become border dwellers, adopting a multi-perspectival standpoint. They need to gain confidence in crossing over real and imagined lines of demarcation and in cooperating with those with differing degrees of unfamiliarity. This is essential because engaging with diversity is not something they *may* need to do but has instead become something that they *will* need to do. As educators, our responsibility is to ensure that students are given the opportunity to gain the knowledge and skills that will equip them to be leaders of the future. This raises a number of questions for those tasked with the responsibility of guiding learning. It calls on us as educators to interrogate our practices and assumptions. It requires us to unpack the way in which we have done things until now and consider how we might adapt them for this new reality.

In this book, these considerations are placed in the context of higher education. Internationally, 196 million students were enrolled in a higher education in 2011. This number is growing fast, rising from 99.5 million in 2000 (UNESCO Institute for Statistics 2015a). We can be sure that it is even higher now. Although the student bodies of higher education institutions are increasingly diverse, the majority of students are in transition from childhood to adulthood. Moving away from parental influences for the first time,

2 *Global citizens*

they are in the process of constructing self, determining how their future lives will come to pass. In a critical stage of their development, higher education students are open to external influences and willing to try on new identities to find the best fit. Their nascent selves are searching for beacons to guide their way forward and for fellow travellers to accompany them on their paths. In parallel, students are exposed to an academic environment in which they can accumulate skills and knowledge. Gaining proficiency along the way, they are hoping to be granted admittance to their chosen professional community.

For educators, the level of responsibility represented by more than 200 million higher education students is enormous. These are the engineers, doctors, lawyers, teachers, scientists, thinkers and doers of the future. But most of all they are the leaders of the future. And not of some far off distant, unimaginable future but of the near future, a future in which many of us will still be alive, and in which our children will live out their lives. If higher education institutions do one thing, that thing should be to educate great future leaders. And this means that as educators we need to have a clear vision of what sort of future we would like to see. A future of tension, distrust, violence, terrorism, war and the threat of annihilation? Or a future in which everyone learns to 'rub along' pretty well with everyone else, enough so that we can devote our collective energy to more constructive pursuits? We cannot push diversity back into the bottle, it is here, whether we like it or not. As Appiah (2006: xxi) so eloquently suggests, 'conversations across boundaries can be delightful, or just vexing: what they mainly are, though, is inevitable'. The inevitability of blurred boundaries and cross-cultural dialogue calls on higher education institutions to reinvent themselves. We need to, we must, ensure that what we do, the curricula we develop, the pedagogy we use, the behaviour we model, embodies the values that we want to see in our world.

Higher education institutions are not, and have never been, value-free institutions. They are forever shifting their policies and practices to reflect what is going on in the world around them and the prevailing power dynamics. The decisions made by institutions equally influence broader society. But they are slow, lugubrious beasts. Nothing moves rapidly, layer upon layer of bureaucracy stifles innovation and the resistance to change encountered in their hallowed halls is legendary. So how does change happen? It occurs when visionary educators have the courage to reflect on what they are doing and to change their practices, one class at a time. One student at a time. One choice at a time. This book is for those visionaries and its objective is to throw them a lifeline. If we are to respond to the changes we see in the world around us, if we are to ensure that students are prepared to be great leaders, then it helps to have something to support us. This book makes the case for the value of cosmopolitan thought in informing contemporary higher education practice. Cosmopolitan scholars have weathered hundreds of years of turbulent history and the approaches they promote have been strengthened

Global citizens 3

by the challenges the world has faced. The power of cosmopolitan thinking lies in its simplicity: we are all different yet we are all the same. And if we can help our students to approach those they interact with, both now and in the future, with this basic understanding, then imagine what can be achieved. Imagine what kind of world our students, informed by this insight, could create in the future.

Everything changes, everything stays the same

The world we live in is undergoing fundamental change in every way imaginable. The degree of interconnectedness at all levels, from everyday human interactions to business to trade to government has become an inevitability that few can – or even attempt to – escape. As the web of connectivity becomes ever denser, the number of ties that bind us to familiar and unfamiliar others grow increasingly hard to shake. We are creatures defined by our networks – both real and virtual – and receive a non-stop barrage of messages about who we are and how we should view the world around us. We consume what has been created in a space-time continuum that goes far beyond our experience and understanding. The movements of money, goods, ideas, information and power are the most commonly referred to features of globalisation. They are shapeless, impermanent and ever evolving and their very intangibility confounds our ability to comprehend or name any or all. As they whirl around us we feel unable to do more than be swept along by a tide, iPhone in hand, increasingly vulnerable to forces that remove our agency and give it to faceless corporations. Globalisation feels both totally normal and totally alien and we lose ourselves in its clutches.

Easily forgotten, but of enormous importance, is that globalisation is fundamentally expressed not in vague and incoherent terms but in the coming together of one human with one or more others. As we interact across metaphorical and physical divides, we give the faceless forces of globalisation a human form. To focus on humans and the way in which we engage with each other is to see the forces of globalisation play out at the level of the individual and the social. In considering the coming together of humans we also remind ourselves that within globalisation lies considerable continuity with the rest of human history. If we look back in time we see a human evolution that has involved the mixing of races, cultures and religions over millennia. There is little evidence of geographically bound cultural purity anywhere in the world (Said 1995). Instead, we are all descended from a common gene pool and whether our own particular family trajectory has led us to be pale or dark skinned, tall or short, green or brown eyed, straight or curly haired, those factors that unite us have always been far more powerful than those which divide us. As such difference and diversity are not something external to humans. Instead, as Fine (2007: x) asserts 'The human species can be understood only if it is treated as a single subject, within which

4   *Global citizens*

all forms of difference are recognised and respected but conceptualised as internal to the substantive unity of all human beings'.

Higher education institutions have not been impervious to the forces of globalisation. Students have increasing options about the way in which they choose to engage with their chosen institution. Online learning is ever-more prevalent and an increasing number of students have little physical contact with the institution at which they are enrolled. Nevertheless, lectures, tutorials, laboratory sessions and seminars continue to define the experience of the majority of higher education students around the world. Whether higher education occurs literally or virtually it is characterised by person to person interactions. Listening, explaining, talking, debating and negotiating all require the engagement of one human being with one or more others. In this lies the power of educators to help students prepare themselves for the actualities of the world they will inherit. With power comes enormous responsibility. And it is not clear that all higher education institutions use their power in the best interests of their students.

In grappling with the challenges and opportunities wrought by globalisation, the responses of higher education institutions have been uneven. Many institutions have turned their attention to international affairs and have begun to incorporate an international perspective into many areas of institution life. In marketing their offerings to potential students, slogans such as 'Think Global, Study Local' have become all the more common. These would seem to indicate an understanding of the need to equip students with skills that will enable them to thrive in an international context. It is true that there are many examples of excellent practice, and these will be highlighted throughout the book. For many institutions, however, the rhetoric remains unfulfilled. Yet many institutions would claim that they are 'international'. What does this imply? In many cases it suggests the presence of international students. Indeed, the increasingly global mobility of students is frequently held up as a sign of success in international education. In 2012 more than 4.5 million students were enrolled in tertiary education outside their home country (OECD 2014a). At first glance, physical movement during higher education appears to be an ideal way for students to gain exposure to different cultures. Through physical movement they are able to broaden their horizons, both metaphorically and literally. Indeed, there are many examples of international mobility having a profound impact on those who partake of it. At the same time, however, it can lead to significant contradictions.

The paradox of student mobility is that much global mobility takes students from their familiar environment into environments that are, well, pretty familiar. It is no coincidence that highly culturally diverse nations – the USA, UK, Canada and Australia – are also those that host the largest numbers of international students. This is significantly influenced by the ability to study in the English language. But at the same time the presence of large diasporic communities enables students to travel physically while also being able to rely on the reassurance of familiar cultural attributes, including

Global citizens 5

food, language and media. Moreover, the large clusters of, for example, Chinese students who study in Australia – more than 90,000 in 2011 (OECD 2014b) – ensure that there is no need for students who cross borders to confront difference in more than a limited number of transactions. Beyond diasporas, many students move from one country to another that, while 'foreign', is imbued with many of the same assumptions and cultural characteristics. The two top destination countries for globally mobile students from the US are Canada and the UK, for example. And these patterns are repeated around the world.

Not only is student mobility paradoxical in its practice, the very fact that physical mobility is regarded as a precursor to exposure to contrasting cultures assumes that difference is 'out there'. It forgets that our communities are the embodiment of diversity and that our own surroundings are rich with cultural resources. Student mobility certainly has the potential to generate benefits for the individual, but using up precious fossil fuels to fly to another continent may actually generate fewer benefits than a bus ride to an adjacent suburb. It is certainly true that student mobility has become an important export revenue for a number of countries, as well as providing crucial income for many institutions. But as a consequence many governments, institutions and educators are blinkered in regarding the international aspects of higher education as market based, phrasing the up-front and long-term yields in the language of trade and exchange, rather than the enrichment it can provide to students.

Through emphasising international mobility, the industry of international education interprets global citizenship in instrumental terms, overlooking the potential for transformation that lies within, and in close proximity. And student mobility is also socially divisive. The assumption that physical movement generates benefits that non-movement does not reinforces divisions between those with the resources to partake in movement and the vast majority for higher education students for whom this is not a possibility. The reality of many contemporary students is that participation in higher education requires part-time employment and, as student populations in many countries get older, an increasing proportion of students have family commitments. Neither of these are ties that can be carelessly jettisoned for the sake of a foreign sojourn. By suggesting that international exposure can only be gained through studying in another country, more than 190 million students are disenfranchised. This is clearly not an acceptable response to the need of *all* students to be prepared for global lives.

Tomorrow's leaders

As the realities of life in a global era pervade every element of our lives, it is increasingly important for higher education institutions to ask themselves whether the education they offer students is adequate for the realities of the third millennium. In preparing the leaders of tomorrow, institutions must

6 *Global citizens*

carefully scrutinise the characteristics of the tomorrow the students will inherit. It has become rare in any profession, however place bound, to encounter clients, suppliers, contractors, contingencies or transactions that are purely local in scope. This underscores the necessity of being able to engage with people and processes different to those with which we are most familiar. At the same time, an increasing proportion of higher education graduates are likely to work outside of their home country. More and more will experience careers that take them to locations and cultural environments that are in stark contrast to the one(s) in which they have been raised.

The increasing normality of heterogeneity requires leaders who are well versed in viewing diversity as an asset rather than a problem. Leaders need to have dispositions that not only accommodate and celebrate cultural diversity, but also the ability to devise solutions that harness the strength that lies in difference to generate benefits for all. In a future in which increased competition over scarce resources seems to be a likely scenario, the ability to work with those whose standpoints are fundamentally opposed and to search for mutually satisfactory outcomes is an imperative for those who wish to assure the security of the world around them. Higher education institutions thus have a fundamentally important role in ensuring that their graduates develop an appropriate set of skills, skills that are directly applicable to the challenges they will be called on to help solve in a world characterised by diversity, mobility and adaptability.

A number of terms are used with reference to the need for higher education graduates to be able to function in a global world. 'Intercultural competence' refers to the ability to use 'effective and appropriate behavior and communication in intercultural situations' (Deardorff 2011: 66). This encompasses reflection, critical thinking, openness, curiosity and the ability to utilise diverse perspectives through deep cultural knowledge. While fundamentally sound, intercultural competence has been interpreted in a number of ways. Most worryingly, it is frequently used with reference to interactions between unitary 'cultural' groups. Examples such as 'cultural tips for doing business in China' assume that Chinese culture is somehow homogeneous and that all Chinese people are alike in their dispositions. While such directions may act as a useful shortcut for time-poor business people hoping to make an impression with Chinese clients, they do not bring us to a deep sense of understanding that diversity is found among all humans. Another common term is 'global citizenship'. This is a very different take on global skills, focusing on social responsibility, global competence and global civic engagement (Morais and Ogden 2011) and refers to the 'capacity and disposition to understand and act on issues of global significance' (Boix Mansilla and Jackson 2011: xiii). Again, this approach is imbued with many positive characteristics, but it focuses more on the outcomes than the understanding that prompts them. Both approaches have a great deal of value. But they can lack depth – focusing on the 'what' in isolation from the 'why' and 'how'.

Global citizens 7

This book utilises an approach that delves into the cosmopolitan canon. It draws on hundreds of years of thought to identify the underlying cosmopolitan insights that can usefully be applied to the higher education context. It looks at the tensions in contemporary higher education through a cosmopolitan lens and diagnoses their impact on students. And it explores ways to to translate espoused goals and references to global preparedness into pedagogy and curricula. The term 'cosmopolitan' echoes ruminations and debates that have travelled from one generation to another over thousands of years. Cosmopolitan is a much used and abused term, perhaps most commonly associated with a magazine for young women and a cocktail. It has also lent its name to an endless parade of cafes, bars, restaurants and hotels. There is even a 2003 film of the name, directed by Nisha Ganatra. While its wide usage has blurred the underlying concept, it has also kept the term alive, with a general connotation of 'openness'. This is, in fact, not far from the core concept of cosmopolitan that will be used in this book, defined by Szerszynski and Urry (2002: 468) as 'a cultural disposition involving an intellectual and aesthetic stance of "openness" towards peoples, places and experiences from different cultures, especially those from different nations'.

In this book 'cosmopolitan' is not viewed as an abstract monolith that must be regarded with awe, or as a prescriptive recipe for universal love and happiness. Instead, it is seen as a resource that when used to inform educational practice can yield beneficial outcomes. As higher education institutions grapple with the challenges presented by increasingly diverse student bodies and their need to be appropriately prepared for the global environment in which they will live and work, cosmopolitan insights can help guide and shape the approaches educators adopt. Not only does a cosmopolitan approach provide a means for understanding the ways in which global forces have transformed our everyday lives, it also allows us to acknowledge that we have affiliations and allegiances to multiple groups, some within national boundaries and some across them. In some ways a cosmopolitan approach can be regarded as a moral education, which Cheng (2006: 560) defines as 'education for becoming a human being capable of sustaining and fulfilling his [sic] humanity and creating a social context of inter-human relationships of trust and respect'.

One of the strengths of cosmopolitan thought, and its benefit in considerations of the education of future leaders, is that it does not gloss over the complexities of cultural diversity. Cosmopolitan theorists do not approach contemporary challenges with banners proclaiming the path to peace, love and harmony. Instead, they acknowledge the significant cultural divisions that characterise many contemporary societies. Rather than trying to brush these under the carpet, those who apply cosmopolitan tools consider cultural divisions as opportunities in which negatives can be transformed. They look for ways in which human agency, whether individual or communal, can be brought to bear on seemingly intractable problems. As such, the emphasis is on reshaping the world through social action, and finding positive ways forward through an application of what Delanty (2006: 42) terms

8 *Global citizens*

'socio-cultural mediation'. The implications of the approach adopted by cosmopolitan scholars for the practice of higher education are profound.

If the notion of cosmopolitan sensibilities is regarded by some as being taken straight from ancient Buddhist philosophy, their application is more akin to the Harvard Business School of the twenty-first century. Increasing evidence shows that truly great leaders are what Boyatzis and McKee (2005) term 'resonant' – they practice mindfulness, hope and compassion. In leadership terms, mindfulness means that leaders have a highly tuned awareness of themselves and those around them, as well as the contexts in which they are operating. Hope means that leaders are optimistic about the future, have a clear vision and inspire others. Compassion means that leaders understand the desires and needs of those around them and are motivated to help them through a genuine concern for their best interests. Resonant leadership is particularly well suited for a climate of transformation, complexity, instability and change (see also Goleman 1998; Goleman et al. 2002). These are exactly the characteristics that leaders of the future will face. And this suggests that cosmopolitan attributes are not only about being able to 'rub along' well with those who are different, but are also of central importance to contemporary leadership.

The challenge for higher education

Higher education systems have been shaped by decades of government policy, reflecting a host of stakeholder priorities. In turn, institutions are shaped by the interests of leaders and the multitude of players that come together to determine institutional policies and practices. Together, these forces determine the 'what' and 'how' of the higher education that students experience. The expression of a modern-day higher education reflects the myriad of assumptions that influence decision-making processes. There are also persistent tensions that lie within much of higher education thinking. For example, a constant tug-of-war takes place between those who believe it is the function of higher education institutions to supply skilled professionals to meet economic needs versus those who think that a vocational approach is flawed and that institutions should instead focus on cultivating the intellectual capacities of students. Another area of disharmony lies around the development of discipline-specific versus generic skills. These debates are part of the higher education milieu and strengthen its contribution in many ways.

When it comes to preparing students for global contexts, however, the debate is both less pronounced and less visible. In the last two decades, it has become increasingly common for educational leaders to include references to global contexts and conditions in their espoused priorities. Many institutions include 'global citizenship' (or a variation on the theme) in their definition of graduate attributes. But the assumptions that underlie these constructs often fail to be articulated. The vagueness of these references, and

Global citizens 9

the fact that they have failed to awaken strident debate among higher education stakeholders around what kind of world we are preparing students for, is in marked contrast to other key outcomes of higher education. And this is arguably because a focus on what kind of global attributes students need is yet to filter down to everyday institutional practice. There is the odd 'international' case study here, an exchange programme to a partner institution there and a growing number of international students on campus. But other than in a small number of cases the concept of global attributes has yet to percolate down into higher education practice in a whole-hearted way. Of course, some institutions, some educators and even some policy makers are extremely proactive and are doing excellent work. We shall meet some of these later on in the book. But the importance of ensuring that students have the attributes they need to prosper in the contemporary world is yet to profoundly shape higher education practice. As a senior academic was kind enough to explain to me (his emphasis):

> It's a *uni*versity, Sarah, not a *multi*versity.

The notion he was expressing – that an institution is locally located and serves a local context – has profound implications. It is likely shared by many educators in institutions around the world. Even when notions of the necessary global attributes of graduates are explicitly addressed they fall into the same category as employability skills. Even if educators agree that they are important, there is less agreement on whose job it is to help students gain them. At the same time, they seem to be regarded as somehow external or tangential to the core role of higher education, rather than central. This approach suggests that a higher education that does not ensure that students are ready to be global citizens has nevertheless achieved other useful educational goals. In the twenty-first century it is increasingly questionable whether this can be regarded as a justifiable standpoint. The challenge faced by higher education institutions and educators should not be about whether to impart appropriate global preparedness but how to do so. And this starts with the question of what attributes they need to help students gain. As Brustein (2007: 383) suggests, 'if the training of globally competent graduates is accepted as one of the chief goals of our system of higher education, our curricula will have to be redesigned to ensure that outcome'. And in his powerful essay *The Loss of the University*, Berry (1987: 12) argues that:

> what universities ... are mandated to make or to help to make is human beings in the fullest sense of those words - not just trained workers or knowledgeable citizens but responsible heirs and members of human culture .... Underlying the idea of a university ... is the idea that good work and good citizenship are the inevitable by-products of the making of a good – that is, a fully developed – human being.

10 *Global citizens*

In the second decade of the twenty-first century, surely fully developed human beings are those ready to live, and lead, lives as global citizens.

Communities of learning

If 'international education' that is narrowly interpreted as the physical crossing of borders is problematic, what is the alternative? The most obvious resource for higher education students is their peers. In the contemporary era, many higher education campuses are microcosms of intense cultural mixing, with students from a plethora of cultural backgrounds. Indeed, Hopper (2006: 68) suggests that the student bodies of higher education institutions in many nations have become 'primary sites of cultural interaction and exchange'. The influence of their peers has the potential to profoundly alter the way in which students view the world around them and their place within it. If utilised to inform education, diversity can upset assumptions, challenge beliefs and help students gain a subjectivity that is oriented to the global (Matthews and Sidhu 2005).

It is always a mistake to regard learners of any kind as blank slates. Every student who comes into an educational environment brings with them a whole host of prior experiences that have coloured their approach to learning and disposition to the learning environment. Parental expectations, familial beliefs and community values ensure that young people are primed with partially constructed selves, which develop as they move through an educational system. Here they encounter institutional definitions of success and failure, good and bad, normal and abnormal, which may, or may not, gel with their prior expectations. One of the important lessons that young people learn is to regard difference with acceptance or rejection. Through exposure to those who are different – in how they look, what they wear, how they talk, what they eat and the rituals they engage in – young people can learn either that there are many kinds of different, all of which are of equal value, or they can learn to regard some (or all) forms of difference as inferior or alien.

In the past, many students would have left difference behind at the school gates and gone home to a reasonably homogeneous community. This is still the case for some, particularly in rural areas. In the modern world, however, information technology ensures that exposure to difference penetrates all facets of the lives of young people. It is estimated that there are more than 3 billion internet users worldwide, with internet penetration varying from 26.5 per cent in Africa to 87.7 per cent in North America (Internet World Stats 2014a). In the US it is estimated that among 8–11 year olds, 61.5 per cent of boys and 58.4 per cent of girls access the internet at least once a day (Statista 2015). While internet usage is for multiple purposes, one impact is that young people are able to maintain strong connections with relatives and friends many miles distant, with country, continent and hemisphere divides rendered irrelevant. For diaspora children, the impact is profound. Despite being geographically remote from their former peers or close relatives, there is no need to jettison close friendships and relationships – contact can be maintained on a daily, or even hourly, basis with real-time interactions. The ubiquity of satellite and cable TV, in addition to the wealth of online media, ensures that those who live away from their roots can remain connected to their culture and language in a way that their forebears could never have imagined.

Taken together, modern communications ensure that engaging with difference has become a regular occurrence for an ever growing proportion of young people around the world today. An increasing number are straddling borders on a daily basis – retaining bilingual or multilingual, national and cultural identities and engaging in a range of cultural practices within any 24-hour period. Migration no longer means making a clean cut and casting off former networks. Those networks simply become fellow travellers. In terms of identity, then, as well as their connections, young people are fully cognisant of the demands and benefits of maintaining multiple allegiances. While this is particularly the case for those living in diaspora, it is increasingly becoming the norm for many young people. That many within the student bodies of higher education institutions are both well practiced and adept at crossing real and virtual borders is an extremely important fact for higher education leaders and educators to understand. A high degree of familiarity with the everyday expression of multiple allegiances inevitably primes students with a particular take on the world they will adopt an increasingly powerful role in. They expect to encounter a variety of international perspectives and approaches in everything they do and many are expert at border crossing.

For educators this is both a wonderful resource and a challenge. Their global connections mean that many students are primed for an introduction to cosmopolitan attributes. Their lived experiences enable them to experiment with what they have learned in their everyday interactions. At the same time, their expectations for educators are high. They can access 'facts' on the internet without going to class. Thus they are looking for an educational experience that does a great deal more than present them with information. Students increasingly expect to be co-developers of knowledge with educators. And they expect to have the freedom to interpret what they learn as they see fit. This calls for more attention to be paid to the process of education, and to aligning the formal and informal curricula. It calls for educators to utilise the diversity in the classroom as a resource rather than as something that needs handling. And it calls for the learning community, the institution, to model engagement with difference.

Navigating the book

This book considers the importance and implementation of cosmopolitan education in a series of steps.

Chapter Two considers the way in which higher education practice has evolved over time in response to economic, social and political changes,

12   *Global citizens*

both nationally and internationally. This is done with reference to Frijhoff's (1996) focus on learning, utility and virtue as the guiding forces of the evolution of higher education institutions, both in the past and the present. The discussion goes on to consider the position of higher education institutions with regard to globalisation and frames 'virtue' in this context. Focusing on the human interactions across boundaries that are at the heart of globalisation, consideration is given to possible approaches for higher education that hold out promise for enhancing global understanding. Drawing on the thinking of Paolo Freire, Chapter Two concludes with a consideration of the needs of contemporary higher education students and introduces the critical moments in the educational process for introducing cosmopolitan elements.

Chapter Three begins with a description of the growth of cosmopolitan thought through the ages, from the Ancient Greeks, through the Enlightenment and up to the present time. Discussion then moves on to critically consider previous attempts to apply cosmopolitan principles to practical challenges in the realms of universal norms and global governance. The danger of cosmopolitan thought becoming a universalism imbued with Western assumptions is highlighted. Indicating the need for cosmopolitan thought to be rehabilitated, the chapter goes on to suggest that its application to higher education embodies greater potential for a return to the underlying principles from which it developed. The chapter concludes by suggesting that the application of cosmopolitan values to the practice of higher education could be done in such a way as to negate inherent limitations and emphasise the strengths that cosmopolitan approaches have to offer.

Chapter Four considers international higher education, with a particular focus on student mobility. It draws on empirical evidence to consider the drivers of mobility and then critically evaluates the espoused benefits of mobility for employability, language competence and society more broadly. It examines the role which student mobility plays in reinforcing status and access to opportunities and questions its accessibility for non-elite students. It then goes on to consider an alternative to physical mobility of students in which the benefits of risk taking through social interactions with those from different backgrounds can be attained without the need for movement.

Chapter Five draws on empirical evidence gathered from higher education students in Australia to consider what students hope to gain from an international education. It then draws on empirical evidence from a second group of students to contrast students' hopes with their lived experiences of international education. It highlights the social schisms that characterise much international education through mapping the social interactions of students and draws on the social capital literature to identify why this is problematic for students in both the short and long terms. It finishes by drawing on the cosmopolitan canon to consider how it can inform educational practice that enhances students' experiences and outcomes.

Chapter Six looks at contemporary higher education practice to consider how much of an opportunity students have to gain cosmopolitan attributes during their studies. With a focus on curricula, it considers the increasing interest in international elements of education and evaluates how they are implemented in practice. It then goes on to consider a number of concrete forms of international curricula in the shape of foreign campuses, collaborative programmes, a whole of institution approach and short-term study abroad. Each one is considered with reference to the elements of a cosmopolitan education defined in Chapter Five in order to evaluate the extent to which it represents an expression of cosmopolitan education. It suggests that while curricula are important, the way in which they are implemented is perhaps even more critical to optimising cosmopolitan opportunities during a higher education.

Chapter Seven goes beyond curricula to consider the essential elements of pedagogy, the skills and knowledge of educators and assessment to promote the opportunity for students to gain cosmopolitan attributes during their higher education. With reference to pedagogy, it considers a number of current approaches to pedagogy that are particularly suitable for adapting in order to achieve cosmopolitan outcomes. For educators, it considers the experience, background, institutional context and professional development that can position educators to play a key role in helping students gain cosmopolitan attributes. In terms of assessment it touches on the characteristics of good assessment practice and looks at how these can be implemented to measure the cosmopolitan achievements of students. It also evaluates assessment of cross-cultural competence in terms of its value for cosmopolitan education.

Chapter Eight considers the increasingly important role of online modalities to higher education, whether students are classroom based or are studying via a distance mode. Charting the evolution of online pedagogies it considers the potential they have to offer to education that gives students the chance to gain cosmopolitan outcomes. It looks at the essential elements of online learning that are required if it is to yield cosmopolitan benefits for students and what can happen when these are not implemented appropriately. It highlights pertinent considerations for the design and facilitation of online learning and the positive outcomes for students that these can help generate. It finishes with a consideration of the value that games and simulation could offer in providing cosmopolitan opportunities for students.

Chapter Nine considers the need for appropriate educational responses to the complex and challenging global contexts we are facing, and the role that higher education institutions can play in focusing on social expansion rather than containment. It restates the benefits to be gained from applying cosmopolitan insights to educational practice in order to give students the opportunity to gain cosmopolitan attributes during their studies, and considers key considerations for educators in implementing such an approach. It concludes by suggesting that the application of cosmopolitan thought to higher education practice generates insights that can be used to counter some of the criticisms aimed at cosmopolitan thought, and to reinvigorate cosmopolitan theory.

2 Transforming the academy

Introduction

Higher education institutions have been around for more than a thousand years. And this does not take into account the myriad forms of advanced teaching and learning that have been practiced over a much longer period of time around the world. As the form and function of higher education institutions have evolved, many elements have remained stable. A fundamental role has been, and continues to be, the provision of an environment in which students can gain new skills and knowledge. Why, what and how students learn, however, has altered dramatically, and continues to do so. At the root of this transformation lies the context in which learning takes place. Social, political and economic dynamics alter the rationale that underlies gaining a higher education. They change the characteristics, needs and expectations of students. They modify the way in which learning occurs. And they reshape the world that students will inherit and for which they thus need to be prepared. In order to understand the role of contemporary higher education institutions as institutions designed to serve a specific purpose in society, it is necessary to understand their origins (Rohstock 2011). This chapter considers the development of higher education institutions over time, from the foundation of Al Qarawiyyin University in AD 859 to the present day. It looks at the contexts that have shaped the development of institutions in different parts of the world. In structuring the discussion, Frijhoff's (1996) suggestion that three elements – learning, utility and virtue – are the guiding forces behind the development of higher education institutions is used, both in the past and to the present day. Clearly, each element is profoundly shaped by its context. Nevertheless there are powerful commonalities that give institutions shared characteristics.

Advancing scholarship, both through research and teaching, remains a defining characteristic of higher education institutions, one that few would dispute. A further fundamental objective is to provide students with knowledge and skills that are useful to society, even though in the contemporary world their utility may be expressed in the enhanced earning power of graduates. Virtue – which Frijhoff (1996: 43) defines as 'preparation for the observance of a code of social, moral and religious conduct' – is another matter. Many contemporary institutions would suggest that they are value neutral. But, as will be discussed, emphasising the moral code of the time remains a defining feature of higher education. When we consider cosmopolitan education, all of these three elements are relevant, but it is this third role that is of particular interest to the present discussion. The sections below do not present a comprehensive comparative overview of educational history. For that you will need to look elsewhere. Instead, they establish the context against which contemporary forms of higher education can be understood. They chart the transformation of institutions from narrowly focused entities serving the specific needs of a small number of elite students to catering for the demands of ever-growing student bodies, ones with increasingly diverse characteristics. In establishing the foundations on which contemporary higher education institutions have been built, this chapter makes the case that ensuring relevance to the demands of our contemporary and highly globalised world is of paramount importance. It concludes by introducing the qualities that make cosmopolitan education a solution to the demands and challenges of the modern era.

The first universities

Deep in the heart of the labyrinth of the Fez medina in Morocco lies the Al Qarawiyyin Mosque. Its immense studded doors guard one of the world's oldest institutions of higher education. For more than 1100 years it has provided intellectual succour for generations of students. It has spanned tremendous changes in human existence. It was founded in 859 at a time when voyages of many months were required to disseminate information from one part of the globe to another, and it continues to educate students when the same transaction takes just a fraction of a second. It sits as a monumental reminder of another time and place. And yet it is recognisably a place of higher learning today. Its claim to be the oldest university in the world (at least of those that continue to exist to this day) is challenged. The University of Al Azhar in Egypt (972), the Nizamiyya Academy in Baghdad (1065) and the University of Bologna in Italy (1088) are among the rivals. But Al Qarawiyyin is unbowed. The echoes of students from more than a thousand years ago set the scene for their contemporary peers. And while iPads and laptops may have found their way inside, the form and function of education are remarkably unchanged.

A close look at Al Qarawiyyin yields insights into the history of higher education more broadly. In exploring its foundation, emphasis and the purpose it played in society it is possible to see echoes of developments around the world, both a thousand years ago and also in the present day. The establishment of Al-Qarawiyyin itself drew from earlier expressions of higher education. In ancient Egypt, the per-ankh could be regarded as a prototype higher education institution. A per-ankh was the library of papyrus

16 *Transforming the academy*

in the inner part of a temple. It played host to those studying law, architecture, astronomy and medicine alongside those destined for the priesthood. The per-ankh tradition ended with the fall of the Egyptian empire. But scholars such as Lulat (2005) regard it as the model on which Al Qarawiyyin and other institutions were established. If Al Qarawiyyin took its structure from ancient Egypt, it took its focus from Islam. Learning is a fundamental part of the Islamic tradition, enabling students to gain the knowledge and under-standing they require to become an embodiment of spirituality. Friday prayers and relatively informal dialogue between those who had knowledge of specific disciplines and those who wished to learn more about them had been used as a form of education in the Islamic tradition for many centuries. In terms of stimulating advances in knowledge this approach was highly productive. As Talbani (1996) recounts not only were works of science, philosophy and literature translated into Arabic as early as the 800s, but countless original works were also produced.

The spiritual dimension that under-laid the development of Al Qarawiyyin was equally prevalent in the foundation of higher education institutions in other parts of the world. In Lao, for example, Vat Vixun was established as an important centre for religious study in 1506. Students gained an introduc-tion to disciplines such as philosophy and medicine, alongside a deep focus on religious texts (McDaniel 2008). In Ethiopia Lulat (2005) points to the conversion of the royal family to Christianity in the fourth century as an important factor that led the way to the establishment of higher education institutions. In China, Lee (2000: 11) considers higher education to have evolved from the confluence of a number of forces, religion among them. He suggests that an emphasis on the development of 'moral uprightness' for the greater good of society was a defining factor of Chinese education, both in the Confucian era and thereafter. Cheng (2006: 559) refers to this as the 'Confucian model of onto-cosmology of self-cultivation' and suggests that this is a means of achieving balance in society through the development of the individual. In Europe Rüegg (1996) describes the Catholic papacy as providing the adhesion around which higher education institutions were established, at least until the Reformation.

Spirituality alone, however, was not enough to spark the creation of higher education institutions. Indeed, a major motivating factor was prosaic in the extreme, namely taxation. For rulers to be able to efficiently collect tax from populations spread across wide areas, they had a need for people to manage the bureaucracy of power. This required the offspring of the elite to expand their learning beyond the purely spiritual and to gain skills in the emerging disciplines. Medicine, cosmology, philosophy, architecture, science and governance were of particular importance. Thus ruling elites established institutions of higher learning that balanced spiritual awakening with the other knowledge and skills required of administrators. This does not indicate a democratic form of education. As Talbani (1996: 71) stresses, insti-tutions were an 'important instrument of social and ideological containment'.

Secular education was limited to those fields deemed necessary for administration (Anzar 2003). Questioning and critique were kept to a minimum. Knowledge was not accrued for its own sake but needed to have functional value (Halstead 2004).

While Al Qarawiyyin may lay claim to its status as the oldest university in existence today, its development as a centre that balanced the accrual of secular and spiritual learning for the sake of enhanced administration was not unique. Indeed, similar developments took place around the world. Vat Vixun in Lao was established for a very similar purpose and gave students an introduction to disciplines such as philosophy and medicine (McDaniel 2008). Similarly, in pre-Islamic Persia, Gundeshapur is an example of an institution that became a centre for religious and secular learning. As Farhang et al. (2012: 1006) suggest, it was established to 'foster obedient to govern the realm whereby the kings could improve and expand their kingdom [sic]'. In the Sung era in China, academies were established by Chu Hsi to enable intellectuals to become accomplished in both the skills and knowledge needed to pass civil service examinations and to pursue individual moral advancement. Lee (2000: 8) suggests that this emphasis could be summed up as 'how to balance one's life in official service, which meant elite status and its accompanying heavy duties, with a life of meditation and writing'.

In Europe, the first universities were established in particular conditions in the Middle Ages that reflect those around the world. These included a desire to utilise law to legitimate territorial claims and, like at Al Qarawiyyin, to produce people with the right skills to support governance and administration. These motivations arose from an increasing emphasis on trade and urbanisation. They were underlain by divinity and the need to serve the church, whether Catholic or Protestant (Scott 2006). Rüegg (2004) suggests that early European universities were remarkably uniform in both their breadth and depth. Religion was not just important in orientation but also in focus. Either universities came under direct supervision from churches or they retained a strong connection through them due to the importance of religion in practical matters – such as considerations about which students were admitted and which educators were appointed – as well as what Rüegg (2004: 6) refers to as 'the ideological orientation of academic studies and careers'. Inevitably, the need to prepare the elite to govern led to a degree of cross-fertilisation between intellectual developments from different regions. Due to its geographic location this was particularly the case in Islamic Spain and Anzar (2003) reports some scholars combining their Islamic studies with Greek and European thinking, and others bringing together Jewish and Islamic thought to develop knowledge in fields such as mathematics and medicine. On this basis significant higher education institutions developed and Ahmed (1987) recounts one of Al Qarawiyyin's contemporary institutions as containing a library of 6,000 books on subjects as diverse as astronomy, architecture and philosophy.

18   *Transforming the academy*

If religion lent its focus on education as the guiding force behind the establishment of institutions of higher learning, it was also the organising structure around which pedagogy was enacted. To this day, many Islamic higher education institutions balance religious instruction with teaching in other subjects. In their twenty-first century study of teaching at Al Qarawiyyin, for example, Hardaker and Sabki (2012) find that religious knowledge remains taught with a focus on memorisation and oral repetition, something that aims to help students 'embody' the sacred. While other forms of knowledge (such as medicine and mathematics) are taught in ways that would be more familiar to Western students, Talbani (1996) notes that they should only be studied to the extent that they are necessary. And secular subjects can be removed if religious leaders feel vulnerable. As Muslim empires declined, scholars began to 'shun any pursuit of worldly knowledge' (Anzar, 2003: 4). In the present day, Talbani (1996: 66) points to Pakistan and reports that in response to Western influences revivalist Islamic education movements are turning back the 'secularization and modernization of knowledge'.

Towards contemporary models

The history of Al Qarawiyyin speaks volumes about the way in which the three forces of learning, utility and virtue combined to stimulate the development of early universities. But it does not explain their proliferation, nor the role they play in the present day. Until the Middle Ages, a handful of higher education institutions catered to the elite and were predominantly interested in the administration of power. Advances were made in many disciplines but the seed of the shape of contemporary higher education institutions was planted less than 500 years ago. As Rüegg (1996: 5) suggests it was at this time that the influence of European exploration and discovery of the 'new world' led to a 'changed conception of time and the world'. The era of European colonial expansion called for massively increased ranks of civil servants, those who could be sent all over the world to administer new sovereignties. Universities in the centres of empire expanded hugely, with the universities of Amsterdam, London, Madrid and Paris all being established to meet this need. Exploration and discovery were not the only factors shaping universities. The notion of 'nation' was beginning to take hold and the power of religion declining, resulting in a move from a feudal, agrarian society to secular, centralised administration. In the void left by the decline of religious authority, the leaders of nascent nations established universities to continue the tradition of shaping the minds of the elite, and preparing them for governance. As Rüegg (1996: 8) argues, universities were preparing the elite 'to live and act in society in accordance with the norms of civility'.

For universities this meant increased interest in matters such as civilisation and also a growing role in contributing to their respective nations. The national focus was such that in many parts of Europe universities became an extension of the public service, charged with preparing teachers, doctors, clergy and bureaucrats. For example in Norway the first university marked not only a degree of independence from Danish rule but also make it possible for Norwegian civil servants to attend a university in their own country (Langholm 1995). The number of universities remained small, however. Frijhoff (1996) records that between 1500 and 1790, 137 universities were founded in Europe. Events around the French revolution caused many to close, however. The number of European universities dropped from 143 in 1789 to just 83 in 1815 and still numbered less than 100 in 1850 (Rüegg 2004).

Across the Atlantic Ocean, American universities were developing in patterns that both reflected and contrasted with European models. The first American university, Harvard, was founded in 1636 and most Ivy League institutions had been founded by 1781. Thelin (2011) suggests that they were a product of Anglophilia, with the romance of Oxford and Cambridge influencing the style in which they developed, and were strongly Protestant in their make-up. In terms of pedagogy Thelin (2011: 18–19) points to 'a mix of classroom recitations and oral disputations' that aimed to prepare future statesmen with the 'critical analytical skills that defined political economy as a discipline'. As this definition suggests, even though the context was the 'new world' in the 1600s, the focus on learning, utility and virtue was similar to that at Al Qarawiyyin 800 years earlier.

Inevitably the industrial revolution and the spread of manufacturing and new forms of employment exerted an influence on the shape and remit of universities. Advanced engineering skills were required, both for manufacturing itself and associated transportation and communication infrastructure. Mass migration from rural to urban living led to outbreaks of disease that called for advances in medical science. As schooling became more and more widespread, ever-greater numbers of teachers were required. Little by little higher education expanded beyond the most elite to include the offspring of the upper-middle classes. As such, Pruneri and Bianchi (2010) note that in the eighteenth and nineteenth centuries universities in Italy consolidated their role to become almost a monopoly in preparing students for professional careers, with education expanding from medicine and law to encompass up and coming professions such as engineering. No longer were universities solely preparing the elite to govern. In England, Oxford and Cambridge had long been training a very small number of upper-class men for leadership of the church and state. Unlike France and Germany, the expansion of universities in England had been extremely limited with just three more established by the middle of the nineteenth century. But this all changed at the very end of the nineteenth century when seven new universities were established in the great northern industrial cities such as Liverpool, Manchester and Leeds. This was partly a result of the quadrupling of the English population in the nineteenth century (Walsh 2009). But it was also a consequence of rapid economic expansion in which England had become one of the world's largest producers of manufactured products.

20 Transforming the academy

The new universities were founded thanks to the munificence of rich industrialists who were concerned at sustaining industrial growth in the light of competition from other European powers. Walsh (2009) notes that the role of the state in universities was extremely limited until the two world wars when universities were valued for stimulating scientific and technological advances and, latterly, for absorbing returning servicemen. The role of universities as producers of a skilled workforce marked a radical shift in their remit. Nevertheless, they maintained a traditional style of education with a focus on the classics, philosophy and literature alongside more modern fields (Walsh, 2009). As Wright (1979: 92) suggests, this approach was based on the 'inculcation of facts' in order to achieve mental discipline. In contrast, Scottish universities focused more on professional skills. The intent of both was to create men who could both think and articulate but the difference in approach reflected competing views on education. Across the Atlantic, US universities increased in number, recruited more students, added professional education, became more specialised and began to emphasise scientific research (Nidiffer and Cain 2004). By 1910 seven American universities had close to 5,000 students each.

If universities in Europe and America began to turn their attention to the new areas of science, engineering and technology, universities in other parts of the world maintained a focus on preparation for civil administration. In the colonies of European powers universities were grudgingly established when it became clear that highly educated members of the local elite could assist to administer colonies and spread Christianity (Roberts et al. 1996). At the same time, colonial leaders realised that the provision of higher education would help to secure support from chiefs, whose offspring would be given a chance to further themselves (McKenna 2011). As Persianis (2003) notes, however, this was done very cautiously. First, students had to be possessed of the 'right temperament'. Second, there were concerns that an overexpansion of universities would lead to more graduates than were actually needed to exercise colonial rule. Thus in East and West Africa, for example, the decision was made not to establish universities but instead to use colleges of higher education that gave only a limited form of university-type education to a small number of elite students (Persianis 2003). Needless to say, where universities were established the model used was imposed on, rather than reflective of, local circumstances. The approach used has had a lasting impact and even in the late twentieth century Brock-Utne (1999: 91) reported that in Africa 'there are hardly any examples ... [of] African universities that are consciously trying to restore the African heritage'.

In China universities went through a series of political changes that reflected those in broader society. In 1911, for example, Tsinghua University was established to prepare elite Chinese students for study in America. As Shi (2011) describes, it used a balance of Western and Chinese approaches. After the 1949 communist revolution the Chinese government adopted the Soviet approach to higher education, with control centralised and higher education seen as a tool of national policy (Wang and Liu 2011). After 1978, reforms led to a pattern of decentralisation, commercialisation and expansion of the higher education sector (Ennew and Fujia 2009; Liu 2007). After 1982 private provision was allowed and has grown to a situation in which there are a significant number of ventures with Western providers (Ennew and Fujia 2009). In response to the Asian economic crisis of 1997–1998 China, similarly to Malaysia, expanded the higher education sector in order to stimulate economic growth (Postiglione 2011; Wang and Liu 2011). Postiglione (2011: 800) suggests that China views higher education as 'a national endeavour that strengthens capacity to participate effectively in an increasingly competitive global knowledge economy'.

As the preceding paragraphs indicate, a great confluence of factors led to higher education institutions gradually becoming part of the landscape in most parts of the world. This was the same whether a country was a colonial power or was colonised, whether it used institutions as a tool of national social policy or left their evolution in the hands of philanthropists, whether the key aim was to ensure religious adherence, stimulate technological advances or prepare 'gentlemen' to govern. While higher education institutions became more common and enrolments grew, they long maintained a specific role in almost every society in which they were established. Schofer and Meyer (2005: 902) explain that the focus of universities was on 'creating a limited set of national elites required by closed national societies and occupational systems'. Those who were neither male, nor the offspring of small elite groups, were excluded.

In the last century a revolution has taken place. In 1939, Europe had 200 universities and 300 institutions of higher learning (Rüegg 2004). In 2013, there were 850 universities in Europe (European University Association 2013). In 1900 just half a million students around the world were enrolled in higher education institutions (Schofer and Meyer 2005). One hundred years later there were 100 million students in tertiary education institutions and by 2011 this had risen to almost 200 million (UNESCO Institute for Statistics, 2015a). The gross enrolment ratio in tertiary education worldwide had reached 18.95 by 2000 and 32.01 by 2012, with this higher than 90 per cent in some countries (UNESCO Institute for Statistics 2015b). This means that in some parts of the world tertiary education participation is reaching universal levels. Female students now account for around half of all tertiary students around the world and outnumber their male counterparts in many countries.

The global trend of expansion in higher education can be explained by a confluence of factors. These include expanded secondary education, the spread of democracy, increased interest in science, strong international connections and economic development (Schofer and Meyer 2005). More important than the causes, however, is the impact. If more than a third of young people around the world are gaining a higher education, what is the implication for society, both that defined by national boundaries and that which is global in scope? If the role of higher education institutions is no

22 *Transforming the academy*

longer to simply prepare the elite to govern, but now extends to preparing ever-growing proportions of young adults for lives in the contemporary world, what implication does this have for curricula and pedagogy? And does the notion of virtue play any role in a modern higher education?

Virtue and globalisation

Frijhoff's (1996) suggestion that three elements – learning, utility and virtue – define the development of universities was introduced at the start of this chapter. At Al Qarawiyyin it is clear that virtue remains a core element of the education experienced by students. Outside of higher education institutions that overtly set out to provide students with a religious education, however, this approach may seem archaic. Is a higher education not simply a means to gain the skills and knowledge required for employment in a chosen field? Is not the broader social role of higher education institutions simply to enhance the ability of young adults to contribute to economic growth and development? With this understanding it would be tempting to regard higher education institutions as value neutral, as institutions in which discussions of virtue, morality and ethics have their rightful place within the philosophy department. But this would be to deny the role of higher education institutions as social institutions of immense influence, and their importance in both mediating power and achieving consensus. Their ability to exercise power so effectively is precisely because it is invisible to most stakeholders.

Some believe that any discussion of higher education institutions as mechanisms of social conformity is a leap too far. That it requires lurching into the territory of conspiracy theories. This is not the case and it is important to unpack the values that contemporary higher education imparts to students. This needs to be done in order to determine whether the 'virtue' promoted by contemporary higher education institutions is a good fit for life in a global era, and to consider whether a cosmopolitan approach would have greater value. Many scholars view higher education institutions as what Readings (1996: 11) terms 'an ideological arm of the state'. Influential thinkers such as Gramsci (1971) have discussed the historically specific circumstances and social relations in which young people are prepared for professional lives. The professions on offer are determined by the needs of the social order and Gramsci (1971: 12) calls those who enter them 'functionaries'. The role of functionaries is to ensure that the population as a whole gives consent to 'the general direction imposed on social life' by the dominant social group, i.e. to exercise hegemony. To prepare young people for their 'functionary' roles, educational processes must ensure that students can promote the interests of the dominant group in society and conform to social norms. This means that they must be convinced that their interests are shared with the dominant group. Foucault (1984: 248) suggests that education passes on the 'great anonymous, almost unspoken strategies' to the next generation. Because individuals gain so much from a higher education they are loath to criticise the values it represents. As such, higher education institutions are a key instrument for eliciting consent where, as Boli et al. (1985: 149) suggest, individuals gain the capacity of 'making suitable choices and engaging in proper action'. 'Suitable' and 'proper' are defined by the context in which institutions are located, underlying the specific forms of virtue that higher education institutions promote.

In previous eras the virtue required of students and graduates was clearly defined. It was determined by local needs and dynamics and required those with university degrees to serve the interests of tangible elite groups. This might mean administering power for a Moroccan regent, serving in one of the colonial outposts of European empire or contributing to enhanced manufacturing efficiency for the benefit of the nation state. The expansion of university education in nineteenth century Europe and its colonies, for example, was a 'consciously articulated progress-oriented project' (Meyer et al. 1992: 129). Universities ensured that social and political objectives were met and their legitimacy maintained. In contemporary times many elements of this relationship are less clear. Who are the dominant elite groups in society in today's world? Which forces control economic, political and social dynamics? In an era of globalisation it sometimes seems as if the answers to these questions are impossible to find. The world in which human lives play out has undergone significant transformation as a consequence of the forces of globalisation (see Bauman 1998, 2000; Hopper 2007; Robertson 1992; Scholte 2000; Waters 2001). While globalisation is viewed by scholars as highly contested and contradictory, its impact is familiar to most. Capital, goods and ideas are increasingly fluid and mobile, production and the division of labour have become integrated on a world scale, nation states are reconfigured to attract global capital and neoliberal ideologies seem to run rampant. No longer is the locus of power place bound. Instead the 24/7 global market seems a blur of intangible energy that controls our lives for better and for worse. Tertiary education itself is increasingly viewed in market terms, with institutions needing to reinvent themselves to generate revenue and students recast as consumers in search of private goods.

In this context, what virtue do higher education institutions imbue their students with? The ability to serve the global economy seems paramount. In 2010 the broad field of social science, business and law was the most common area of study for students around the world. In the top economies alone enrolments in this field varied from 27.7 per cent of all tertiary students in the US to 40.3 per cent in Brazil (UNESCO 2013). This suggests that disciplines such as accounting, business, economics, finance, management and marketing dominate the tertiary sector. This is not surprising, given a global environment in which market forces, commerce, trade, consumption, competition, progress and the individual are emphasised. Some scholars claim that higher education around the world has become increasingly uniform, serving the needs of the same global market, ensuring that graduates have more in

24 *Transforming the academy*

common with each other than with those in their local communities (Schofer and Meyer 2005). Other disciplines have not lost all their ground of course. There remains a need for engineers, doctors, teachers, scientists and demographers. But the prestige has shifted to business, and bankers have become the kings and queens of the world.

Virtue and humanity

Globalisation is about far more than money. Ultimately, the whirl of energy that characterises contemporary life is expressed in the bringing together of people from around the world. As travel, both physical and virtual, becomes ever more accessible, opportunities to encounter those who look, talk and act differently to ourselves are increasingly common. And whether a tertiary graduate becomes a banker, a farmer, a teacher, a marketing executive or a nurse, cultural interaction and exchange has become an everyday reality. In this context it is vital that higher education graduates go out into their careers and future lives equipped not only with skills and knowledge about their chosen disciplines but also with the competencies required for life as a global citizen. This opens up another set of questions about the virtues that higher education institutions imbue.

Considerations of global citizenship open up alternative approaches to education. Beyond being a force for normalisation and conformity, education can also be a force for change. For within it lie the seeds to challenge that very same social order that it serves, disputing prevailing ideologies and clarifying the contradictions of our lives. Gramsci (1971) argues that dominant social forces can be challenged through 'counter-hegemony', which Carroll and Ratner (1994: 6) define as a 'disorganization of consent, a disruption of hegemonic discourses and practices'. In the contemporary world this means arguing against elements such as the power of financial markets, global capitalism, patriarchy and neo-colonialism to develop new ways of thinking about the world. Counter-hegemony requires a critical approach to education, and the ultimate critical education theorist is Paulo Freire.

Freire's (1970) book *Pedagogy of the Oppressed* has sold more than a million copies and has been translated into multiple languages. Much of its power, and its popularity, lies in its simplicity. Freire regards education as a form of 'cultural politics' and suggests that it exhibits a powerful dichotomy. It can be a force that 'reproduces existing social formations'. Equally, education can constitute 'cultural practices that promote democratic and emancipatory change' (Freire and Torres 1994: 101). Freire considers that education which stems from the interests of those in power, while it may be disguised as benign, actually dehumanises those who experience it. To counteract this, it is necessary to 'confront' the dominant culture through a process in which manipulative structures are recognised and then transformed. This often requires individuals to recognise that they are themselves part of the powerful elite, and to acknowledge the impact which their actions have on others.

Much of Freire's vocabulary – oppression, exploitation, violence, dehumanisation – sits uncomfortably with discussions of higher education in the twenty-first century. In the contemporary world, discussions of social revolution can appear naïve. But without looking through a critical lens at higher education, we fail to see the power of each of its elements in shaping the way students think and view the world around them. Neither curricula, nor pedagogy, nor decisions made by institutional leaders are value free. And if we want to ensure that students graduate with the skills and knowledge they will need to succeed in a highly complex and interconnected world, then it is worth unpacking the assumptions that comprise each of these elements.

As part of the elite, whether local or global, it is imperative that higher education students can critically reflect on their positions of power, and the impact of their beliefs and behaviour on the world around them. Critical elements include the assumptions inherent in each theory, approach, model, thought and expression that they encounter during their studies. The vocabulary they use to characterise the world around them is another important element, as is the impact of their actions and decisions on different constituents and stakeholders. When we consider that the professional lives of students will play out in a global stadium, each of these elements is imbued with cosmopolitan undertones. The ideas, theories, approaches and thinking that students confront during their studies are geographically place bound. They emanate from a particular time and are heavily laden with assumptions that reflect the context in which they arise. Without a critical understanding, however, they can seem inanimate and neutral. If students lack the skills to critically unpack and reflect on all of the elements of their studies, they will gain a view of the world that perpetuates the dominant view, is unquestioning of the power structures that shape reality and fails to recognise alternative ways of thinking. They may gain a degree but will not gain an education, will not have the skills to think for themselves as they negotiate the complex reality of the modern era.

Freire suggests that one of the key components of enlightened pedagogy is to recognise the prior experience and knowledge of students. He describes a 'banking' approach to education as one in which 'knowledge is a gift bestowed by those who consider themselves knowledgeable upon those whom they consider to know nothing' (1970: 53). It is not too large a step to suggest that this approach characterises much higher education, in which 'experts' pass on their insights, frequently – with the use of large lecture halls – to nameless, faceless recipients. As Freire suggests, this approach negates the notion that education is a 'process of inquiry', it precludes the opportunity of knowledge exchange between educator and student. It also denies the need to question the power relations present in the classroom, and the positioning and assumptions of the educator. It impedes the realisation that there is no such thing as 'the truth' but, instead, different ways of viewing the world. The solution is critical consciousness for all involved, unpacking the

26 Transforming the academy

contradictions inherent in both the subject matter and their own subjectivities, and then facilitating a process in which all participants are active in co-creating knowledge through dialogue. In a multicultural classroom this approach needs to take into account the cultural positioning of both the educator and students. This is particularly critical in a situation where there is a clear dichotomy. For example international education unashamedly uses the language of 'local' and 'international' students. This sets up a binary situation in which students and educators regard those in the classroom as comprising two distinct groups. Unless this way of thinking is named, critiqued, confronted and discussed, its role in shaping the way in which teaching and learning take place is made invisible and those in the minority are silently subjugated by the majority.

Freire refers to a 'constant unveiling of reality' (1970: 62) that occurs in 'problem posing' education through dialogue, which he defines as 'the encounter between men [sic], mediated by the world, in order to name the world' (1970: 69). Freire sets out a number of conditions for true dialogue: love for the world and people, humility, faith in humanity, trust between participants, hope and critical thinking. As the following chapter will indicate, these conditions find great resonance in the cosmopolitan canon. Freire considers dialogue as essential because this is the way in which the world – both tangible things and intangible ideas and beliefs – is created. Freire explains that 'an epoch is characterised by a complex of ideas, concepts, hopes, doubts, values and challenges' (1970: 82). Thus, in transforming reality we transform all of these through dialogue.

One of the key concerns Freire addresses is that of 'cultural invasion' in which one group 'penetrate[s] the cultural context of another group, in disrespect of the latter's potentialities: they impose their own view of the world' (1970: 133). In his naming of 'culture', Freire is referencing a way of viewing the world, whether it is one bound by place or by social position. In a move towards a cosmopolitan education the notion of cultural invasion takes on a particular pertinence. Globalisation is often criticised for transfusing 'Western' values into 'non-Western' societies. While this notion is premised on questionable categorisation, it does hint at the danger inherent in dominant approaches repressing those more marginal. In the higher education sector this concern takes a number of tangible expressions. Take, for example, concerns about linguistic hegemony versus the extinction of local languages. International rankings of higher education institutions tend to take account of publications in the English language only. And the international education market is largely premised on the desire to acquire proficiency in English, the international language of business. While students (or their parents) may make a rational choice to pursue higher education in an English language medium, this does not, and should not, mean that they are willing to jettison their own way of looking at the world. It is essential that students enter an educational environment in which multiple perspectives are valued. If not, there is a risk that they will begin to internalise attitudes about superior and inferior knowledge and, as Freire warns, this would make it all too easy for individuals to begin to regard themselves as inferior.

Cosmopolitan opportunities

To transform Freire's insights into progress towards a cosmopolitan education requires us to acknowledge the critical moments in the educational process, moments in which choices are made about the form and content of teaching and learning. A specific intent is required to ensure that decisions are made that encourage critical reflection, value the knowledge and experiences of students, emphasise the co-creation of knowledge through dialogue and avoid cultural invasion. Determinations about what to teach students, how to teach it and the shape of the environment in which teaching and learning will take place are laden with values. Thus a cosmopolitan education begins long before students come into contact with a learning space. Indeed, many of the critical moments in a cosmopolitan education are remote from the teaching learning dialogic.

Some of the earliest choices are about curriculum and syllabus. These are meta choices that shape how students will engage with their degrees, and the subjects or courses within them. They reflect assumptions about what it is important for students to learn in a particular context. Decisions about what is relevant for a particular cohort's level of study. Judgements about what is appropriate for students to learn in that time and place. Curriculum and syllabus are usually set by senior and experienced educators. They reflect prevailing norms and influences within a particular academic discipline. These choices reflect critical moments in setting up an educational approach that is conducive to cosmopolitan values. Ensuring that a range of perspectives are included, that students are encouraged to question underlying assumptions, that knowledge can be constructed in a dialogue between students and teaching staff are all premised on the decisions made about curriculum and syllabus. This requires those educators tasked with devising and designing curricula and syllabi to themselves be able to critically reflect on their values and to be open to challenging, and even contradicting, them.

Each time a student commences a new subject or class they are presented with resources carefully selected to help them advance towards specified learning objectives. They commonly receive a list of topics and a reading guide, often pre-prepared readings uploaded or copied and bound. They may be given the name of a set textbook. They are likely to be directed to additional resources, materials, online depositories, databases and websites to enhance their understanding of the topic material. All of these have been chosen by one or more educators with preconceived notions about what students should read, study and refer to as they come to grips with the material at hand. Once again, the decisions made are critical moments to ensure that opportunities for cosmopolitan thinking are included. It is important that those responsible are aware that their decisions are imbued with a set of

28 Transforming the academy

cultural assumptions about what is 'best' for their students. While students have the agency to select their own learning resources, the vast majority will simply follow what they are given. Thus the scope, values and perspectives that learning resources embody need to be carefully considered.

Once curricula have been set, syllabi defined, learning materials selected and class outlines prepared, the next step is for those responsible for teaching to determine the best method of engaging students. PowerPoint and Prezi may have replaced overhead projectors and blackboards in many cases, but beneath the choice of presentation medium lies a whole set of decisions about the best way to communicate with students about the key points of a given lecture, seminar or tutorial with students. How do educators view themselves and their roles? Do they position themselves as the holders of knowledge and students as recipients? Do they instead follow Gramsci's (1971: 350) suggestion that 'the relationship between teacher and pupil is active and reciprocal so that every teacher is always a pupil and every pupil a teacher'?

Much of this depends on the environment in which they teach. Are they giving a lecture to 700 students, or interacting with students entirely online without adequate infrastructure, or trying to engage students in critical reflection when there are insufficient chairs to go around? Conscious decisions made by senior administrators – frequently on financial grounds – have a marked impact on the context in which learning takes place. Setting up situations in which students cannot engage in dialogue, whether face-to-face or virtual, with either each other or teaching staff establishes a model in which banking education is almost inevitable. Large classes are not in themselves unconducive to active engagement but it requires a degree of pedagogical skill to make them come alive. But even a small class can fail to stimulate students if handled poorly. Thus another critical component is the nature of training that educators receive. In many cases there is none, and thus they can only replicate the pedagogy that they themselves have experienced. And when a shortage of qualified educators and budgetary considerations mean that second-year undergraduates are tasked with teaching first-year undergraduates, the pedagogy used is likely to be rudimentary at best.

Some academic staff are natural educators, able to engage students with stimulating, exciting and entertaining classes in which they are able to communicate their passion for the topic and their concern for students' learning. They are able to, in Freire's words, 'bear witness to the student about what knowing is, so the student will know instead of simply learning' (Freire and Torres 1994: 103). They are willing to learn from their interactions with students and to recognise the rich knowledge that students have about the world. Others cannot find it within them to do this and so retreat to didactic inertia. The action that higher education institutions choose to take when this occurs speaks volumes about their valuing of the learning dynamic. Are struggling educators provided with support, professional development and mentoring to improve? Or are they given the impression that as long as their research output is maintained their teaching does not really matter?

Conclusion

Overall, it would seem that the secret to transforming the academy into a sanctuary for critical reflection, co-creation of knowledge and valuing of multiple perspectives is multilayered. It involves not just those at the coalface of teaching but those who make decisions about what is to be taught, and how. Each learning experience is redolent of the institutional approach to education, whether top down or bottom up, democratic or autocratic, unidimensional or multidimensional. To ensure that students have the opportunity to encounter, and take on board, a cosmopolitan ethos, it is essential that all of the parts work together. This requires everyone who serves a higher education institution, from the uppermost echelons to the troops of casual teaching staff, to understand what a cosmopolitan perspective is, and how it can be interpreted in practice. In the following chapter the evolution, characterisation and expression of cosmopolitan thought are laid out, providing a path through the theoretical maze for those who are interested in giving all students the opportunity to gain cosmopolitan attributes during their higher education studies.

3 Cosmopolitan thought

Introduction

'Cosmopolitan' is not a term that has yet gained much traction in discussions of higher education. This is despite the fact that scholarly interest in cosmopolitan thought in the social sciences is growing, with Hollinger (2006: xxi) referring to it as 'one of the prominent political and cultural movements of the turn of the twenty-first century'. As this chapter outlines, cosmopolitan thought has much to offer the practice of higher education in the contemporary era. The strengths of the cosmopolitan approach lie in the insights it gives us to understand the human consequences of globalisation. These understandings enable us to investigate the contradictions inherent in our contemporary lives and the ways in which shifts at the global level are expressed in everyday human interactions. For educators this approach raises pertinent questions about the new demands that life in a globalised world places upon us and informs us of ways in which young people might be prepared for their careers and lives – lives in which otherness is normalised and the ability to transcend difference has become essential.

As higher education institutions and educators grapple with new realities and are motivated, whether extrinsically or intrinsically, to reappraise the extent to which their practice has relevance in the contemporary world, they cannot do so in a vacuum. The cosmopolitan approach provides them with an intellectual prism that has both deep historical roots and contemporary intellectual vigour. While cosmopolitan thought has much to offer educational practitioners, it is still at a relatively nascent stage of development, without a significant catalogue of empirical data with which to support its contentions. Until recently the naiveté of the cosmopolitan approach has tended to render it overly normative, with only limited considerations of the ways in which cosmopolitan influences play out in the human experience. As such, cosmopolitan philosophy is frequently understood to be prescriptive (Nowicka and Rovisco 2009), viewed as a shopping list of what human behaviour *should* be, but with limited connection to what human behaviour *is*. Of late, however, scholars have begun to explore the ways in which cosmopolitan ideals are expressed in real-world encounters and practices.

Cosmopolitan thought 31

This both expands the approach's horizons and also presents it with new possibilities and challenges. Education is just one of the arenas in which cosmopolitan practices can be expressed.

By exploring what is happening in contemporary higher education institutions, the philosophical approach is able to be both sharpened and deepened. At the same time, everyday incidences of the application of cosmopolitan practices in the arena of higher education reinvigorate the concept and enable its proponents to better grasp new realities. In this way, bringing cosmopolitan theory and the practice of higher education together has the potential to enhance both. In order to demonstrate the value of cosmopolitan thought for higher education practice, this chapter outlines the evolution of the cosmopolitan concept, and the context in which this has occurred. It identifies the three main strands of cosmopolitan thought and then focuses on the social project and its potential for higher education practice. It summarises the main ways in which cosmopolitan thought helps us to understand contemporary reality and then discusses its potential value for higher education.

The origins of cosmopolitan thought

The word 'cosmopolitan' is a combination of two Greek words – κόσμος, or 'cosmos', meaning universe, and πολίτης, or 'polités', meaning citizen. Cosmopolitan thought is generally viewed as having originated with the Cynics in the fourth century BC. Diogenes the Cynic is famously quoted, in response to being asked why he was living in a barrel, '*civis mundi sum*' (I am a citizen of the world). This was an expression of both his refusal to be bound by local origins and also his interest in defining himself by universal concerns. In this way, as Appiah (2006) suggests, he was rejecting the notion that each 'civilised' person needed to be a member of a particular community. Diogenes made this statement at a time when humans were becoming increasingly aware of the existence of other societies around the world. Even though inter-regional trade and human movement date back thousands of years, an intellectual awareness of the consequences of what Nederveen-Pieterse (2004: 25) terms 'ongoing intercultural traffic' had not previously been recorded.

The Stoics (300 BC onwards) further developed the notion introduced by the Cynics, rejecting the Greek focus on 'polis' as the only legitimate community by suggesting a notion of belonging that was universalistic (Boon and Delanty 2007). As Held (2005) notes, the Stoic Zeno of Citium suggested that humans belong to two communities at the same time – their local one and also the broader community of humanity. Using Hierocles' circular model of identity, the Stoics suggested that individuals are at the centre of a set of concentric circles that expand out from the family, to the local neighbourhood and on to the widest reaches of humanity. Nussbaum (1996: 7) stresses that the Stoics argued that not only should we recognise our shared humanity with others, but also that we should 'give its fundamental ingredients, reason and

32 *Cosmopolitan thought*

moral capacity, our first allegiance and respect'. The implication of this approach is that humans need to transcend differences in order to view the basic humanity in all others, including those we might otherwise regard as our enemies. Beyond this, there is a need for humans to actively work together in order to achieve outcomes that are beneficial to all. These sentiments were, unfortunately, subject to biased interpretation by ancient Greek society. Rather than being applied to political, legal and social structures in order to transform conditions for all (Delanty 2006), the underlying principles were, as Malcomson (1998) suggests, applied as a licence to dominate the world around them in an egregious form of colonisation in which the realities of slavery, conquest and the exploitation of other peoples were accepted. Nevertheless, the cosmopolitan ideal remained potent as a principle and both Appiah (2006: 111) and Nussbaum (1997: 9) quote Publius Terentius Afer in Rome in the second century AD stating '*homo sum: humani nil a me alienum puto*' (I am human: nothing human is alien to me).

For substantive innovation in cosmopolitan thought, however, it is necessary to move ahead 1,600 years to Germany in the Age of Enlightenment. Intellectuals at this time took the notion of freedom and incorporated it into a range of political theories including republicanism, liberal nationalism and legal cosmopolitanism. Prominent among thinkers at the time was Immanuel Kant. Influenced by men of stature such as Cicero, Seneca and Marcus Aurelius (Nussbaum 1997), Kant developed the notion of a 'Weltbürger', or world citizen. In his eyes, a 'Weltbürgerlich' society was one in which all had the right to participate (Held 2005). Despite the historical precedents of his thinking, the distinguishing feature of Kant's philosophy was what Harvey (2009: 258) refers to as a 'doctrine of progress'. Kant appears to have been strongly influenced by both Basedow and Rousseau (Cavallar 2014). Like Basedow, Kant did not regard being a patriot as at odds with being a cosmopolitan and both saw cosmopolitanism as encompassing tolerance and openness as well as political change. Like Rousseau, Kant's notion of cosmopolitanism has strong moral underpinnings and Cavallar (2014: 377) suggests that Rousseau's *Émile* focuses on 'the formation of a moral and cognitive cosmopolitan, who avoids the deformations of a commercial society influenced by processes of globalisation'.

It is important to consider that the context in which Kant wrote was one in which the world was being reconstituted, particularly as a consequence of conflict. Kant's concerns about the physical and psychological cost of conflict led him to write *Idea for a Universal History from a Cosmopolitan Point of View* in 1783. In this influential work Kant claimed that 'after devastations, revolutions and even complete exhaustion, [nature] brings [men] to that which reason could have told them at the beginning … to step from the lawless condition of savages into a league of nations' (1963: 18–19). He went on to argue that 'a universal cosmopolitan condition' is the only way in which the 'capacities of the human race can develop' (1963: 23). Kant's argument was developed further in *On the Common Saying*, written in 1793, in which he argued that 'the

Cosmopolitan thought 33

need arising from the constant wars by which states in turn try to encroach upon or subjugate one another at least bring them, even against their will, to enter into a cosmopolitan constitution' (1996b: 307). Both of these essays foreshadowed the one for which Kant is perhaps most famous, *Perpetual Peace*, which he wrote in 1795. In this essay he developed his thinking further, suggesting that when people are 'too exhausted to continue the war' (1891a: 80) states ought to 'proceed in their disputes that such a universal International State may be introduced thereby' (1891a: 76). Kant's statements about the progression of war to a 'cosmo-political relation' were based on a strong belief in the 'principle of right, as to what relations among human being and states ought to be' (1996b: 309), suggesting that 'the position therefore holds good, that what is valid on rational grounds as a Theory, is also valid and good for Practice' (1891b: 76).

Kant's interest lay in the creation of universal laws that would limit the behaviour of states by making them submit to an international order, finding a way to bridge the contradiction between universalistic rights and the nation-centric model that protected rights. In *The Doctrine of Right*, written in 1797, Kant explicates cosmopolitan right (*ius cosmopoliticum*) as 'the rights of citizens of the world to try to establish community with all and, to this end, to visit all regions of the earth' (1996a: 21). Fine (2003) suggests that Kant was searching for a way to create concrete forms out of the philosophy of universality and wished to stress the failings of nationalism. Perhaps Kant's most crucial contribution was to highlight 'universal hospitality' as the most profound right held by people in their status as 'citizens of the world in a cosmo-political system'. As he famously stated: 'All men are entitled to present themselves thus to society in virtue of their Right to the common possession of the surface of the earth, to no part of which anyone had originally more right than another' (1891a: 101).

Kant argued that the 'right to common possession' derived from the fact that from the beginning nature had allowed humans to live all over the world and it was only conflict that had driven particular groups out of certain areas. In a situation in which humans were fed up with conflict, it was necessary for them to find other ways to relate to each other. As Kant wrote in *Perpetual Peace* (1891a: 103):

> social relations between the various Peoples of the world, in narrower or wider circles, have now advanced everywhere so far that a violation of Right in one place of the earth is felt all over it. Hence the idea of a Cosmopolitical Right of the whole Human Race, is no phantastic or overstrained mode of representing Right, but is a necessary completion of the unwritten Code which carries national and international Right to a consummation in the Public Right of Mankind.

Tragically, while Kant suggested that the lure of commercial benefits would cause humans to forego war and result in long-term peace, Europe once

34 Cosmopolitan thought

again descended into war not long after he wrote these lines and this continued for decades, eventually culminating in the horrors of World War II. Ironically, two of the targets for the Nazi policy of annihilation were Jews and Gypsies, and one of the reasons that they were so despised was precisely because they were regarded as 'cosmopolitan'. Beck et al. (2009: 114) suggest that these groups were seen as 'rootless', with their presence in political communities across Europe 'calling into question the premises of homogeneity' and therefore regarded as a destabilising influence. Indeed, Beck (2006) suggests that suspicions of those who consider themselves cosmopolitan remain prevalent, with rootless, mobile people often regarded as a threat to social balance. This is reflected in contemporary policies towards asylum seekers. At the same time, however, the two world wars clearly illustrated the interdependence of societies around the world and emphasised questions about identity that were solely determined in terms of territory and geography. Following World War II, the great empires of the European powers began to dissolve as independence movements swept through their former territories. The post-colonial movement, in combination with the rise in the phenomenon of globalisation, and the pressure it has exerted on the nation state, led to the resurgence of interest in a cosmopolitan approach in the 1990s.

The phenomenon of globalisation has led to a particularly heightened interest in cosmopolitan thought and its real-world applications, largely as a consequence of an intensification of global interconnections. While it is clear that such links are not entirely new, globalisation has significantly lessened geographical constraints on human behaviour, hence increasing the global interconnections within which individuals play out their social lives (see, for example, Giddens 1990; Robertson 1992; Spybey 1996; Waters 2001). As Marginson (2008: 218) eloquently suggests, 'globalization multiplies sojourners and journeys; encourages multiple place-making as well as the one way journeying and renders more complex the record of cultural encounters'. The result is a contemporary reality in which human activity proceeds in a complex web of what Held et al. (1999: 2) term the 'widening, deepening and speeding up' of global ties, which has led to increasing cultural differentiation (Nederveen-Pieterse 2004). Inevitably, the degree to which this is true is unequal, with people in some regions more affected than those in others. The overall result, however, is that every single human being in the world today is more connected to every other human being than they have been at any point in the past, and there is no indication that this is a pattern that will be reversed.

Crucially, this means that there is no need to physically cross borders in order to participate in, or be affected by, global interconnections. Instead, global influences are all around us, wherever we happen to live, and encounters with those unlike ourselves are increasingly normalised (Anthias 2006). As such, those whose lives are constrained to the local are regarded as being socially deprived (Bauman 1998) and there is a need for us all to be able to navigate lives in which external influences and cultural diversity have become the norm. While political responses to this phenomenon tend to be polarised into those who view cultural diversity as a threat or an opportunity, the reality for individuals is that if we wish to live successful and peaceful lives, whether in our birthplaces or elsewhere, interaction with those who are different to ourselves cannot be avoided. Hybridity is an increasingly common characteristic of our lives (Nava 2007) and, as we have already seen, Appiah (2006) regards interactions across difference as inevitable.

Three strands of cosmopolitan thought

While the evolution of cosmopolitan thought over time, which Skrbis et al. (2004: 115) term 'its Stoic parentage, Kantian upbringing and postmodern spoiling', has led to an approach that can seem confusing, contradictory and excessively normative, there are nevertheless three fairly robust strands that are now being applied to real-world challenges. By elucidating the philosophical, political and social projects of a cosmopolitan approach, it becomes clear that rather than fragmenting a cosmopolitan approach, as Rumford (2007) suggests, they all focus on different iterations of the same underlying idea. The 'philosophical project' of a cosmopolitan approach is closely linked to the transnational political project, building on Kant's ideas to create political processes that allow us to separate 'the demos from the ethnos' (Post 2006: 8). Seyla Benhabib is one of the major proponents of this approach and locates herself amongst those who view a cosmopolitan approach as 'a normative philosophy for carrying the universalistic norms of discourse ethics beyond the confines of the nation-state' (2006: 18). As Brock and Brighouse (2005) highlight, however, it is one thing to accept that we have moral obligations to all other humans, but it is another to decide how these can be put into practice.

In the political understanding of a cosmopolitan approach, scholars such as Held (2005) are interested in a global form of governance that recognises eight principles of a cosmopolitan approach: equal worth and dignity; active agency; personal responsibility and accountability; consent; collective decision making about public matters through voting procedures; inclusiveness and subsidiarity; the avoidance of serious harm; and sustainability. Held (2005: 21) argues that the basic unit in the world is not nations but individuals and proposes that 'it is possible to have a modern democratic rendition of the Stoic aspiration to multiple forms of affiliation'. This is a particularly interesting notion in the European context and a great deal of attention has been paid to the political and philosophical implications and opportunities of the EU (see Beck and Grande 2007; Delanty and He 2008; Rumford 2007). Held (2005: 27) suggests that a cosmopolitan approach gives us a relevant political philosophy and reality that is most suitable for 'living in a global age' and allows us to be simultaneously citizens of national, regional and international communities. Despite these declarations, some feel that

36   *Cosmopolitan thought*

Held and his peers utilise a notion of rights that is 'far too close to the neoliberal ethic for comfort' (Harvey 2009: 89).

While this book will not deal with the philosophical or political projects of a cosmopolitan approach, it is important to state that in many ways they are the most questionable aspects of cosmopolitan theory. Their most problematic features derive from a reluctance to fully critique their Kantian legacy. While Kant's scholarly work has had a huge impact on the development of cosmopolitan thought, it is dangerous to consider his contributions without fully unpacking the context from which they emanated. While Kant's most famous writings have been translated into English and pored over by scholars, others, such as his *Geographie,* have not and, as Harvey (2009) points out, this is a book that makes clear some of Kant's more contestable arguments, at the same time as demonstrating the context in which he understood the world. One of the more illuminating statements was made by Kant in relation to race, about which he said 'Humanity achieves its greatest perfection with the White race. The yellow Indians have somewhat less talent. The Negroes are much inferior and some of the people of the Americas are well below them' (cited in Harvey 2009: 26).

As this statement suggests, it is vital to remember that Kant's work on a cosmopolitan approach was, as Hall (2008: 349) explains, 'embedded in a certain form of historical particularity'. If Kant is to be regarded as one of the major proponents of a cosmopolitan approach, there is a pressing need for greater critical attention to be paid to Kant's works than has so far taken place. Kant's Western-centric partiality carries over to both the philosophical and political approaches of cosmopolitan thought, which have a tendency to preach an approach that is universalistic and to promote individual rights at the expense of collective ones. As a result, critics such as Harvey (2009: 84) accuse these approaches of acting as a mask for 'hegemonic neo-liberal practices of class domination and financial and militaristic imperialism'. Whether or not this accusation is justified, there has clearly been a lack of success in combating outrageous social inequalities around the world, despite the considerable emphasis on regimes of individual rights and participatory democracy. This alone points to the need to critically unpack the assumptions on which these discourses are built.

Beyond his inability to consider non-Western perspectives, which is to a great extent a reflection of the context in which he wrote, Kant is also criticised by Hegel for failing to question the notion of a nation state, with Hegel (1952: 134) suggesting that 'a human being counts as such because he is a human being, not because he is a Jew, Catholic, Protestant, German, Italian, etc.'. While Hegel argued that it was of 'infinite importance' to be conscious of this fact, he did not think that it was useful to create an abstract monolith from it, arguing that 'it is only defective when it is crystallised'. Fine (2003) points out that Hegel criticised Kant for separating cosmopolitan right from the reality of everyday life, suggesting that discussing rights is only useful in trying to meet real needs. Habermas (1998: 166) too finds fault with Kant, concluding that his contributions are 'beset with conceptual differences' and sit awkwardly with twentieth-century experience. For Habermas what is needed is a reformulation in order to bring Kant's ideas up to date and to take into account the changes wrought by globalisation. As Habermas (1998: 28) argues:

> any attempt to project a universally binding collective good on which the solidarity of all human beings ... could be founded runs up against a dilemma ... an intolerable degree of paternalism ... an empty conception that abstracts from all local contexts and undermines the concept of the good.

Habermas explains that Kant fails to fully consider history and thus inadequately takes into account the ways in which identities are built up over time, a process that takes into account traditions and practices, and in doing so fails to acknowledge that in order to shape a universal norm, all different perspectives need to be incorporated. This position is reinforced by Cheah (2006: 486), who emphasises the persistent power of the nation as a medium for solidarity and the danger of cosmopolitanism being merely 'an intellectual ethos of a select clerisy, a form of consciousness without a mass base'. He points to the exploitation of some groups of people by others as a core component of globalisation and suggests that political cosmopolitanism can become a 'symbolic marker' of a state that has gained the position of the exploiter rather than the exploited.

Kant is not the only cosmopolitan thinker who failed to consider normative contributions from outside the West. Indeed, this is a failing that continues to the present day. Despite the claims of cosmopolitans to be truly interested in the needs of *all* humans, there is a marked tendency to continue to rely almost solely on European normative roots. Consequently, this leaves the cosmopolitan approach wide open to the accusation that it is a view that Mignolo (2000: 735) suggests comes from the 'heart of Europe' and inevitably undermines its claims to truly universal notions. In order to overcome this bias, it is vital to move beyond the exclusive focus on European developments in order to consider historical advances in other parts of the world. While there are some interesting examples of the development of cosmopolitan thought in Persia during the Muslim period in Spain, in the Middle East (Zubaida 2002) and in the Confucian tradition (Chan 2002; Delanty and He 2008), these are rarely discussed.

A further accusation that is made of cosmopolitan thought is that it is elitist. Scholars such as Kuhling and Keohane (2007) claim that cosmopolitan thought is based on the assumption that individuals have the requisite economic and cultural capital to be able to move around the globe. Moreover, Anderson (1996: 270) warns that the cosmopolitan desire to transcend national boundaries could be seen as a form of detachment that leads to the creation of 'a rootless, intellectualised managerial class'. A similar

38 *Cosmopolitan thought*

concern is shared by Fardon (2008: 249), who questions the way in which cosmopolitans view what he calls 'the uncosmopolitans'. Fardon points out the danger of a privileged cosmopolitan class looking down upon those who are not, warning of the danger that 'to be on board the cosmopolitan project … you have to have been on board already'. This unease is connected to another criticism of a cosmopolitan approach, that it has a tendency, as Calhoun (2002: 875) argues, to downplay tensions present within the multiple realities of globalisation and to insufficiently distinguish its various forms. In this sense there is the danger of failing to value place-bound traditions and the ways in which 'people are moved by commitments to each other' in particular contexts. Calhoun (2002: 893) suggests that the necessary solidarity for 'mutual commitment and responsibility' is created on the basis on local conditions.

While all of these criticisms are valid, most are immediately rendered less potent when we consider the third project of a cosmopolitan approach – the social approach. Indeed, the premise of a social cosmopolitan approach, that humans need to return to the Stoic notion of being citizens of the world and learn how to interact with each other on a one-on-one basis, expressed by Habermas (1998: 40) as 'a non-levelling and non-appropriating inclusion of the other in his otherness', does not provide much scope for domination by any particular standpoint – Western, universalist, elitist or other.

Multiple allegiances

For many of us, simply investigating our own genealogies, as Mitchell (2007) recognises, is enough to make clear that the notion of cultural homogeneity is what Bauman (1999: 200) terms 'cognitively misleading'. In setting itself up as an alternative to a view of human society as 'recalcitrantly divided' (Post 2006: 9), however, the cosmopolitan approach does not adopt universalism (Delanty 2006). Instead, as Hollinger (2006) argues, it is inter-ested in the diversity among humans. In contrast to multiculturalism, an approach that Beck (2006: 67) describes as viewing individuals as 'merely epiphenomena of their cultures', the cosmopolitan approach embraces the enormous complexity of multiple identities and 'posits the individual actor as existing beyond particular communitarian arrangements' (Rapport and Stade 2007: 225).

By focusing on multiple allegiances, the cosmopolitan approach avoids what Puwar (2006: 82) terms 'categorical reductionism' and accepts that not only do people belong to multiple groups at any one time, but also that, as Hollinger (2006) recognises, these groups are not just those defined by their ethnicity or nationality. Indeed Anthias (2006: 20) points out that not only do we find the 'coexistence of different identities within one person', but the identities of individuals often depend on the various spaces and contexts in which they live their lives, all of which are constantly in a process of change. This 'intersectionality' means that we experience a number of positions depending on the context, and experience each of these positions differently. For example our positions at work, with our families and when we socialise tend to vary considerably, as does the way we experience each of these. Consequently, we define our identities by creating what Beck (2006: 5) terms a 'progressively inclusive self-image', with the result that Fine (2007: 135) suggests 'no one actually coincides with what the sociologists call their social identity'.

The ways of referring to identities, which are based on the 'both/and principle' (Beck 2006: 57), are many and varied. Hybridity is one that is increasingly popular, despite the negative way in which it has been used in the past to denote racial impurity. Hybridity encompasses our shifting identities, ones that are not restricted to a nation but are tied to a 'transnational social fabric' (Anthias 2006: 25). The cosmopolitan approach allows our sense of belonging to be open, equipping us for lives that are lived in a period of great transition and that may take place in a range of geographic locations in which our 'subjectivity, modes of action and strategies for social visibility' are altered (Introduction to Ossman 2007: 2). Rumford (2007: 2) points out that this focuses our attention on the 'fluid and evolving' nature of human relationships, both on the micro and macro scale, without pretending to know what the ultimate outcome will be. It allows for us to have an array of loyalties that coexist with each other and accepts that our ways of life are increasingly diverse and transnational. Furthermore, Beck (2006: 2) suggests that it emphasises the 'real, internal cosmopolitanization' of our lives.

Allowing for the fact that individuals have multiple affiliations, and acknowledging what Hollinger (2006: xvii) refers to as the 'endemic human need for intimate belonging', this approach allows for the notion that cultures and traditions are not unitary and separate but that they 'interpenetrate, interconnect and intermingle' (Beck 2006: 7). It allows people to articulate multiple allegiances without losing their identity as a member of a particular social, cultural or political community (Vertovec and Cohen 2002). Crucially, the cosmopolitan approach is not against nationalism. It does not ask us to choose between loyalty to our nation of origin and loyalty to the human race, but allows us to feel both at the same time (Pollock et al. 2000). While some cosmopolitans do indeed argue that nationalism is profoundly incompatible, and suggest that, as Nussbaum (1996: 15) contends, 'becoming a citizen of the world is often a lonely business', there is little truth in this assertion. While the cosmopolitan approach is certainly against the dark forces of extreme nationalism (Beck 2006; Cheah 2006), the notion that it is antithetical to nationalism derives from a misplaced and highly Western assumption that nations were once culturally homogeneous (see Fardon 2008; Kahn 2008).

Instead, Cheah (1998) asserts that the cosmopolitan approach is not about detachment from our origins. Instead, the place in which we are born, our family, our roots are 'essential attributes' that help to define who we are (Himmelfarb 1996: 77). To ignore them would be to disregard 'the actualities,

40 *Cosmopolitan thought*

particularities and realities of life that constitute one's natural identity'. Moreover, it is particularly important in the face of globalisation that our national identities are used to resist its homogenising influence, which Falk (1996: 54) refers to as 'stultifying convergence'. Instead, the cosmopolitan approach demands that we acknowledge all our attachments, both national and otherwise, in order to recognise that our community extends further than our immediate reality (Delanty 2006). Indeed, both the cosmopolitan approach and nationalism provide individuals with what Cheah (2006: 489) calls 'alternative vehicles for the actualization of moral freedom'. Therefore, Appiah (1998: 91) calls for a 'rooted cosmopolitanism' or a 'cosmopolitan patriotism'. While at first this may appear contradictory, this gives us the ability to juggle multiple frames of reference and to view the world from multiple positions (Rumford 2007).

A cosmopolitan disposition

Beyond focusing on multiple allegiances, the cosmopolitan approach also requires us to become competent in a particular mode of practice – in the ability to move among cultures with respect and understanding (Vertovec and Cohen 2002). It encourages us to engage those different to ourselves in 'an intellectual and aesthetic stance of openness toward divergent cultural experiences' (Hannerz 1990: 239). This is an aspect that is frequently referred to as a 'cosmopolitan disposition' (Nava 2006: 47), but an alternative would be to adopt the suggestion of Skrbis et al. (2004) that we use Bourdieu's notion of 'habitus'. The use of the term 'habitus' focuses attention on the ways in which people relate to one another within particular contexts and the principles that guide them in doing so. Bourdieu (1977: 214) himself uses the term 'disposition', when he defines habitus as 'a system of dispositions', including the 'result of an organising action', 'a way of being' and a 'predisposition, tendency, propensity or inclination'. Woodward et al. (2008: 211) suggest that this relates to 'a consistent set of simultaneously cognitive and cultural structures of thought and action'.

Whether termed 'disposition' or 'habitus', this element of a cosmopolitan approach demands more than a passive acceptance of the diversity in which we enact our lives. Instead, an appreciation of, and interest in, diversity is viewed by Mignolo (2000) as the fundamental momentum in a cosmopolitan approach. Cosmopolitans value the various expressions of human lives and, as Appiah (1998: 111) suggests, assert 'that sometimes it is the differences we bring to the table that make it rewarding to interact at all'. Moreover, as Beck (2006: 89) affirms: 'the cosmopolitan outlook and sensibility opens up a space of dialogical imagination in everyday practice ... [and] forces us to develop the art of translation and bridge-building'.

It would be wrong to assume that globalisation inevitably leads to a cosmopolitan approach. Indeed, there is nothing about movement or about contact with those different to ourselves that turns us into cosmopolitans.

Beck (2006: 89) refers to this as the 'cosmopolitan fallacy', arguing that just because our lives are being altered by globalisation does not mean we are all becoming cosmopolitan. Simply being in contact with people and practices from around the world, or 'a bit of dabbling in, or desire for, elements of cultural otherness' does not make us cosmopolitan (Vertovec and Cohen 2002: 8). Even those who are globally mobile and operate transnationally are not necessarily anything more than 'parochial cosmopolitans' (Hopper 2006). In the safety of their expatriate communities they resist the differences around them, engage only with others like themselves, fail to learn the local language and see the local culture as an unfortunate imperative to which their global marketing campaigns must adapt. Their pseudo-exposure to other cultures does not alter their consciousness of themselves and their place in the world. They may have 'cultural worldliness' or a 'cosmopolitan aesthetic' but lack 'moral worldliness' or 'cosmopolitan ethics' (Sypnowich 2005: 56–57).

In research with United Nations professionals across 40 countries, for example, Nowicka and Kaweh (2009: 64) found that while their subjects were geographically mobile, linguistically versatile and considered them- selves 'cosmopolitan', they 'prefer the comfort of familiar facilities over the stress of discovering new people and places ... they often observe rather than participate in local life'. This finding supports Hannerz's (1990: 242) contention that for many people travel simply involves a search for 'home plus' – that which is familiar plus an added dimension. He suggests that those forced out of their countries of origin are often searching for 'home plus safety, or home plus freedom', without much desire to engage with the differences that they encounter, although they 'may reluctantly build up a competence'. Hannerz (1990: 243) describes the way in which 'a surrogate home is again created with the help of compatriots, in whose circle one becomes encapsulated'.

It is vital to remember that, as Kofman (2007) points out, there is no need to leave home in order to become cosmopolitan. Whether we leave home and expose ourselves to other cultures, or remain at home and experience the impact of living in communities with diverse populations, the contemporary world certainly gives us more and more opportunities that have the potential to lead to what Vertovec and Cohen (2002: 14) term a 'fundamental change in attitudes', and this is the moment at which a cosmopolitan approach becomes a possible reality. It is not enough, however, to enjoy eating food from around the world, watching world movies and listening to world music. While these practices may be 'associated with those who hold deep or reflex- ive cosmopolitan values' (Woodward et al. 2008: 212), cosmopolitan practice demands more than a superficial engagement with unfamiliar cultures.

Limitations to the social cosmopolitan approach

While a social cosmopolitan approach denies many of the criticisms that are levelled at the political and philosophical variants of a cosmopolitan

42 *Cosmopolitan thought*

approach, it is still weak in one particular regard. Scholarly interest in social cosmopolitanism continues to overemphasise normative dimensions, while providing too little empirical evidence of the ways in which a cosmopolitan approach plays out in the everyday actions of normal people. It suggests that 'sharp oppositions between "us" and "them"' may be lessened (Beck 2006: 90–91) but fails to indicate the ways in which these oppositions can become 'blurred'. Much of its empirical evidence is based on the personal experiences of academic authors who, while providing a rich seam of interesting narrative, fail to engage with what is occurring in wider society. While there have been recent attempts to demonstrate the ways in which cosmopolitan sensibilities are embodied (see the edited volumes Nowicka and Rovisco 2009; Werbner 2008), these remain more descriptive than substantive and lack analytical rigour.

Examples from the Malaysian women's movement (Stivens 2008); Indonesian feminists (Robinson 2008); Dalit Tamil women in India (Ram 2008); Maasai activists in Tanzania (Hodgson 2008); African migrants in Cape Town (Sichone 2008); Europe-wide protests about the US-led invasion of Iraq (Delanty and He 2008); steel workers in India (Parry 2008); East European building workers in London (Datta 2009); Cubans in Spain (Berg 2009); working-class men in the USA and France (Lamont and Aksartova 2002); skilled migrants in Manchester (Kennedy 2009); and globally dispersed Sindhis (Falzon 2009) have all been used by scholars to argue that a cosmopolitan approach is embodied at the local level and that cosmopolitan dispositions are nurtured and created through daily practices and interactions in which individuals negotiate post-national identities.

Despite the richness of these narratives, they fail in several regards. First, the extent to which these examples demonstrate a wholehearted commitment to a cosmopolitan approach is questionable. It is likely that many of the subjects are 'ambivalent cosmopolitans' (Skrbis and Woodward 2007) for whom a cosmopolitan approach is a practical mode of functioning 'amid cultural uncertainty' (Calcutt et al. 2009: 182). Second, these examples fail to uncover patterns of interaction between individuals in these contexts, or to consider rationales that may underlay such patterns. This is a critical weakness of the cosmopolitan approach. If it cannot give us the tools with which to comprehend patterns of behaviour in social contexts of great diversity, it renders any observations superficial. Consequently, suggestions that there is evidence of the existence of cosmopolitan dispositions in any context are highly questionable and open to critique. Finally, they are, with notable exceptions, accounts written by Westerners about 'the other' and this positioning renders the telling and the understanding inevitably tinged with the perspective of the observer, reducing their authenticity and adding to the absence of clarity that permeates the cosmopolitan literature. Overall, there is clearly an urgent need for cosmopolitan theory to develop a methodology that can help us to understand what happens when, in Malcomson's (1998: 238) terms, 'individuals ... enter into something larger than their immediate cultures'.

Conclusion

As detailed in this chapter, cosmopolitan theory has grown up as a response to the need for humans to have allegiances that transcend national borders. In the contemporary world, the profound changes wrought by globalisation have intensified movement, diversity and the interpenetration of nations by international forces. In this context the focus of a cosmopolitan approach has increasing relevance. While the political and philosophical projects of a cosmopolitan approach receive more attention, it is the social project that is considered in this book. The social cosmopolitan approach focuses attention on the ways in which individuals negotiate their lives in an increasingly complex world. It does this by considering two increasingly common characteristics of contemporary society. In the first instance, it recognises that nearly every person alive is likely to have an increasing number of encounters with those unlike themselves, and consequently needs to develop the skills to successfully negotiate such encounters. Second, it demonstrates that individuals can have multiple allegiances, including to humanity as a whole, without needing to choose between them. As such, a social cosmopolitan approach is of profound importance to a world in which there is a pressing need to enable diverse communities to function in ways that are inclusive and in which tensions are ameliorated.

Despite the strengths of the social cosmopolitan project, the potential that it embodies to help humans to find solutions to social challenges is undermined by a shortage of rigorous empirical investigations and a lack of methodological tools. In bringing together the normative insights of cosmopolitan theory and needs of higher education students, this book aims to tap into the 'fertile energy' (Woodward et al. 2008: 210) that exists among contemporary students and to find ways to help them gain the skills and attitudes they will need to succeed in a global world. This requires educators to give students opportunities to move towards a 'tip off point' (Phillips and Smith 2008) at which cosmopolitan dispositions are likely to begin to develop. Doing so is a highly worthwhile endeavour. Higher education graduates will go on to participate in, and ultimately lead, heterogeneous communities. If their experience of higher education can give them 'the skills of inter-culturality' (Rizvi 2005: 9), the ability to appreciate diversity (Hannerz 1990: 239) and proficiency in engaging with difference with mutual understanding and respect, they may be able to lead their communities to overcome the distrust that is so often found in heterogeneous contexts. Such an outcome would not only enable higher education institutions to 'serve broader, more progressive aims' (Rizvi 2004: 36) but would also fulfil the ultimate wishes of cosmopolitans everywhere and greatly enhance the likelihood of establishing 'planetary conviviality' (Mignolo 2000: 721).

4   In search of a global education

Introduction

As previous chapters have established, it is inevitable that many nuances of graduates' work and lives will be pervaded by global forces. This is the case regardless of whether they choose to criss-cross the globe or to remain in their home town. Preparing students for this reality requires higher education institutions to assist students to gain a certain set of skills and competencies. These need to enable them to function successfully in a global context and include elements such as cultural awareness, flexibility and adaptability. Governments and societies are increasingly recognising that global competencies are an important aspect of graduate skills. And many higher education institutions refer to some variation on global competencies in their graduate attributes.

Many would suggest that if higher education students need to be prepared for global lives there is no better way than to spend time abroad. For those with the financial means to do so, nothing speaks more eloquently of global competencies than mobility across national borders. Whether a student wishes to study abroad for their entire degree, or simply undertake an exchange programme for a portion of it, a plethora of options exist to satisfy this demand. Thus the concept of 'international education' has grown into a powerful, and lucrative, industry that promises to give students something that is of increasing value in a globalised world. Among policy makers there is significant faith in the power of international mobility to shape the hearts and minds of students and to impact the choices they make in their careers (Lincoln Commission 2005; Rammell in Fielden et al. 2007).

In this chapter the rhetoric and reality of international student mobility is unpacked to evaluate the benefits that accrue to mobile students. Empirical evidence on the most vaunted gains from international mobility – linguistic skills and enhanced employability – is examined to establish the veracity of these claims. Assumptions about the power of international mobility to provide society with graduating students equipped with global competencies are questioned. And the practical limitations of using international mobility as a means for higher education institutions to ensure students gain global

In search of a global education 45

competencies are teased out. The chapter concludes with considerations of alternatives to international mobility. Drawing on the cosmopolitan canon it discusses other ways in which higher education institutions can help students to prepare to be active global citizens and transnational professionals.

What drives student mobility?

Almost all discussions of international education relate to student mobility. There is something reassuringly tangible about students moving between countries. It is both comprehensible and quantifiable, ticking a number of boxes for governments, institutions, students and employers as a proxy for global skills. As a consequence there is an ever-growing profusion of study abroad, student exchange and international study opportunities. These vary greatly in scope and length, ranging from a week's experience in a foreign country to an entire degree taken overseas. The uptake of opportunities for international mobility has been enormous. As was noted in an earlier chapter, in 2012 more than 4.5 million students were enrolled in tertiary education outside their home country (OECD 2014a). This represents a significant phenomenon, one that is set to become even more widespread in coming decades. There is an extensive literature on student mobility (see, for example, Brooks and Waters 2009; Gürüz 2008; Varghese 2008; Williams and Balaz 2009). King et al. (2010) provide a comprehensive summary. Much of the focus on international mobility is on its financial benefit for institutions and also its impact on graduate employability. In Australia, for example, international students were estimated to have contributed AU$15 billion to the economy in 2012, positioning education as Australia's fourth largest export (Group of Eight Australia 2014). For higher education institutions, the fees from international students have become essential revenue. Research undertaken with Australian higher education leaders (Richardson 2010) indicates the importance of fees to the very existence of many institutions. As one institutional leader interviewed for the research suggested, fees paid by international students have become 'the essential source of income for universities', adding that these fees are 'in fact paying for everyone else's education, they're subsidising everybody else'. The focus on student mobility as a vital source of revenue is compelling and generates easy headlines. But the danger of viewing student mobility from a trade and finance perspective is that its social and cultural importance is underemphasised.

The benefit for students of international mobility is often similarly couched in economic terms. The oft-repeated rationale is that students are globally mobile in order to enhance their employment prospects (Gürüz 2008). This approach focuses on global capitalism and views students as rational economic agents. As graduate numbers grow the competition faced by students is increasingly intense (Byrne 2005; Strathdee 2005; Weenink 2007). In order to identify worthy recruits, employers are looking for more than an average degree. For those with sufficient financial capital, international study can be

46 *In search of a global education*

used to signify that graduates have gained a superior education. Students (or their parents) view international study as prestigious and look to enhance quality, reputation and employment prospects after graduation (Abubakar et al. 2010; Bennett and Ali-Choudhury 2009; Chen 2008; Clayton et al. 2012; Hemsley-Brown 2012; Lee 2008; Pampaloni 2010; Shanka et al. 2005). As such, 'some graduates become more equal than others' (Kivinen and Ahola 1999: 196). The basic underlying assumption is that physical movement, specifically physical movement across national boundaries, gives mobile students a benefit that is not available to their place-bound peers.

But humans are more complex than economists would have us believe and the motivations that underlie student mobility are more intricate than these explanations suggest. Much of this oversight comes about through an overly narrow conception of globalisation and its impacts. It is certainly true that the ability to be globally mobile has become a signifier of status (Rizvi 2005). It is also true that the power of English as the dominant language of global trade and diplomacy ensures that the desire to enhance English language skills is a significant driver of international education, one that reflects the legacy of colonialism (Rizvi and Lingard 2006; Rizvi et al. 2006). But it is important to go beyond explanations that fail to consider alternative aspirations. It is important to take into account other imperatives, motivations, advantages and costs that are involved in the choice to undertake an international education. As emphasised in this book, globalisation has not simply led to a restructuring of the economic sector but has intensified the movement of people around the world. Its physical expression is to be found in the everyday practices and interactions of individuals. Many of the reasons underscoring students' desire to study internationally are social in origin and expression. Indeed, Li et al. (1996) suggest that international student mobility is about 'learning to migrate'.

To inform understanding of international education as experienced by students it is important to collect empirical data. The data used here come from survey research with both undergraduate and postgraduate students at four Australian higher education institutions (Richardson 2010). All students were in the faculties of commerce, selected due to the very high proportions of international students enrolled. All four institutions were located in the city of Melbourne but varied significantly, from an elite institution in a leafy campus to an 'international campus' located in a city skyscraper. The 627 students research participants in the population held citizenship in 47 countries, with students from China, then India and then Australia the most numerous. Those students with international student visas were asked why they had chosen to study in Australia and out of a range of options, including cost, academic standards, career enhancement, improving English skills and gaining permanent residency, the multicultural nature of Australian society was selected most frequently, with 85 per cent of respondents agreeing that this was an important factor.

Digging a little deeper, it becomes clear that the multicultural nature of Australian society was deemed particularly important by students from India and China. Both countries are large sources of migrants to Australia. This finding is thus indicative of the importance of diaspora in mobility. Students are choosing both to leave behind their country of origin and also to move towards those who are from it. This indicates one of the important social drivers behind student mobility – pre-existing social connections. A number of students referred to relatives living in Australia, indicating a form of chain migration (Johnston et al. 2006; Omelaniuk 2005). Chains, or social networks, are crucial in the dissemination of information and often provide active encouragement to follow. Thus international education becomes a form of cultural circulation, with students entering into a cultural context that is outside their experience but also finding themselves part of a pre-existing cosmopolitan expression (Malcomson 1998).

This apparent contradiction is an essential element of cosmopolitan reality (Beck 2006). It is possible that students who arrive into established diaspora retreat into what Appiah (2006: 103) terms 'pockets of homogeneity'. But alternatively, diaspora help students to develop a 'broader sense of "we"' (Putnam 2007: 139). Thus students learn that they do not need to throw off former allegiances in order to make new ones (Himmelfarb 1996). This is an indication of the need for humans to combine the constituent parts of their identities (Appiah 1998). Crucially, to gain cosmopolitan sensibilities, individuals do not need to cast off their loyalties but to extend them. They need to be adept at balancing transnational attachments, identities and social networks (Anthias 2006; Hollinger 2006; Nava 2007; Ossman 2007). By engaging with diaspora, students find that culture exists along a continuum. They are developing the ability to maintain multiple loyalties and cultural understandings (Kuhling and Keohane 2007) while stretching out the richness of their identities (Singh et al. 2007). They are experiencing lives that transcend multiculturalism.

Some of the respondents in the study indicated that the chance of gaining permanent residency in Australia (at the time a reasonably straightforward process after graduating from an Australian institution) was an important reason for study in Australia. This does not necessarily imply a permanent move, however. As one respondent stated, 'Australia is just a stop-over destination to something else'. This suggests a multi-mobility perspective on their future lives and echoes research by Rizvi (2005) that finds that intentions among students towards mobility are highly heterogeneous. Thus the possibility of gaining permanent residency in Australia represents an investment in a world characterised by what Beck (2002: 63) terms 'fundamentally ambivalent contingencies, complexities, uncertainties and risks'.

Enhancing employability

If the drivers of student mobility are highly nuanced, so too are the outcomes of cross-border movements. Language learning and enhanced employability are two of the most commonly referred to benefits of international mobility.

48 In search of a global education

Perhaps the most well-known programme for student mobility is the European Union's Erasmus programme, with the acronym standing for European Community Action Scheme for the Mobility of University Students, although mobility is actually only one component. The size and reach of Erasmus means that it is an ideal case study for the outcomes of mobility. And all evidence points to these being mediated by a complex series of interactions. Since 1987, almost 3 million European students have participated in Erasmus, with the programme having grown to encompass more than 4,000 higher education institutions in 33 countries. German, Spanish, Italian and French students comprise 55 per cent of all students who have participated in the Erasmus programme since its inception and continue to dominate to the present day (European Commission 2013b). In the 2010–2011 academic year the most popular destinations were these same four countries, plus the UK (European Commission 2013c). The popularity of the UK as a destination is demonstrative of the power and importance of the English language in defining global success in the contemporary world (Rodríguez González et al. 2011).

European policy makers regard student mobility as an important means of developing a trans-European skilled labour force, encouraging links, connections and a greater likelihood of working internationally during a graduate's career (Maiworm 2001; Rodríguez González et al. 2011). Politically, Erasmus is regarded as one of the most successful elements of EU policy (Altbach and Teichler 2001) and student mobility has thus gained widespread acceptance (van der Wende 2001). There is no doubt that for many European students the opportunity to study in another European country is invaluable. And this benefit also extends to students in countries such as Turkey (Tekin and Hiç Gencer 2013). As a European citizen myself, and one who benefited from the opportunity to gain a postgraduate degree in another European country from the one in which I was raised (albeit not under the auspices of the Erasmus programme), the benefits are not something I wish to downplay. Much of the rhetoric around Erasmus is about creating an elite trans-European workforce with appropriate skills to contribute to greater cohesion and cooperation within the European Union. This assumes both that mobility is something that employers value, and also that a certain skill set is gained from mobility. The scale and policy importance of Erasmus ensures that significant data have been collected on its impact on participating students sufficient to support or refute these assumptions. It is clear that many of those who participate in Erasmus do have employment outcomes that are indeed better than average students (Bracht et al. 2006). Crucially, however, students who participate in Erasmus are anything but average students. Thus, the unit of comparison is an essential element of this argument.

There is clear evidence that students who participate in Erasmus are from middle and upper-middle class backgrounds, relying on parental support to supplement the grants they receive (House of Lords 2011; Souto Otero and

McCoshan 2006). There is nothing about Erasmus that is particularly unusual in this regard. In a comprehensive study on student mobility around the world, King et al. (2010: 27) conclude that the evidence for social privilege as a determinant of student mobility is 'persuasive, even overwhelming'. The requirement for private economic capital to enable mobility, or to supplement any grants available, ensures that the majority of mobile students are from relatively wealthy backgrounds. Due to the high socioeconomic status of participants in Erasmus, it is difficult to use statistics on employment to demonstrate enhanced outcomes unless relevant groups for comparison are used. In the absence of these data, alternative approaches are required. A valuable perspective comes from employers. There are numerous claims that internationally mobile students are regarded preferentially by employers (Fielden et al. 2007; King et al. 2010). While this is a widely held belief, empirical evidence of the impact of mobility on employment is actually quite rare. A major European Union investigation found evidence that while there is some 'general' attraction of mobility to employers, this is not as much as students expect, with the employment opportunities of former Erasmus students not noticeably better than students who have not participated in Erasmus (Bracht et al. 2006).

Moreover, data suggest that employers do not value international mobility for its own sake, but for what it represents, and then only when it is relevant to a particular field of work. This is confirmed by a Finnish study (Garam 2005: 6) that finds that 'international skills and abilities are not an undivided whole that is either valued or not by employers'. For example the research finds that Finnish public sector employers tend to value international abilities and attitudes while language skills are regarded with more weight by the private sector. Crucially, the interpretation that employers place on experiences of international mobility is filtered through the activities of the employer and the domain of employment. Companies with international dealings view international mobility and linguistic ability as important in employing graduates (Archer and Davison 2007; Fielden et al. 2007). Thus they may view mobile students as being 'active, courageous and open-minded' (Garam 2005: 7). Mobility seems to be a particular advantage for business, management and social science graduates, or for those who wish to have an academic career (Brooks et al. 2012). This is only the case, however, if applicants are able to explain their motivation for, and experience of, study abroad and its connection to their area of study. As the head of the Association of Graduate Recruiters in the UK explains, 'the value that employers will put on it depends on how the graduates themselves articulate the added value that overseas study has given them' (Fielden et al. 2007: 15).

Garam (2005) finds that employers are unimpressed by what amounts to little more than 'academic tourism'. Furthermore place-bound organisations can view international experience as irrelevant to their operations, viewing mobile students as restless and having difficulty staying in any one place (Archer and Davison 2007; Garam 2005). In addition, a degree from another

50 *In search of a global education*

Western country is not necessarily as valued as a domestic degree (Brooks et al. 2012). Overall it would seem that for some students who participate in Erasmus, as in other forms of international mobility, employment prospects are enhanced, while for others they are not. And it is likely that this pattern is equally true of mobile students around the world. Hence, enhancing employability is something that can be done without the need to study in another country.

Linguistic gains

If enhanced employability is not necessarily an outcome of international student mobility, then the other much-lauded benefit is the ability to gain language skills. This is based on two assumptions, first that mobile students go to a country in which the dominant language is other than the one in which they are most proficient. Second, that they undertake their studies in the language of the country in which they are studying. Both of these are questionable assumptions. Patterns of circulation in the Erasmus programme do suggest that gaining proficiency in another major European language is an important element of this programme, and this is something that makes sense in a common European market. For example King et al. (2010) highlight that the largest groups of UK students who participate in Erasmus are enrolled in language degree programmes. Outside of Erasmus, however, the dominant patterns are language acquisition in some cases but language reinforcement in others.

Certainly, the desire to improve English language skills is very important in shaping international student mobility. English proficiency is important in the contemporary world not only for gaining employment but also for social interaction (Crystal 2003). As more and more interaction goes online, it is informative to note that 28.6 per cent of those who use the internet do so in English, making English by far the most dominant internet language (Internet World Stats 2014b). This means that to communicate across national boundaries, English is often required. Moreover, English is in widespread use in elite global networks and in fields such as business, research, politics and law, and thus facilitates access to these networks (Grewal 2008). As people move around the world in ever-increasing numbers, English maintains its dominance. In many cases it is the only way in which people from diverse cultural backgrounds with mutually incomprehensible languages can communicate with each other. The inability to speak English proficiently hinders individuals who wish to emancipate themselves from local ties. And as Bauman (1998: 2) suggests, 'being local in a globalised world is a sign of social deprivation and degradation', while mobility signifies success.

Many of the students who cross borders to study in English language-speaking countries already speak very good English, however. For example students from countries such as India, Malaysia and Singapore are likely to already speak good English as a result of British colonial rule. Despite this,

In search of a global education 51

a desire to improve their English skills remains an important motivating factor in their decision to study in an English language-speaking country (Richardson 2010). This reflects the existence of different 'Englishes' around the world. For example, English speakers in Singapore or Malaysia refer to 'Singlish' (Ho 2006), and those in Hindi-speaking areas of India to 'Hinglish' (Bamgbose 2001). These variants reflect a language that has thrived due to its ability to adapt and change, becoming the third most-spoken first language in the world (after Chinese and Spanish) and also perhaps the most widely spoken second language in the world (Lewis et al. 2013).

Beyond a desire to enhance already existing language skills, language is also a strong predictor of mobility patterns. The US hosts the largest number of international students, with more than 700,000 in 2011 (OECD 2013). Three of the six countries in which international students comprise more than 10 per cent of all tertiary enrolments are also English speaking (Australia, New Zealand and the UK). The dominance of English as a global language is certainly important in shaping these patterns. It is also important among English speakers. Indeed, among students for whom English is the dominant language in their country of origin, the attraction of English-speaking countries continues to dominate mobility patterns. In illustration, consider five English language-speaking countries in the Organisation for Economic Co-operation and Development (OECD) – Australia, Canada, Ireland, UK and the US. More than 60 per cent of students from each of these countries who studied abroad in 2011 studied in one of the other four countries in the group, with this percentage rising to 87 per cent of Canadian students and 91 per cent of Irish students.

English is not the only language for which these patterns can be seen. The fourth of the six countries with more than 10 per cent international students is France, with almost two-thirds of international students coming from Africa and Asia, reflecting the power of former colonial ties and, once again, language (OECD 2013). The fifth and sixth are Austria and Switzerland, in both of which more than 70 per cent of international students come from European countries (with more than 50 per cent from France, Germany or Italy). A further example is Russia, the destination of large proportions of those students from Armenia, Azerbaijan, Belarus, Kazakhstan, Kyrgyzstan, Tajikistan, Turkmenistan, Ukraine and Uzbekistan who study abroad. There are obvious practical reasons for these patterns. Remaining close enough to home to enable regular visits, comparability of curricula (and hence recognition of study points), ease of obtaining visas, reductions to the cost of study, the availability of scholarships, and so on. What these patterns do mean, however, is that when students study abroad they do so either to improve their English skills, or in a country in which the dominant language is one with which they are already extremely familiar. The dominance of English as a global language, particularly in commerce and politics, makes the former pattern inevitable. The latter pattern opens questions about the linguistic pay-off of student mobility. The other assumption – that students tend to

52 *In search of a global education*

study abroad in the language of that country – is also flawed. Study in the English language is possible in a large number of countries. As research from the USA suggests, 'many American students are pursuing English-taught degrees in countries where English is not the official language' (Belyavina et al. 2013), citing the fact that more than 5,700 English-taught masters courses are available in European countries other than the UK and Ireland. Similar patterns are found in Asia (Gill and Kirkpatrick 2013) and Dapous (2012) refers to the 'exponential growth of English-taught programmes'.

Overall, these indications suggest that international mobility can no more be associated with linguistic gains than with enhanced mobility. Certainly, some students do improve their skills in a second or third language. But many travel abroad to study in their first language, or at least one in which they are already highly conversant. And while studying a language is made easier in a country in which it is the lingua franca, there is no need for mobility to gain proficiency in another language.

Social benefits

If international mobility does not necessarily lead to enhanced employability or to expanded language skills, surely it must benefit societies as a whole by enabling higher education institutions to produce graduates with high-level global skills? The problem with this notion is that the elite nature of mobility ensures that its benefits only extend to a small proportion of graduates. As such, international mobility reproduces, intensifies and entrenches social differences among graduates (Marginson and van der Wende 2007; Waters 2012). The importance of social segmentation in graduate employment cannot be overestimated. In a model proposed by Findlay et al. (2012: 121), graduates are vertically segmented into the transnational elite at the top, then the national managerial class and then other professional employees. The trajectory from elite secondary education to world-class tertiary education to the top of the graduate hierarchy is clear, while those from standard secondary education move to mass higher education institutions and then the bottom of the hierarchy in terms of professional status. As Christie (2007) reports, students from working class backgrounds are more likely to live at home and attend local higher education institutions. Depending on the calibre of institution available, this puts them at risk of being trapped in the lower echelons of graduate careers.

The search for superior higher education means that mobile students rarely direct their gaze beyond Western institutions. Many have previous experiences of mobility that influence their choice of destinations. For example, there is evidence that more than 40 per cent of British students studying abroad have previously lived in a country other than the UK (Findlay et al. 2012). Others may have experienced mobility through school activities such as a school exchange. Such activities tend to be concentrated among the more elite secondary schools (Findlay et al. 2012). The focus on Western education means that Asian higher education institutions are only just beginning to be seen as valid choices. This is partly because there is an added element of cultural capital to be gained from studying in a Western institution, regardless of where in the world someone originates; cultural capital that resonates in elite transnational society and that sets up those who possess it for elite careers (Deem et al. 2008).

For students whose elite status might have been expected to provide them with access to the top institutions in their country of origin, intense competition for places may lead mobility to be viewed as a fall-back position. For example, Brooks and Waters (2009) find that many British students who choose to enrol in overseas institutions do so because they have not been admitted to Oxford or Cambridge universities. Despite being able to enrol at other high-quality institutions in the UK, the highly stratified higher education sector and graduate employment market leads students to consider that overseas study would represent better compensation. When students participate in exchange schemes they tend to come from elite institutions. Fielden et al. (2007) find that British students who study abroad tend to be from institutions with higher entry grades and a stronger research emphasis, generally the 'pre-1992' elite institutions. This is partly because these institutions take in a higher proportion of students from elite secondary schools than other institutions, schools in which language teaching tends to be emphasised above that in less elite schools. Hence, more students are linguistically flexible and open to study overseas.

Conclusion

As we have seen, international student mobility is much valued by policy makers and institutional leaders. But simplistic claims about the importance of mobility for enhanced employability, language skills and broader social benefits do not stand up to careful scrutiny. Mobility tends to be socially exclusive, providing opportunities to elite students to enhance their distinctiveness from other students but remaining inaccessible to many. While some employers may value mobility, there is no guarantee that mobility enhances employability, with the value of student mobility to employers determined by the type of work and the type of mobility students undertake. And student mobility does not necessarily extend students' language skills as they tend to study in either their mother tongue or in a language with which they are already familiar.

For those who already partake in mobility as students, and for the parents who likely fund that movement, these conclusions are unlikely to be of concern. Elite patterns become self-perpetuating, and for particular social groups in many countries study abroad has become an expected pathway to adulthood. For the majority of non-mobile higher education students, however, the suggestion that mobility is not as advantageous as it is often made out to be should be reassuring. In learning to be a global human, in

54   *In search of a global education*

gaining a broader sense of us (to paraphrase Putnam 2007), in expanding their identities to encompass diversity and in learning to live in a contingent and uncertain world, students do not need to be physically mobile. As such, this opens up new opportunities. Most of all, it calls on institutions and policy makers to turn their attention away from a myopic focus on movement as the holy grail in helping students to gain a global ethos. Instead, a holistic approach that focuses on what can be achieved in place-bound education is encouraged. This turns the attention of institutions towards the classroom, lecture hall or tutorial space, with a need to find ways to inculcate cosmopolitan assets in the everyday practice of institutions.

But this does not mean that mobility should be abandoned, simply reconsidered. Rather than focusing on the physical dimension of mobility, we instead need to shift our attention to the affective element of mobility. As Papatsiba (2005) suggests, the espoused benefits from mobility do not derive from the act of crossing borders but instead from two other factors. First, the encounters that students have. And second, the influence on their psychological make-up of responding to these encounters. This suggests a realm of mobility that transcends the physical. One of the factors that causes employers to maintain a degree of caution towards the gains from mobility for individual students is that mobility is not experienced in a uniform manner. This is partly due to the circumstances in which mobility is conducted, and partly due to the psychological make-up of the individuals concerned. Some students may choose to take social risks when they have the opportunity of mobility. They may specifically choose to place themselves in an unfamiliar environment. They may select a mobility experience in which they are required to fall back on their own ability to cope with uncertainty, strangeness, novelty and a degree of dissonance. They may go out of their way to avoid contact with those from a similar background to themselves. They may search out a context in which their lack of proficiency in a language means that they will spend much of their time in a fog of confusion.

For these types of students mobility can yield enormous dividends, including insights into hitherto unknown contexts. In these circumstances students are well able to demonstrate that they are comfortable to step outside their comfort zone, to engage in risk taking and adaptation, to take social risks. Above all, they can show their propensity and aptitude for social and psychological mobility. But how much student mobility is characterised in this way? How many mobile students choose to go to a country similar to their own in which a language they are fluent in is spoken? How many students select an institution to where many of their peers are also bound? How many students will spend their mobility seeking out the familiar and the comfortable? This is an approach to mobility that does not demonstrate an interest in stepping outside their comfort zone. It fails to indicate that students are able to take risks or to adapt to unfamiliar contexts. It shows neither a desire for social and psychological mobility, nor the capacity to engage in it.

Some forms of mobility could be encompassed by the first description and others by the latter, although in reality many mobility experiences probably fall somewhere between the two. What this does illustrate, however, is that much of the value that mobility can offer is a consequence of the orientation of an individual student toward the experience. Hence this suggests that an emphasis on learning experiences that challenge students' assumptions about the world around them can help them to gain cosmopolitan assets without the need for mobility to do so. The following chapter explores what happens when students are placed in an environment in which engagement with difference is required, and examines the range of responses they demonstrate. And it then indicates the necessary constituents of a cosmopolitan education.

5 Learning to become part of the global tribe

Introduction

Thus far the book has considered the changing context for which students need to be prepared and a relevant theoretical underpinning to inform educational approaches. It has also been shown that although mobility may yield certain dividends to those who experience it, claims about its transformative potential are somewhat overstated. This opens up the potential for helping students gain cosmopolitan attributes without the need for physical mobility. Instead, we need to move our attention to the affective elements of mobility and this calls for a focus on how international education at home could be implemented. Before this is explored, however, it is first important to consider students' perceptions of the skills and attributes they need to gain or enhance during their higher education studies.

This chapter draws on two pieces of research with Australian higher education students to investigate their responses to studying in an international environment. It considers their experiences and the patterns of social connections that arise. It then goes on to reflect on the conditions required to build connections with those unlike ourselves in an environment in which social risk is prevalent. Finally, the chapter concludes with a consideration of the key elements that comprise a cosmopolitan education.

Students' hopes for international education

What do contemporary higher education students need and want to gain from their higher education? To what extent are they aware of the global nature of the world that they need to be prepared for? What do they think that their institutions should be doing to help them achieve desired outcomes? The only way to answer these questions is to ask students to express their own thoughts. In this section data from a small empirical study are used (Richardson 2010). The study used a convenient sample of first- and second-year higher education students at an Australian higher education institution. No claim is made for generalisability of these results. Instead, they should be seen as a snapshot in time of the attitudes of a particular

Learning to become part of the global tribe 57

group of students towards their experience. Nevertheless, the themes they raise are of relevance to the discussion here. And they come from students who are experiencing international education first hand.

In the contemporary world, Australia is the ideal context in which to consider the ways in which international education plays out. In 2013, 25 per cent of higher education students in Australia were classified as 'international' (Department of Education and Training 2014). Moreover, in some fields of study and in some institutions, international students make up more than 45 per cent of all students. This situation has evolved out of the confluence of a number of social, political and economic forces. These include a concern post-World War II about communism reaching Australia through Southeast Asia (Oakman 2004), growing diplomatic and trade engagement between Australia and countries in the Asia-Pacific, and increasing social and cultural diffusion through Australia's active migration programme. The impact has been significant.

Inevitably the presence of more than 300,000 international students in the Australian higher education sector, a sector with a total of just 1.3 million students overall, is significant. The 'default' international education experienced by those students who attend higher education institutions in which international students make up a large proportion of the student body should not be understated. Opportunities for default international education are particularly pronounced when the local population is already highly diverse, as occurs in countries with long histories of migration such as Australia. 'Local' students attending Australian higher education institutions are among the most diverse on the planet, reflecting a population characterised by a high degree of cultural differentiation. Many Australians have what Nederveen-Pieterse (2004) terms 'mélange identities'. Migration continues to this day with net overseas migration of almost 300,000 in 2008–2009 (Australian Bureau of Statistics 2013a).

In this context a short survey was disseminated to 350 first-year undergraduate students at the University of Melbourne in October 2005. All students were enrolled in the first-year subject 'Global Politics'. This subject was specifically chosen for two reasons. First, it had the highest enrolment of any subject being taught in the Faculty of Arts at that time, which gave access to a large group of potential respondents. Second, given the subject matter being taught, it was hoped that students would have an ability to comment on international education through a global lens. Surveys were disseminated via educators for students to complete and return to the departmental office, along with consent forms. A total of 186 survey forms were returned, a response rate of 53 per cent. Of the respondents, 153 identified themselves as local students, indicating that they were Australian citizens or permanent residents and 33 as international students, indicating that they held international student visas. Of the respondents, 52 per cent were female and 48 per cent were male. Students were asked to provide responses to a number of open and closed questions. They were asked to estimate the proportion of

58 *Learning to become part of the global tribe*

students in their classes that were international students and were then asked about the advantages and disadvantages of having international students at their institution. They were also asked what their institution should do to integrate international and local students, and to comment on any ways in which the institution should become more international by the time they graduated. All comments are verbatim.

Results showed that on the whole students were impressed by the multicultural atmosphere that they experienced on campus, citing this as the greatest advantage of the presence of international students. Students were clear on the advantages of the 'opportunity to meet people from different places' for both social and career reasons. Many students reported the social benefits that they gained from studying alongside students from a range of backgrounds. This included the enjoyment in 'meeting and making contacts with international and new people', the ability to make 'worldwide friends' and having 'friends to visit overseas'. Beyond friendships, a number of students mentioned the opportunities that existed for 'overseas networking' and the sense that 'creating a broader network' and 'making good contacts around the world' will 'help in my career' and 'allow me to work in a diverse environment in my career in the future'. One of the major benefits that a number of students felt would assist them in future work environments was the opportunity to enhance their communication skills. As one respondent reflected, they were 'learning the ability to communicate technical ideas to people with which I have variable ability to communicate'. The ability to communicate well across national and cultural differences was seen by many students to be essential 'in this era of globalisation'. As several students made clear, they understood the need to equip themselves with skills that would enable them to function in contexts of great heterogeneity, and one explained that studying alongside students from other countries 'enhances sensitivity of students that will eventually come across such multi-ethnic and multi-cultural situations in their working life etc. in today's globalised world'.

Beyond personal relationships, they viewed an advantage in exposure to different perspectives. An element of the 'multicultural learning' environment in which students found themselves was the opportunity to learn that there is more than one way of looking at any given issue and many respondents emphasised the 'different perspectives on issues discussed' that they encountered. One benefit that students highlighted was that it is simply 'interesting to get different views on issues'. Many students found the range of perspectives to be a really enjoyable aspect of their studies, with one commenting that it is 'fantastic to get a more worldly view through international students' opinions and stories'. Others felt that they were gaining the ability to be able to 'think out of the box' and to learn that 'different thought processes can lead to different solutions to the same problem'. Several respondents commented on ways in which the ability to incorporate a range of perspectives would 'help in future if doing business internationally' and thus 'helps you throughout the career'. Other students focused on the broader social benefits such as the 'finishing of blatant ignorance' or that it 'promotes tolerance'. Others simply reflected that exposure to a range of perspectives 'adds to education experience' and 'makes a university diverse'. As one respondent commented: 'It creates the opportunity to hear a variety of perspectives when discussing political and moral issues rather than being limited to one's own mind-set that is influenced largely by the country in which the person grew up'.

Not all students were convinced of the benefits, however. There were a number of references to segregation between students from different backgrounds (a theme explored in more depth below). And a number of students pointed to the contrast between the theoretical advantages of being part of a multicultural student body and the inability of educators or the institution to realise these in their everyday practices. Nevertheless, overall students emphasised the connection between the multicultural student body and growing 'global interdependence'. Students referred to the need to 'embrace diversity', which involves an 'acceptance of others' and 'adaptability'. As one explained:

> I think it is important to have a wide variety of students with different backgrounds at the university. Diversity should promote tolerance and it provides Australian students like myself with an opportunity to ask questions of students with different cultural perspectives, and how they view our society.

Overall, these comments suggest that the students surveyed had an acute intellectual understanding of the need to engage with students different to themselves from around the world. This does not necessarily translate into behaviour that leads to actual engagement, however. Most of the students' comments were about exchanging views and making social contacts. This is very much at the level of Hopper's (2006) 'parochial cosmopolitans', dabbling in difference (Vertovec and Cohen 2002) but not considering the need for deeper change. This suggests that a challenge for higher education institutions is to leverage the willingness to learn from students different to themselves that exists among some of their student body in order to achieve powerful outcomes. Thus, the following section includes consideration of a second study of Australian higher education students, one that looked in more depth at the social connections they reported developing during their experience of international education.

Lived experiences of international education

The discourse of international education is premised on the added value that accrues to those who study in an international environment. Clearly this is not due to the quality of the air they breathe in, but comes down to tangible, lived experiences. If students are to truly enjoy an international education,

60 *Learning to become part of the global tribe*

one that renders cosmopolitan attributes, it is essential that they practice certain skills. Deep engagement with others unlike themselves is a core element of this learning, perhaps more so than the formal curriculum. Whether they are students who have chosen to study outside of their home country or students experiencing a default international education, interactions with those unlike themselves are a vital part of the experience. The heterogeneous environment of contemporary higher education institutions provides an opportunity for cosmopolitan practices to be 'formed, instilled or bolstered' (Vertovec and Cohen 2002: 21). Hannerz (1990: 245) terms sites such as higher education institutions 'bridgeheads' for this reason. For this to be achieved, however, there is a need to consider the practices that are most likely to lead to successful outcomes. In this section the social connections between students from different backgrounds are explored to chart the social connections which they choose to make.

Grayson (2004) describes the passage of a student through a higher education institution as involving the enhancement of their existing skills, knowledge and personality with additional skills and knowledge as well as new social contacts. The students inevitably bring with them a host of socially conditioned behaviours, beliefs and predilections that govern the ways in which they interact with their new environments and peers. Students enter into a number of spaces during their higher education. The first of these focuses on the formal curriculum in which they attend lectures and tutorials, experience various forms of teaching, work their way through the prescribed academic curriculum and interact with their classmates. Increasingly, much of this is mediated by online modes. The second space is found outside of class where students have the opportunity to join clubs and societies, play sports, meet for coffee, attend parties and other social events, and interact with their peers. If students undertake long hours of paid work their ability to engage in either of these spaces is curtailed. But they are forced to engage with the third space, that of the institution, which determines who is able to access higher education, as well as modelling the environment in which social activities and learning take place.

Much of the focus of the higher education experience is on the learning that students experience in order to gain their desired degree. This is regarded as an essential stepping stone towards their career and future success. But it is important to acknowledge the importance of the social connections that they make at the same time. These are valuable in two ways, first in what students learn from them and second in their inherent value. Putnam (2004) argues that the learning that students gain from their peers is greater than that from formal teaching. This suggests that if students are to gain cosmopolitan attributes during their higher education studies then their interactions with their peers are absolutely vital. Furthermore, social connections represent powerful resources and Lin (2001: 21) considers that 'social resources far outweigh personal resources in their potential usefulness to individuals'. Leveraging the insights of Putnam and Lin, and

Learning to become part of the global tribe 61

without delving too deeply into the social capital literature, it might be considered that students can gain important attributes that will set them in good stead for their future lives from interacting with their peers. In a multicultural student body the choices that students make about who they interact with are thus of great significance in determining their outcomes. Exploring their social connections in the higher education space can therefore tell us a great deal about the potential for the development of cosmopolitan attributes.

Before moving to consider the connections between students from different backgrounds, it is worth unpacking the labels 'local' and 'international' in relation to students in the study. The limitations of these labels are particularly emphasised in a multicultural context such as that found in Australia. Despite the continuing domination of a white public, Australia's population base is becoming increasingly diverse. More than a quarter of the Australian population were born overseas (Australian Bureau of Statistics 2013b), and 20 per cent speak a language other than English at home (Australian Bureau of Statistics 2012). Consequently, the student bodies of Australian higher education institutions are already highly international, before any of the students classified as 'international' are counted. In illustration, an analysis of the total student intake of one Australian institution in 2005 was undertaken (Richardson 2010). Of 10,457 commencing students, 28 per cent were classified as 'international' and 72 per cent 'local'. 'International' students held citizenship in 100 countries, had been born in 90 countries and spoke 76 first languages. But 'local' students were also highly diverse: they had been born in 107 countries, held citizenship in 25 countries and spoke 6 first languages. The reality of such enormous cultural diversity renders the classification of students into the categories of local and international relatively meaningless, constraining identities and underestimating diversity (Beck 2006; Falzon 2009; Puwar 2006). This diversity also suggests that for students attending Australian higher education institutions, however they are categorised, the opportunity to gain cosmopolitan attributes and to experience a truly international education should be unsurpassed. The conditions could not possibly be more optimal.

Mapping student's social connections requires acknowledging the common social situations in which contemporary students find themselves. Schemas developed for use in the past demonstrate how quickly social activities evolve. Situations defined by Bochner et al. (1977) for use in the 1970s include 'going on a picnic'. A decade later, Furnham and Alibhai (1985) listed activities including 'go to a disco or party'. Bringing these up to the present involved long discussions with students at a residential college for those from multiple cultural backgrounds (Richardson 2010). This resulted in six key activities, in rising order of intimacy: study together; meet for a coffee; go to a party; invite to your home; go on holiday; and go on a date. Although students gave a great deal of prominence to chatting online, this was excluded in order to focus on activities that involved direct, face-to-face, corporeal contact. Survey instruments were distributed to 740 undergraduate

62   *Learning to become part of the global tribe*

and postgraduate students in the faculties of commerce at four Australian higher education institutions and a response rate of 90 per cent was achieved by limiting the number of questions and encouraging students to complete them *in situ*. In the instrument students were asked to indicate which of four categories of students they *normally* did each of the six activities with. They could choose from 'someone who is from your home town or city', 'someone from a different city in the same country', 'someone from another country with a similar culture' and 'someone from another country with a different culture'. Respondents were instructed to circle as many responses as they wished.

Results were very clear – students reported that they were more likely to do all of the activities with those most similar to themselves, with this pattern becoming increasingly marked as the level of intimacy of activities rose. Even for the most neutral activity (studying together), more than half of respondents reported studying together with those from their home town or city against just 37 per cent studying with those from another country with a different culture. Overall, almost half of all students (49 per cent) reported having little contact with those from another country with a different culture. While disappointing, this result does not come as a surprise. Research from each decade of the last half-century, and across Canada, New Zealand, the USA and the UK, has found that there is significant social segregation between students from different backgrounds on higher education campuses (Bochner et al. 1977; Bochner et al. 1985; Choi 1997; Furnham and Alibhai 1985; Liberman 1994; Sawir et al. 2008; Tajfel and Dawson 1965; Trice and Elliott 1993; Zheng and Berry 1991). As Smart et al. (2000) conclude, close proximity of students from different backgrounds does not necessarily yield any more than highly superficial contact.

These findings are confirmed by institution leaders (Richardson 2010) who acknowledge the problem but are unable to suggest a solution. As one leader remarked, 'there's always been a high degree of what I call "racial cleavage" on campus ... so international students don't interact very much with local students'. Another leader suggested that 'there are these Asian kind of enclaves' and a third commented that students who come from overseas to study in Australia are frustrated at their 'inability to make friends with Australians'. In terms of solutions, most higher education leaders interviewed had good intentions, with comments such as 'we've just got to do something about it'. Ready solutions were not forthcoming, however. Several leaders commented on integration between students from different cultural backgrounds being an intractable problem, one which is almost insoluble. As one leader summarised: 'We don't do a good job at all in integrating our overseas, international student body with our domestic one. How do you do that? We've tried everything. The fact is, we don't do a good job – nobody else does, by the way'.

Students were also asked to comment on their experience of the international education environment. Many commented on there being insufficient integration between different groups of students suggesting that institutions are 'kind of multicultural but we don't seem to be engaging with those other cultures, nor them us'. Some students pointed the finger at incoming students' 'self-imposed segregation' and, inversely, others at unwelcoming Australian students. A number of students, however, suggested that higher education institutions themselves were to blame. Students suggested that their institutions failed to encourage integration between students from different backgrounds, or to organise activities that would encourage students to mix with each other. Students expressed considerable concern that by failing to create an environment that facilitated integration, higher education institutions were complicit in actually increasing the degree of segregation on campuses. As one student explained, 'there isn't a concerted effort by the university to highlight the importance of being open to interacting with different nationalities'.

Overall, the research reported here seems to indicate that the potential for students to gain or enhance cosmopolitan attributes during their studies at culturally diverse higher education institutions is unable to be optimised as a consequence of social schisms and the underlying assumptions and prejudices on which these are based. While institutions may put enormous resources into competing with each other to recruit students from other nations, they seem to struggle to find ways to ensure that their heterogeneous student bodies are fully integrated. These divisions undermine the potential that institutions embody. The opportunities that an international higher education should generate for all students to learn about difference and to appreciate a range of perspectives are stymied. And this is likely to have long-term consequences.

Risk and social connections

One of the skills increasingly valued by globally agile organisations is the ability of individuals to 'step outside their comfort zone'. While a hackneyed phrase, it is one that suggests having both the confidence and courage to place oneself in unfamiliar and challenging situations, and the capacity to handle these with poise. In other words, it indicates the willingness to take a risk and the ability to deal with the consequences. Risk taking is one of the reasons why mobility during higher education studies is so valued by institutions. It is more than the prestige of having studied at an institution with international pedigree, or of having polished English-language skills. In addition, graduates who have studied overseas are regarded as being able to provide employers with tangible evidence of their ability to put themselves in a foreign environment and cope with whatever they encounter. 'Foreign' sums up a host of differences. But while the climate, buildings and food may differ from what is familiar, the ultimate embodiment of 'foreign' is the people encountered. Thus the fundamental principle of global mobility during an international education is the opportunity for students to have sustained interactions with people unlike themselves. Risk taking is defined by the social.

64   *Learning to become part of the global tribe*

If students are to optimise what they learn from their peers, they need to take social risks. While physical mobility is only available to those students with financial means, social mobility is not similarly constrained. It is open to all students, and particularly to those who study alongside peers from different cultural backgrounds. Thus everyday encounters with others offer higher education students ample opportunities to take social risks. Of course, building connections with those from a similar cultural background does offer reassurance. But it can seriously constrain the opportunities available to students, both while they are learning and when they graduate (Woolcock and Narayan 2000). Without contact, without building up social ties and networks that cross social and cultural divisions, students miss out on the learning opportunities that abound, ones that require them to take risks. As Marginson (2014) emphasises, higher education is a critical time of self-formation in which adjustment involves students who travel internationally 'achieving harmony' with the destination country. The same can be said for social risks, in which students need to achieve harmony in interacting with those who are different to themselves as part of their process of evolution as individuals and members of a global community.

The missed potential of international education is not only important for the time in which students attend higher education institutions. If we return to Lin's (2001) contention about the importance of social resources, this suggests that the student experience of higher education is an opportunity to do something that is of equal importance to gaining a degree. The relationships students make, and connections they form, will arguably be of great significance in their future lives. When they find themselves part of a multicultural student body, the connections that students establish, and the choices that they make about who to build these connections with, have the potential to radically alter the way in which they view the world around them, and their place in it. And they may also shape the opportunities open to students after graduation. Social connections with those who are dissimilar are vital to students who wish to transcend the opportunities available to them locally. Building these requires the skills so valued by employers – critical thinking, reflexivity, active thinking and risk taking (Gurin 1999). In order for social connections which cross cultural difference to be built, however, trust is required. This means that higher education institutions need to provide the right context for trust to be built, one that encourages students from diverse backgrounds to engage in sustained social interaction.

Higher education institutions promote the ways in which gaining a degree will generate career prospects. There is overwhelming evidence from around the world that suggests that students will be disadvantaged in accessing career prospects, however, unless they have built suitable social connections during their studies (Field 2003; Franzen and Hangartner 2005; Rebick 2000; Try 2005). Moreover, there is significant evidence that if graduates rely on connections with only those similar to themselves this can disadvantage their career search (Belliveau 2005). This suggests that building connections with

Learning to become part of the global tribe   65

those different to themselves is essential for higher education students, both in enhancing their learning and in providing a kick-start to their career. Moreover, there is evidence that the value of diverse social connections continues to yield dividends throughout people's careers (James 2000).

While finding employment is an important outcome of a higher education, it is not the only one. It is essential to remember that students do not merely enhance their employability during their sojourn at a higher education institution. Instead, while working towards gaining a degree, students are mainly young adults who are in a transitional phase from reliance on their parents to independence. They are still in the process of discovering themselves and establishing their identities, and this leads them to use the interlude that their studies offer to form a range of relationships. Some of these will, indeed, be 'instrumental', giving them access to new people, new resources and new opportunities, including for employment. But others will be 'expressive' (Lin 2001). Students can choose whether their self-expression requires the reassurance of reinforcing their identities by building connections with those similar to themselves. Alternatively, they can express their ability to challenge their identities and transcend their cultural contexts. As future leaders of increasingly diverse and complex societies, students will benefit from finding ways to view the notion of identity holistically, one that encompasses a whole range of backgrounds, allegiances, cultures and ties. In order for this to occur, the social connections they make while studying are crucial.

If students are to take the risk to connect with those different to themselves, this requires a mindset that is open towards difference. A key component of making connections with others is trust. It is an essential social lubricant that enables individuals to come together for mutual gains. Generally those we trust are part of our 'moral community', while those whom we do not trust are outside of this. Evidence from studies in culturally diverse communities around the world indicates that those most likely to distrust people who are different to themselves have certain characteristics in common (Alesina and La Ferrara 2002; Glaeser et al. 2000; Hurtado et al. 1994; Rosenthal et al. 2006). First, younger people tend to be more hesitant about those who are different than those who are older. Second, women tend to be more hesitant than men in trusting those from different cultural backgrounds. Third, people from the dominant cultural group tend to be less trustful than those in minorities. Given that young women are increasingly the dominant group at higher education institutions, this indicates an even more pressing need for institutional leaders and educators to find ways to build trust between students.

The good news is that levels of trust appear to be malleable (Dinesen 2012). Social trust increases when people are part of informal social networks (Delhey and Newton 2003). It increases when institutional staff treat all individuals equally, with their behaviour regarded as indicative of the moral standards of the community (Kumlin and Rothstein 2007). Social trust also

66   *Learning to become part of the global tribe*

increases when individuals engage in shared experiences and social activities that, in turn, motivate participation in more shared experiences (Richey 2007). Higher education staff – from leaders, to administrators to educators – can influence students' experiences and behaviours in many ways. They can strive to ensure that the higher education environment – both physical and virtual – is conducive to trust and social connections across cultural differences. Given the limited time that many contemporary students spend on campus outside of class time (James et al. 2007; Rosenthal et al. 2006), however, the impact of a focus on the environment may have only limited impact.

This brings us to the importance of what happens during the formal curriculum. Research reported here indicates that students are most likely to choose to interact with those who are different from themselves during class and in other study-related activities. In these circumstances, if guided well by the educators responsible for facilitating their learning, students can begin to overcome any hesitation they may have towards those whose characteristics are different to their own. Those most reluctant may begin to view the heterogeneity around them as a resource rather than a threat. As students engage with each other they become aware of their differences and similarities, and conscious of the range of different positions and alternatives that are available to them (Strydom 2012). Forced to recognise that each other's positions are different, and may be conflicting, they can choose to focus on what is in disharmony and thus turn to feelings of enmity, conflict and dislike. Or they can consider the commonalities and instead choose to reflect on unifying factors. The choice that is made will reflect prior experience, ethics, beliefs and assumptions. The latter choice is a cosmopolitan one. Those who are already disposed towards cosmopolitan encounters can enhance the value that they gain from interacting with their peers. With appropriate guidance students are more likely to reach the 'tip-off point' of gaining cosmopolitan attributes (Phillips and Smith 2008).

Achieving this outcome means establishing the learning environment as what Anderson (2004: 18) terms a 'cosmopolitan canopy'. He defines these spaces as places where the distrust and wariness that people often display in a heterogeneous society are reduced, where differences are 'salient but understated'. Instead, communities form in which people from different backgrounds build trust for each other. In this context the differences between students are rendered less relevant and their commonalities are highlighted. Students become more open to surmounting the invisible barriers between them and to developing what Paquet (2008) terms 'a growing social sophistication'. This means that students learn that differences, while important, are not actually as profound as they may at first appear. In many ways higher education students are primed to accept these notions, with so many already having experienced realities that have prepared them to be 'intellectually invested global citizens ready for curriculum that encourages them to cultivate cosmopolitan habits of mind' (DeJaynes and Curmi 2015: 75).

As such, institutional leaders and educators are duty-bound to establish learning spaces where students can learn to understand and critically assess situations they encounter on a daily basis as well as how to engage with their peers as members of a shared global humanity. In the following chapters approaches to turning classrooms, lecture theatres, seminar rooms, laboratories, libraries and online study communities into cosmopolitan canopies are considered. Initiatives from around the world that aim to encourage students to feel sufficient trust to deconstruct social divides and to build respect and cooperation with their peers are evaluated.

Using cosmopolitan insights to inform educational practice

Returning to cosmopolitan thought it is possible to identify the components that might make up a cosmopolitan education. Nussbaum (1996: 6) suggests that students need to be taught that 'they are, above all, citizens of a world of human beings'. Beck (2006: 90–91) defines the context in which this is most likely to occur, characterised by a space in which 'seemingly sharp oppositions between "us" and "them" become blurred and a conflictual and cooperative culture of transnational openness and reconfiguration of the local arise[s]'. We can also see the relevance of Robbins' (1998: 261) comment that a cosmopolitan approach can teach us 'that there is no right place to stand' in relation to the development of a cosmopolitan education. Similarly, Mignolo (2000: 743) refers to the need for 'border thinking' in order to learn from the experiences of others. Finally, Appiah (2006: xiii) argues that the key challenge we face today is to 'take minds and hearts formed over the long millennia of living in local troops and equip them with ideas … that will allow us to live together as the global tribe that we have become'. As he goes on to affirm, this requires more than simple engagement, demanding also curiosity and intelligence. Held (2002: 57–58) calls for 'dialogue with the traditions and discourses of others' and Harvey (2009) emphasises that it is essential to take into account specific local contexts.

Cavallar (2014) draws on writing by Kant, Rousseau and Basedow to suggest that all three regard cosmopolitan education as an element of practical philosophy. In this way they see education as akin to religious education in terms of moral formation but with the religious element removed. Instead, the focus is on personal virtue that emphasises tolerance and an interest in the common good for all humans. As Cavallar (2014: 385) argues, Kant viewed the development of a cosmopolitan disposition as 'a long-term result of helping adolescents to form their own moral characters', helping them learn to act for the benefit of humanity. One means of this moral development from a 'culturalist cosmopolitan' perspective is through interaction with others different to ourselves. Papastephanou (2011: 598) highlights that this approach emphasises the need to learn about different traditions of cultures, interacting with others 'as producers of meaning and life experience

68 *Learning to become part of the global tribe*

that might be enriching of one's own or ... subjects who desire as much as we do to learn from the insights accumulated globally or ... recipients of our respect, tolerance and hospitality'.

A key theme arising from the cosmopolitan literature is the need for students to gain an understanding of the nature of multiple allegiances. This incorporates a number of key elements. First, the ability to look beyond the borders of nation states and to understand what Beck and Sznaider (2006: 21) term 'different modalities of situatedness-in-displacement'. This means transcending reductionist categories and acknowledging that identities are multifaceted, contested, hybrid and fluid, varying according to context and tied to a transnational social community. Moreover, it means recognising that cultures are not unitary and distinct but that they 'interpenetrate, interconnect and intermingle' (Beck 2006: 7). Beyond identity, this suggests that students need to gain an understanding of 'sociology of motion' (Ossman 2007: 216) and a world characterised by multiple and diverse forms of social transformation in an elevated state of flux, moving towards 'open and contingent' outcomes (Rumford 2007: 3). It incorporates an insight into the ways in which social realities are being altered and renewed (Delanty 2006), using the 'lens of the local' (Delanty and He 2008: 324) to gain an understanding of global changes, and a multidisciplinary approach that is suited to appreciating, and finding solutions to, global challenges.

Beyond the notion of multiple allegiances, the cosmopolitan literature suggests that students need to be given the opportunity to gain a cosmopolitan disposition. This is underlain by a strong belief that each human being in the world is of equal value and importance (Held 2005) without any requirement for sameness (Beck and Grande 2007) but with a refusal to value one over another (Parry 2008). In contrast to a cosmopolitan aesthetic, this calls on students to transcend a superficial engagement with unfamiliar cultures and to develop an ethical position towards difference. In this way a cosmopolitan disposition is chosen and conscious, combining thought and action and incorporating not only an awareness of ambivalences but also what Beck (2006: 3) terms a 'sceptical, disillusioned, self-critical outlook'. Instead of presupposing universally applicable values, Appiah (2006) suggests that a cosmopolitan disposition involves us in the assumption that we can learn from everyone with whom we come in contact, not only about them but also about ourselves. It is an approach that calls on us to relate to all those we meet in our homes, families, neighbourhoods, schools, workplaces and social groups with feelings of 'empathy, attraction and hospitality' (Nava 2006: 47). In this way, a cosmopolitan approach is not a lofty notion of some idealised future society but is embodied in everyday activities as a way for everyone to find common ground with those unlike themselves (Lamont and Aksartova 2002).

A further important insight from the cosmopolitan literature is that contemporary higher education students need to value the interdependence of humans everywhere. The lives we face are ones in which risk is at the

Learning to become part of the global tribe 69

forefront of human concerns. As Beck (2002: 63) suggests, we are in a situation characterised by 'fundamentally ambivalent contingencies, complexities, uncertainties and risks'. This underscores the importance of our reliance on others, making cosmopolitan approaches necessary for mainstream issues (Linklater 2006). Beck (2006: 14) explains that when we are confronted by pressing dangers, old distinctions become increasingly invalid and 'a new cosmopolitan realism becomes essential to survival'. In order to understand perils that endanger the lives of humans around the world, a cosmopolitan approach may well be the best possible response. Crucially, a cosmopolitan approach 'promotes a mediated solidarity between strangers, emerging from our shared humanity' (Paquet 2008: 84). It calls on us to recognise the extensive nature of our community and the ability to juggle multiple frames of references and perspectives.

In converting these insights into a cosmopolitan approach to higher education, it is essential that educators avoid falling into the trap of 'self-indulgence, complacency and closure' that can characterise those who regard themselves as cosmopolitan (Papastephanou 2013). Thus afflicted, there is a tendency to view non-cosmopolitans – or indeed all those with communitarian claims – as somehow inferior and to regard themselves and fellow-cosmopolitans as comprising the moral elite. This self-congratulatory trait can easily lead to an approach to education in which students are to be convinced of the value of the cosmopolitan ethos above all other approaches, closing out all other ways of viewing the world. Equally, this embodiment of a cosmopolitan ethos can render mute critiques of the theoretical underpinnings of cosmopolitan approaches and the expressions of cosmopolitanism in the individual and group. Overcoming this requires open dialogue that enables the exchange of views and that includes a willingness to learn about, and from, others. For educators this means being prepared to adopt a feeling of belonging associated with 'a deconstructive awareness of ruptures, dis-continuities, ambiguities and ambivalences' (Papastephanou 2013: 191). It means being prepared to engage with 'different assemblages of discourses and practices, habits and artifacts' in order to engage in a 'long-term project of intellectual and practical world-building' (Waks 2009: 260). Hansen et al. (2009: 590) suggest that such an approach 'helps spotlight new possibilities for creating meaning and for addressing issues peacefully ... [that] can assist people in engaging the challenges of being thrown together with others whose roots, traditions, and cultural inheritances differ'.

Hansen (2010: 159) suggests that a cosmopolitan approach to education involves us in 'ascending downward: of coming to penetrate or pay attention to local traditions more fully precisely by seeing them in juxtaposition with other traditions'. This allows students and educators to gain a sense of belonging in the world, but it can also be uncomfortable as it requires them to confront their preconceptions of how things are and how things should be. Discomfort also arises from the fact that cosmopolitan insights do not provide any answers but merely suggest that in dialogue with each other people can

70 *Learning to become part of the global tribe*

find the best way to proceed and to address the challenges they face. And it is the willingness to learn from encounters, even those they do not enjoy, that makes a cosmopolitan approach what Hansen (2013: 42) terms a 'philosophy *for* life rather than just a theoretical framework *about* life' (emphasis in original). This does not mean that a cosmopolitan approach can teach students a magical means of creating a perfect life, but that students are better equipped to deal with the complexities and challenges they will face. Hansen's (2008: 296) 'educational cosmopolitanism' is what he defines as an approach that can help students to gain 'a deepening if also at times unsettling connection with the dynamic spaces between the local and the universal'. It focuses attention on the ways in which humans make meaning in their lives and the trajectories that have led to those meanings. It helps students to find common ground and to develop new ways of understanding the differences they encounter – 'a standing back as well as a standing in' (Hansen 2008: 298). In positioning students as both subject and object, this approach to education can be unpredictable. Each student will respond in a unique way and educators need to be skilled in dealing with the non-linear evolution of students' growing awareness as they question what they encounter. For some the outcome will be the development of, or expansion of an already extant, cosmopolitan sensibility or disposition in which they transcend being spectators and instead engage in what Hansen (2008) terms 'participatory enquiry'.

With these considerations in mind, how might these concepts be translated into a framework for application in higher education practice? The British Higher Education Academy has developed an 'Internationalising Higher Education' framework. It is premised on the desire to help institutions ensure that they are 'preparing 21st century graduates to live in and contribute responsibly to a globally interconnected society' (Higher Education Academy 2014) and comprises three key components: knowledge, activities and values. While the framework itself does not go nearly far enough for the purposes of a cosmopolitan education, it is a useful starting point for considerations of a cosmopolitan framework for higher education. At the same time, a cosmopolitan framework should not be prescriptive or static, as this would fly in the face of cosmopolitan theorisations of reality. Instead students and educators need to develop it between them, expanding, enlarging and tweaking as they engage in dialogue and reflection. But what follows may provide a starting point.

In considering activities, a cosmopolitan framework would start with the need for students to engage with difference. This means recognising the diversity in their midst and valuing the number of perspectives that people bring into the learning space. Diversity does not necessarily refer to culture but could indicate any ways in which students vary from each other. Beyond acknowledging and valuing diversity, students need to be guided to recognise their positioning in particular contexts, and the ways in which it varies over space and time. As this chapter has shown, none of these are something that happens automatically or by osmosis. Instead, institutions need to ensure that

Learning to become part of the global tribe 71

their values, policies and practices create a cosmopolitan canopy in which students feel safe and supported to engage with those who are different to themselves. Equally, curricula and pedagogy need to support these endeavours, whether students interact face to face or online – something that will be discussed in the following three chapters. It is also essential that the approach taken to learning embodies a global heuristic that applies multiple perspectives to discovery and problem solving. This requires more than the odd international case study but demands instead a reconfiguration of higher education practice that explicitly draws on insights from around the globe to enrich the experience of students.

Beyond a consideration of the differences that lie within the learning environment, it is also valuable for students to gain an awareness of the diversity in the community, both local and global. A consideration of the notion of society and community and their evolution over time can help students to understand the impermanence and blurred lines of identity. Building on this, critical reflection on the way in which humans define their moral obligations towards diverse groups can help students to apprehend the complexity and contrariness of our ethical stances and to question their assumptions about the ways in which these play out. This can be enhanced by connecting students up with groups outside their immediate institution. Colleges in the United States have a tradition of service learning in which students engage in community activities and assist groups in need of help. This is one approach that could have value in prompting students to consider their positioning towards others but it is certainly not the only one. The internet opens up opportunities for students to engage with communities around the world and this makes possible a host of connections.

Existing knowledge is often presented to students as something that is value neutral but this can never be the case. The creation of knowledge inevitably involves subjective choices about what is worth knowing and which approaches to knowledge construction are valid. Certain traditions are emphasised while others are ignored or downplayed, and dominant understandings render alternative approaches mute. It is important that students are in a position to understand that what they are learning is reflective of a particular place, time and set of assumptions. In gaining this awareness they can begin to consider alternative paradigms and the value that is added when decisions are founded on the acknowledgement of diverse perspectives. It is increasingly recognised that higher education is most effective when educators work with students to create new knowledge. An understanding of the subjectivity of knowledge creation is a valuable starting point for students if they are to embark on this process themselves. Moreover, as educators guide students to create new knowledge it is vital that this incorporates critical reflection on the assumptions involved. Where possible, students should be encouraged to draw on resources and understandings from around the world to advance new concepts, and to consider the impact of advances in knowledge on different communities in diverse contexts.

72 Learning to become part of the global tribe

It is essential that a framework of cosmopolitan education is underlain by values that promote the ethical stance that cosmopolitan theorists espouse. These should encompass openness, reciprocity, empathy, compassion, mindfulness and criticality. Openness refers to curiosity about the world around us and the desire to adopt multiple perspectives. It is a profound desire to learn about human lives in different contexts. It is a willingness to understand the immense diversity of human interactions and expressions, not only those which are pleasurable but also those that are confronting and initially distasteful. It goes far beyond an aesthetic desire to try different foods, clothes and to travel to different countries, and encompasses an intellectual and emotional engagement with difference. Openness allows students to be able to access influences from around the world and to engage with them with respect and curiosity, unpacking their deep-rooted beliefs and examining them with fresh eyes. Reciprocity means that students understand the importance of two-way flows of knowledge and understanding and are ready to interact with others in ways that emphasise cooperation and mutuality. It helps students to learn the importance of listening as well as talking, receiving as well as giving, and to recognise that learning is optimised when everyone is an educator and everyone a student.

Compassion is often considered in relation to the suffering of others but suffering is not a necessary component. It incorporates notions such as interdependence and equality and arises from the notion that all humans are equally important and valuable. Compassion denies that some differences are better than others and calls on us to both understand the concerns and motivations of others and be willing to assist them to achieve their goals. It requires that we dispense with assumptions and recalibrate our standard lenses to view the world through the eyes of others. Mindfulness, as its prevalent usage in Buddhist philosophy and psychology implies, is about being fully aware of the moment. When applied to cosmopolitan education it suggests the need to be aware of ourselves and of the way in which we interpret the world around us. This means critically assessing our preconceptions to question our positioning towards others and the way in which we engage with them. At the same time, mindfulness calls on us to be aware of our interactions with others and to identify ways in which these influence our thoughts and actions. It asks us to consider how others may regard us and how they may interpret what we say and do. It points to the need to be aware of the production of meaning and the way in which the roles we play are informed by context. Criticality means that we should question our own assumptions and beliefs, as well as those of others, with awareness and consciousness. It suggests that we become aware of the multiple approaches to any issue or challenge and are able to assess their utility and shortcomings. Criticality calls on us to acknowledge the cultural conditioning that influences our interpretation of the world around us and to learn from our interactions with others.

Conclusion

Taken together the themes highlighted above reflect the understanding inherent in cosmopolitan thinking and address their application to the educational context. By gaining proficiency in openness, reciprocity, empathy, compassion, mindfulness and criticality, we are granted access to the kaleidoscope of human lives and can see that no one stance is superior to others. We gain a sense of being part of a community of humans in which our commonalities can help us come together to solve problems. This is in stark contrast to an approach in which difference is magnified to the extent that cooperation is stymied. Appiah (2006) suggests that a cosmopolitan ethos is required if humans are to coexist as a human tribe. Inevitably some students will be more open to taking on a cosmopolitan ethos than others. This will reflect their lived experiences and the extent to which they have had the opportunity of deep engagement with those unlike themselves. But whatever the starting point, the likelihood that students will reach the 'tip-off point' towards a cosmopolitan disposition (Phillips and Smith 2008: 398) is enhanced the more that their institution and educators emphasise the elements of a cosmopolitan education discussed here. This depends on certain key elements, in particular the curriculum, pedagogy and background of teaching staff. These are considered in the following chapters.

6 Innovations in global learning

Introduction

The educational space has long been regarded as a metaphorical weathervane of social change. The forms and practices of educational systems, institutions and curricula are indicative of historical and prevailing social, cultural and political currents. As meta-narratives reshape the world in which we live, they are reflected and expressed in how we go about preparing the next generation. Educational institutions are sites in which the external is internalised, shaping the hearts and minds of students. The interactions, thoughts and perceptions of students are moulded by educators, themselves the product of the social and political structures that surround them. In this way, it should come as no surprise that contemporary educational practices in the higher education sector around the world are already strongly influenced by the need to help students gain the skills and attributes that will stand them in good stead as global citizens.

But how far does this go? Even if there is a broad acceptance of the need to imbue students with global attributes (itself a questionable assertion), does this suggest that today's students have the opportunity to gain cosmopolitan attributes during their higher education degrees? If they do, what are the key factors that lead to this outcome rather than to the suboptimal outcomes identified in the previous chapter. Can they be generalised and applied to mainstream practice? To examine these questions, this chapter considers the curricula that frame what students experience during their studies. The following chapter then moves on to examining the way in which curricula are implemented. In considering both the curriculum and its application it is important to acknowledge that these are shaped by numerous external forces, some of which will be addressed. The curriculum itself is something that can be viewed as an encapsulation of institutional policies, the dominant discourses in each discipline and influences from major industries and employers. As the chapter will show, the notion of curriculum is being redefined by modern practices. These include institutions establishing campuses in other countries, where the curriculum draws strongly from the home institution but is inevitably imbued with local influences. Or an institution adopting a policy in which all students are obliged to follow an international curriculum. Or short-term study abroad programmes that aim to expose students to difference.

In considering all of the examples, no attempt is made to present a statistical sample of practices around the world. A huge audit would need to be undertaken to determine which practices are most common in different disciplines and in different contexts. What it does do, however, is put forward some snapshots of contemporary practice that illustrate the key themes on which this book is focused – the need to give all students the opportunity to gain cosmopolitan attributes during their higher education studies, and the ways in which this imperative has been interpreted by a whole host of different actors. There is one significant omission – language learning. Leaving this out does not suggest that it is not important but instead that it is so obvious that there is little to be said. Learning another language is so much more than gaining an instrumental skill, opening us up to new ways of looking at the world. At the same time, the arduous process of learning a language to a degree of fluency provides invaluable insights into the difficulties of operating in another language, enhancing compassion for others struggling with the same challenge. From a cosmopolitan standpoint, every higher education student should be proficient in more than one language.

Curriculum development

The study of curriculum development is a field all of its own and it is beyond the scope of this book to do justice to it. But it is important to briefly consider how judgements are made about what students should learn. The International Association for the Advancement of Curriculum Studies suggests that a curriculum is the 'organizational and intellectual center' of the content, context and process of education (IAACS 2014). But as this broad definition suggests, the notion of what a curriculum is can be interpreted in myriad ways. In any consideration of curricula it is important to acknowledge that there is a difference between the 'formal' curriculum that is intended and the actual outcomes (or 'achieved' curriculum). In this book, a curriculum is considered to be a 'planned educational experience' (Kern et al. 2009). In the context of this book it is also important to distinguish curricula in higher education institutions from school-level curriculum development. At primary and secondary levels curriculum is a product of ongoing and comprehensive processes that consult with hosts of stakeholders to identify what students need to know and be able to do at different stages of their education. This frequently occurs at a national or sub-national level and the end results influence hundreds of thousands of students. Hence we can talk about the National Curriculum in England (Department for Education 2014) and the Australian Curriculum (Australian Curriculum, Assessment and Reporting Authority 2014).

Higher education institutions tend not to use overarching approaches. Instead, they adopt a variation of the following, usually undertaken by a

76   *Innovations in global learning*

curriculum committee. First, a determination of what it is that students need to know and be able to do by the end of their degrees. This encompasses a judgement of what factual learning students should accomplish as well as the skills they will be required to put into practice upon graduation. Ideally, this also takes into account the need to consider 'learning which will influence what occurs in the future, not just for its immediate value' (Stephenson and Yorke 2012: vii). Leask and Bridge (2013) suggest that other considerations that contribute to curriculum design include the assessment of student learning and systematic development across the programme of all students. These considerations are also likely made with reference to the cohort of students in a particular institution and their common strengths and shortcomings. And they are underlain by dominant and emerging paradigms and knowledge in and across disciplines. Given that discipline continues to be the organising structure of the higher education sector, disciplinary assumptions are of particular importance.

Becher and Trowler (2001: 5–6) identify significant shifts in disciplinary boundaries over time and identify a number of sources of influence over curriculum decisions, including external quality assurance, 'performativity' and massification. Together, they suggest, these and other forces have led to an increase in both diversification and diffusion and have led to a situation in which there has been a 'fundamental shift in power relations in terms of who defines what counts as useful knowledge and whose discourses achieve dominance'. Into this mix can be added a whole range of pertinent contexts. Leask and Bridge (2013) point to the importance of forces at the institutional, local, national, regional and global levels. Pinar (2014) suggests that national and regional interest remain predominant in the way in which curriculum is both designed and enacted. This approach reflects policy that views education as a unifying national force (Seddon 2014). At the same time, however, transnational challenges are beginning to be recognised in curriculum design.

This is of particular importance if we consider Autio's (2014: 18) claim that the curriculum has become a site in which educators and students engage in dialogue about 'the worthwhileness of the content and subject matter', both for individuals and collectively. Leask and Bridge (2013) suggest that academic staff are torn between a host of competing allegiances in curriculum design and are forced to make knife-edge determinations about balance. Considerations of particular pertinence include optimising the employability of graduates in the local work context as well as preparing students for a lifetime as global citizens and leaders. Increasingly, the worth is judged in its value to contemporary society, one in which McCarthy et al. (2014: 41) suggest 'young people will have to negotiate a world that is truly cosmopolitan – a world where one must coexist with difference'. Developing curricula for this context suggests a need to combine disciplinary rigour with contemporary social, cultural, environmental and political issues (Slattery 2013). In reality, though, curriculum development occurs through the 'interplay between political and sociological boundary work realised through actors and processes that are differently positioned and scaled' (Seddon 2014: 27).

As is immediately obvious, the process of curriculum development in higher education institutions is highly normative, including many assumptions about what 'should' be gained in order to reach outcomes that have been defined as desirable. Both of these are predicated on subjective beliefs. To attempt to overcome a common disjunction between what institutions teach and what employers want from graduates, institutions are increasingly involving representatives from key employer groups or industries. This is not always the case, however, and curriculum design may simply be done by reviewing pertinent contexts and developments in particular disciplines. Indeed, Clegg (2011: 99) suggests that changes to curricula have 'largely been presented as a matter of common-sense'. The extent to which contemporary curriculum development takes the realities of students' lives into account is highly variable. Overall, curriculum development in higher education institutions tends to comprise a series of ad hoc approaches that crystallise a series of assumptions into learning programmes for students. This process in relation to cosmopolitan education will now be considered.

Bringing the international into the curriculum

For nearly two decades there has been increasing interest in how to ensure that international aspects are included in higher education curricula. In the mid-1990s van der Wende (1997) considered the internationalisation of the curriculum in higher education institutions in the Netherlands and determined that this was a product of social change, policy making, institutional policies and the influx of foreign students. The latter point could be regarded as both negative and positive as it was partly influenced by the 'deficit' model in dealing with international students that dominated international education discourses in the 1990s and beyond (Haigh 2013). Van der Wende identified the need to learn about other countries (particularly in the European Union) as the driving force behind internationalisation of the curriculum, with intercultural learning given much less emphasis. Given the significant changes to the world since that time, it is to be expected that higher education curricula have evolved significantly. Indeed, a decade later Donald (2007: 307) was arguing for the education of '21st century Australian, European or American citizens trying to function as world citizens', with explicit reference to cosmopolitan insights. But how widespread is this way of thinking?

Recent research indicates somewhat frustrating findings. A global survey that reviewed responses from senior staff in approximately 200 higher education institutions around the world on their internationalisation strategies uncovered that they are driven by a range of imperatives (Maringe et al. 2013). When asked about the importance of developing international curricula, just 65 per cent of respondents in Anglophone countries reported that this was important, instead highlighting a much greater focus on student

78 *Innovations in global learning*

recruitment, research collaborations and good positioning on international league tables. In other parts of the world the development of international curricula was regarded as important by between 80 and 100 per cent of respondents, and regarded as the single most important element of internationalisation by respondents in Latin America and Sub-Saharan Africa. But what is meant by the internationalisation of curricula? Research undertaken in the Netherlands by Areden et al. (2013) looked at internationalisation through the lens of what institutions aim to achieve, how it contributes to overall quality and the way in which it is expressed. Across a number of institutions the authors found that international and intercultural learning outcomes tended not to be clearly defined, and neither were institutions able to demonstrate whether they were gained by graduates. This indicates that internationalisation remains inadequately embedded in the curriculum.

The fourth International Association of Universities survey on the internationalisation of higher education (Egron-Polak and Hudson 2014) collected responses from leaders of 1,336 higher education institutions in 131 countries. Results indicate that a focus on developing an international curriculum came a long way behind student mobility and international research collaborations in terms of internationalisation priorities. While some international curriculum elements appeared to be relatively common, these tended to focus on language learning, or some kind of international theme. More profound curriculum elements such as 'integrating the contributions of international students into the learning experience' were ranked second last in terms of their importance, although this does vary by region. Echoing the research by Maringe et al. (2013), results showed that enabling educators to utilise international elements in their teaching was more common in Africa and Asia and the Pacific. Similarly, a study of UK higher education institutions found that while much rhetoric exists around internationalisation, the reality of institutional practices tends to be characterised by weak leadership, unease among teaching staff and underwhelming implementation of strategy (Warwick and Moogan 2013). Energies tend to be focused on the recruitment of students rather than on embedding internationalisation into the curriculum. A particularly noteworthy finding was that where internationalisation of the curriculum was part of the internationalisation agenda this tended to be supported by senior members of the institutional leadership team. Even so, there was commonly a failure to engage teaching staff and a lack of communication about the rationale for internationalisation.

A report on internationalisation among 1,041 US colleges (Center for Internationalization and Global Engagement 2012) found that respondents perceived that internationalisation of the curriculum was becoming increasingly rapid. But this overall positive impression does not live up to deeper scrutiny, and it certainly does not meet Hudzik's (2011: 40) hope that 'globally informed content is integrated into the vast majority of courses, curricula, and majors'. On the positive side, a majority of institutions reported having specific learning outcomes that reference global or international attributes.

But only a fifth of these actually assess whether students achieve these outcomes. In terms of the curriculum, more than half of institutions reported initiatives to internationalise the undergraduate curriculum and the majority required students to take a foreign language (usually for one year). A global focus was most common in the areas of business, humanities and social sciences. While just over a quarter of institutions required students to take classes that *included* global issues, the proportion of institutions that required students to take classes with a *primary* focus on global issues had declined from the equivalent survey in 2006. As the authors suggest, 'the data raises some concern about depth versus breadth ... if current downward trends continue ... the depth and nuance of students' understanding of global issues and challenges may be compromised' (Center for Internationalization and Global Engagement 2012: 12). This concurs with Brustein's (2007: 383) assertion that 'adding a diversity or international course(s) requirement [is] hardly sufficient to instil global competence in our students'.

A 2009 European study considered how to measure and determine the quality of internationalisation. One of the conclusions was that 'developing a comprehensive curricular and co-curricular programme that addresses and assesses global learning, beyond a one-off course or experience of education abroad, is essential if post-secondary institutions are to be truly successful in preparing global-ready graduates' (Deardorff et al. 2009: 34). A problem with determining whether this is being done is knowing how to assess what global learning looks like. As Woolf (2009: 61) suggests, 'the idea of internationalisation through the curriculum is both real and, simultaneously, nebulous. It cannot be easily quantified or necessarily defined'. Indeed, even where a course or programme is taught that appears to indicate an international focus, this may still be taught in a parochial way. Leask and Bridge (2013) report that the limited study of internationalisation of the curriculum ensures that there is no agreed definition across disciplines and institutions, no frame of reference and no benchmarking. Initiatives across various Australian higher education institutions over a two-year period were used by the authors to question how teaching staff interpret the concept of internationalisation of the curriculum. Their research found that a 'reciprocal and uneven relationship between the multiple contexts within which curricula were formulated and enacted in the case studies resulted in a variety of interpretations of internationalisation of the curriculum' (Leask and Bridge 2013: 97).

As the variety of research referred to here has shown, internationalisation of the curriculum remains patchy, poorly understood, interpreted in multiple ways and subject to a myriad of forces and contexts. Nonetheless, it is happening in multiple sites around the world, and the level of interest in preparing students for global lives, and hence in structuring the curriculum to help them achieve this outcome, appears to be on the increase. But to what extent does it filter down into the lived experiences of contemporary higher education students? Haigh (2013) suggests that education for global

80 *Innovations in global learning*

citizenship comprises three key elements – the need to gain multicultural capabilities to succeed in the modern workplace (which is a fairly instrumental approach), education for global citizenship and education for planetary consciousness (particularly influenced by an interest in environmental sustainability). In practice, there are a number of different routes that institutions take towards providing their students with an international education, however that may be defined. In the next section we take a look at a selection of these, at different scales and with different scope. For each one we consider how much it is likely to provide students with the opportunity to gain cosmopolitan assets.

Concrete forms of international curricula

Higher education is increasingly taking place across borders. Student mobility is arguably the most visible form of this activity. But student mobility, as earlier chapters have made clear, is limited to a small proportion of students and leads to contested student outcomes. The interest in providing students with an international education, not only from students and their families but also from governments, in addition to the cost of international study, has inevitably led to alternative solutions. The most dominant ones are considered below.

Foreign campuses

There has been a significant growth in the number of campuses established by foreign institutions in second (or third) countries. Global Higher Education (2014) maintains a database of these and lists a total of 216 as at 1 November 2014. The majority are Anglo institutions, with a domination of those from the US and UK. But others are from countries as diverse as Chile, France, Italy, Pakistan, Sweden, Singapore, Taiwan and Venezuela. Host countries tend to be those in Asia (notably China, Malaysia and Singapore) and the Middle East (notably the United Arab Emirates) but also include those as diverse as Albania, Botswana, Dominican Republic, Kazakhstan, Panama and Tunisia. Foreign campuses differ significantly in size, function and organisation but can be defined as

> an entity that is owned, at least in part, by a foreign education institution; operated in the name of the foreign education institution; engages in at least some face-to-face teaching; and provides access to an entire academic program that leads to a credential awarded by the foreign education institution. (Kinser and Lane 2012: 2–3)

While every campus is different, some of those visited by the author illustrate their international elements. The University of Nottingham from the UK has campuses in Kuala Lumpur in Malaysia and in Ningbo in China. Both campuses are very British in appearance, incorporating the iconic lake and clock tower of the home campus in the UK. Both cater to several thousand students – at the Ningbo campus these are almost all Chinese and at the Kuala Lumpur campus these are approximately two-thirds Malaysian – who tend to be from elite backgrounds. In both cases the University of Nottingham has partnered with local higher education organisations but retains control over all academic elements, with successful students receiving a degree from the University of Nottingham. Teaching staff tend to be expatriates from English-speaking countries, with some key positions held by academics seconded from the UK. Both campuses are quality assured by British and local agencies and the curriculum and teaching materials are identical to those used in the UK (Richardson 2015).

For the University of Nottingham, the establishment of campuses in Asia is part of a clearly articulated strategy of being a 'global university' (University of Nottingham 2014). The university states that 'internationalisation is at the heart of everything we do … [and reaches] into every aspect of university life'. The university views foreign campuses as providing students and staff with the ability to be mobile. Campuses also serve as a hub for research connections with a range of international partners and alumni are distributed around the world. In addition the university is actively working on internationalising the curriculum with an explicit aim to 'develop students who are both prepared and able to be global citizens'. This is defined as giving students the opportunity to undertake components that 'introduce them to a global theme'.

Overall the examples of the Malaysian and Chinese campuses of the University of Nottingham demonstrate an alternative to student mobility, one that gives students the chance to gain an international education without leaving home. A visit to both campuses provides an impression of a higher education institution that not only regards itself as global but is also committed to actualising that, making a tangible and sustained investment in internationalisation. The very large number of branch campuses around the world, a quantity that is likely to expand in the future, certainly exposes a greater number of students to the opportunity to gain an international education in terms of gaining a degree from a foreign institution. But does it provide students with the opportunity to gain cosmopolitan assets?

Let us return to the aspects that would make up a cosmopolitan education and consider the extent to which overseas campuses embody these. Many positive assertions are made about the need for students to become global citizens. But do students studying at foreign campuses do anything more than study a foreign curriculum transposed to their home country? Even if there is a high proportion of international students attending that campus, will this automatically lead to students drawing on resources and understandings from around the world? What activities do students undertake that expose them to situations where the development or deepening of multiple allegiances is made likely? Does a foreign campus automatically imbue an inclusive ethos and promote intercultural engagement? Is there something

82 *Innovations in global learning*

about studying at a foreign campus that exposes students to a true diversity of cultures and paradigms? Do students graduate with cosmopolitan dispositions and an ethical position towards difference? Perhaps most importantly of all, do students at one of the many foreign campuses around the world gain the values of openness, reciprocity, empathy, compassion, mindfulness and criticality simply by attending a foreign higher education institution in their own country?

This all seems extremely unlikely unless a particular pedagogy is utilised. The majority of foreign campuses around the world are at pains to emphasise that the curriculum and teaching resources used are *the same as* those in use in the home country of the institution. This is clearly a smart marketing ploy, and undoubtedly reflects the desire of the target student market to gain a well-respected international education. But it also represents a significant constraint on curriculum innovation at the foreign campus. There is undoubtedly a degree of adaptation of the British/American/Canadian/Australian/French curricula to meet local needs, but this is downplayed by staff in foreign campuses for fear of diluting the claims of sameness that are so essential to their survival. Thus if curricula in foreign campuses are to engage with global issues and to facilitate the growth or expansion of cosmopolitan attributes among students, this relies on advances at the home campus of the institution. In the case of the University of Nottingham, ongoing work that aims to explicitly internationalise the curriculum offers hope for giving students valuable opportunities. But this is not an inevitable consequence of students attending a foreign campus.

There is a striking claim on the University of Nottingham's website that 'those departments with bases in our campuses overseas are *immediately international*' (University of Nottingham 2014, emphasis added). The literature reviewed earlier in this chapter, and discussions in earlier chapters, have made clear that there is nothing immediate or automatic about international education and student outcomes. Efforts to internationalise the curriculum are estimable but what perspective will these offerings take? And what processes will be used to ensure that internationalising the curriculum is undertaken holistically and filters down to the classroom? These questions are particularly pressing for foreign campuses as they commonly attract elite students and openly acknowledge their role in educating future leaders. It is important that institutions ask themselves what kind of future leaders they are educating, and what kinds of skills and attributes their graduates will need to negotiate the pressing responsibilities of the modern age.

Collaborative programmes

An alternative to foreign campuses are collaborative programmes, also referred to as 'highly integrated international curricula' (Spinelli 2009: 50). These can be defined as a degree programme 'that is offered by two or more institutions in different countries and features a jointly developed and integrated curriculum, as well as a clear agreement on credit recognition' (Obst and Kuder 2012: 3). Unlike foreign campuses there is no comprehensive international dataset on collaborative programmes, but research undertaken among eight Asia Pacific Economic Cooperation (APEC) economies (Richardson 2015) suggests that they are far more commonplace than foreign campuses. This is due to the low set-up costs involved in comparison with establishing a campus, and the democratic way in which they are developed (often based on personal connections between academic staff in more than one country). In terms of partners, Kuder and Obst (2009) find that European institutions tend to prefer to have collaborative programmes with either American institutions or other European institutions, whereas institutions from the USA have a broader focus, with top partner countries including Germany, China, Mexico and South Korea.

While many collaborative programmes evolve from connections between teaching staff across institutions, there are also structures in place to support and enhance them. The Erasmus Mundus programme (since 2014 included within Erasmus+) provides support to higher education institutions to assist them to develop collaborative postgraduates programmes across at least three European countries (European Commission 2014). Multiple Erasmus Mundus masters courses have been developed, such as the Erasmus Mundus Masters Course in Emergency and Critical Care Nursing between the University of Oviedo in Spain, the University of Algarve, the Polytechnic Institute of Santarém in Portugal and the Helsinki Metropolia University of Applied Sciences in Finland (University of Oviedo 2014). In addition, Mahidol University in Thailand is an associate partner. A review of 57 Erasmus Mundus programmes found that the greatest success was achieved through 'effective horizontal cooperation' in which all partners were involved in design, implementation and management, and when students could come together (for example in a summer school) (European Commission 2013a).

Collaborative programmes owe their popularity partly to their accessibility. While foreign campuses are generally targeted towards, and primarily enrol, only elite students, the number and diffusion of collaborative programmes ensure that they are more widely accessible to a greater number of students (albeit still elite compared to their peers). Equally, they tend to target post-graduate students, particularly in the disciplines of business and engineering, thus reaching out to those whose needs may not be met by a foreign campus (Obst and Kuder 2012; Richardson and Radloff 2014). Students perceive collaborative programmes as enhancing their employability, giving them access to high-quality education and giving them the opportunity to gain international exposure and enhance their language skills (Knight 2008). While institutions have multiple rationales for establishing collaborative programmes, they tend to be regarded as a tangible element of their internationalisation policies.

In many cases collaborative programmes are based on a desire to give students an international education. Spinelli (2009: 51) suggests, for example,

84 *Innovations in global learning*

that 'the philosophy behind double degrees is that it is desirable to educate graduates who have broader cultural experience and more intense training in their subject areas'. The sheer number of, and significant diversity between, collaborative programmes means that it is difficult to make generalisations about them. But the examination of a case study can help in the identification of the extent to which they represent the use of an international curriculum to provide students with opportunities to gain cosmopolitan attributes.

One example is an initiative between Hanoi University in Vietnam and La Trobe University in Australia. In this case the two institutions collaborate to deliver a Bachelor of Business and a Masters of Business Administration to small groups of students. The business focus grew out of demand from the Vietnam government and from Vietnamese students to drive the development of entrepreneurs. Overall, more than 1,000 Vietnamese students have passed through these programmes (Richardson 2015). Curricula, teaching materials and assessments are identical to those used in Australia and students from Hanoi University are able to take some of their course in Australia if they wish. Efforts to persuade students from Australia to take some of their course in Hanoi are yet to meet with a great deal of interest. This is one of ten collaborative programmes that Hanoi University has with institutions around the world, including in Italy and the UK. This makes sense as Hanoi University specialises in language learning and was previously known as the Hanoi University of Foreign Studies (Hanoi University 2014).

La Trobe University also has a number of collaborative programmes including a Master of International Business with the Foreign Trade University (Hanoi and Ho Chi Minh City) in Vietnam, a Master of Nursing with the Singapore Nurses Association and a Master of Health Administration at Harbin Medical University in China (La Trobe University 2014a). As with the University of Nottingham, La Trobe University has an explicit international focus and is 'dedicated to serving the global community through internationalisation, innovative teaching and learning methods, and research' (La Trobe University 2014b). La Trobe University is also developing an 'internationally relevant curriculum which prepares students to be global citizens, entrepreneurs, employers and employees'. Similarly to the University of Nottingham, the statements made are positive, but it is unclear how they are enacted in the daily life of the institution.

Considering collaborative programmes overall, the same questions can be raised for them as for foreign campuses. Do students studying in collaborative programmes study anything more than a foreign curriculum at their home institution? What makes collaborative programmes different to other programmes in terms of the development or deepening of cosmopolitan assets? Is there something innate about a collaborative programme that gives students some form of enhanced outcome beyond what they could get from a standard programme? Can we assume that collaborative programmes are helpful in imbuing students with appreciation of the interdependence of humans and an ability to consider alternative paradigms? Is there something about them that helps students gain an awareness of diversity in the community? Again, this seems unlikely unless appropriate pedagogy is used. Nevertheless the potential is there if collaborative programmes are approached in a way that enhances their internationalisation. Research with alumni from collaborative programmes indicates that the very fact of experiencing a degree from another culture can help students gain confidence in their ability to operate in a foreign culture (Culver et al. 2012). In addition, alumni report gaining the realisation that a number of perspectives can be used in addressing complex issues. And, as European research has found, a key success factor lies in both genuine international collaboration in design and implementation and the opportunity for students to engage with peers in other countries (European Commission 2013a).

Whole of institution approach

The Institut d'Études Politiques de Paris (known as Sciences Po) is an interesting example of a higher education institution that has taken significant steps towards the internationalisation of its curriculum. Sciences Po is one of the top higher educations in France, specialising in the humanities and social sciences. Headquartered in Paris, it has seven regional campuses and, as of 2010, more than 40 per cent of its students were from outside France (Sciences Po 2014a). Sciences Po has a strongly international focus with a compulsory year abroad for all undergraduate students, teaching in a number of languages and a focus on comparative and international perspectives (Sciences Po 2014b). Each campus has a focus on a different region of the world. Thus the French-German campus is in Nancy, the Central and Eastern European campus is in Dijon, the Euro-Latino-American campus is in Poitiers, the Middle Eastern and Mediterranean campus is in Menton, the Europe-Asia campus is in La Havre and the Europe-American campus is in Reims.

While offering the same areas of study as in Paris, the regional campuses utilise an approach that is highly internationalised and incorporates intensive language study. Students take what could be regarded as a liberal arts degree, encompassing areas such as economics, law, sociology, political science and humanities. Each campus teaches languages of relevance to the area of focus and many general subjects are taught in English, with the objective of ensuring that all students are multilingual by the end of their degrees. For example the Le Havre campus – with a focus on Asia – offers Chinese, Hindi, Indonesian, Japanese and Korean (Sciences Po 2014c). Similarly, the Paris campus with a focus on Africa – offers Arabic, Portuguese and Swahili. In addition, visiting scholars from around the world come to teach at Sciences Po, providing students with an opportunity to learn from those with a wide range of perspectives and experiences.

Beyond a focus on international issues in a range of subject areas, language learning and a regional focus, Sciences Po is also characterised by a highly international student body. Students from other countries tend to attend the

86 *Innovations in global learning*

campuses of direct relevance to their region. And all students are required to spend their third year in another country, either attending a partner institution or undertaking an internship. In the 2014–2015 academic year, 1,360 students from Sciences Po will study abroad, 1,098 of whom are taking part in an exchange programme with one of Science Po's 350 partner institutions (Sciences Po 2014d). Students can choose by language of study and area of study. Thus those studying Arabic can choose between the University of Cairo in Egypt, Yarmouk University in Jordan, the American University of Sharjah in the United Arab Emirates and Al-Quds University in the Palestinian Territories, among others (Sciences Po 2014e). The year abroad is designed not only to enhance language skills but also for students to gain an insight into contemporary realities and also to explore 'global challenges from a non-Western viewpoint'. Examples given include 'what is Africa's view on economic partnership agreements with the European Union?' and 'what are the solutions to conflicts in the Middle East?' Staff at Sciences Po give students a great deal of support to organise their international experience and a range of scholarships are available to support mobility.

Considering the entirety of the offering for students at Sciences Po, it appears that they are a long way down the path towards achieving many of the elements of a cosmopolitan education. In terms of activities, students certainly appear to gain an awareness of diversity, consider alternative paradigms and draw on resources and understandings from around the world. In addition, Sciences Po clearly promotes an environment in which students are connected to groups outside their immediate institution. It is to be hoped that students also critically reflect on the assumptions involved in diverse actions and work together to create new knowledge, but this is unknown. It may also be the case that students have ample opportunities to acknowledge and value diversity and to develop ethical positions towards difference, but this depends on how their learning is structured. On the surface it seems that Sciences Po makes considerable efforts to leverage the potential of diverse approaches to enrich learning as well as to enhance understanding of the interdependence of humans. In terms of values, these are not made explicit, but a close reading of materials produced by Sciences Po suggests that elements such as valuing diversity are encouraged. The organisation of the institution and structure of undergraduate programmes ensures that students should be receptive to diverse perspectives and have opportunities to develop openness, reciprocity, empathy, compassion, mindfulness and criticality. But whether this happens depends on a number of interacting factors and is unknown.

Overall, Sciences Po offers an example of an institution that has specifically set out to structure itself in a way that ensures that students experience an international curriculum. While other higher education institutions have much to learn from this example, there are limitations to this becoming the prevalent model in the higher education sector, most of all because Sciences Po is an elite institution. First, the student body at Sciences Po is relatively small, with

Innovations in global learning 87

just 13,000 students in total, and it appears that the staff–student ratio is very high. Sciences Po also appears to have significant financial resources and its high ranking means that it is able to make collaborative arrangements with the top institutions around the world. Second, the cost of spending an entire year abroad is significant and relies on both the availability of scholarships as well as the financial resources of its students. While these factors mean that what Sciences Po has achieved is not immediately replicable at many higher education institutions, many of the components of its approach are ripe for implementation elsewhere.

Short-term study abroad

Short-term study abroad experiences are a very common way for higher education students to be exposed to global learning. Their attraction for students inevitably lies in their short duration, making them relatively affordable and able to fit around other commitments such as part-time work. For example among 289,000 students from the US who had an international study experience in 2012–2013, 60 per cent were overseas only during the summer or for eight weeks or less, against 37 per cent for a medium term (one semester or one or two quarters) and just 3 per cent long term (for an academic or calendar year) (Institute of International Education 2014). Short-term study abroad programmes vary immensely, in length, type, integration with the broader curriculum and learning objectives. While opening up international mobility to otherwise place-bound students, short-term study abroad programmes often struggle to be given what Woolf (2009: 57) terms 'academic credibility, respectability and recognition', instead tending to be regarded with a degree of derision by academic colleagues as glorified holiday camps.

In a large-scale study that considered the relationship between study abroad during higher education and global engagement in later life, Paige et al. (2010) gathered data from more than 7,000 graduates who had undertaken study abroad between 1960 and 2007. Their findings suggest that the impact of study abroad was profound but while destination and depth of programme had a significant impact on global engagement, duration did not, concluding that 'what really counts is not how long you stay or where you go, but the quality of the program and the nature of deep cultural and learning experiences provided' (Paige et al. 2010: 7) (see also Coryell et al. 2014; Paige et al. 2009; Stoner et al. 2014). But what factors lead to depth in a short-term study abroad programme? Institutions naturally claim that students who return from study abroad do so with an enhanced understanding of global issues, but how do they know this? And what are the key determinants? What factors decide which students are just having a nice time versus those whose thinking is genuinely being confronted? Donnelly-Smith (2009) suggests that success factors include clear learning objectives that are closely linked to the destination; teaching staff experienced in

88 *Innovations in global learning*

experiential teaching; contact with the local community; input from teaching staff from the destination country(ies); and rigorous and facilitated reflective practices.

The discipline of social work is one in which a deal of rigour has been applied to these questions, with a desire to avoid the pitfall of study abroad being 'mis-educative'. Social work educators have a particular interest in this as the context for which their students need to be prepared is one in which global problems impact on everyday dealings (Boateng and Thompson 2013; Collins et al. 2009; Greenfield, et al. 2012; VeLure Roholt and Fisher 2013). An example from the University of Minnesota in the US demonstrates some of the issues involved in ensuring that a short-term study abroad programme has the desired outcomes (VeLure Roholt and Fisher 2013). With a focus on social welfare programmes, the experience involved a group of 14 students spending one week in Amsterdam, the Netherlands and one in Cape Town, South Africa. The experience was established with reference to all of Donnelly-Smith's considerations. Orientation involved information on each country and strategies in optimising learning from the experience, including a guest lecturer from South Africa. Students also set up a site visit in each country in addition to organised activities. In each country the schedule involved visits to a number of social work agencies and participant observation, in addition to visits to cultural sites. Each student completed a self-directed project and structured reflective discussions were regularly conducted. With all this preparation and structure in place the educators found that it was the unexpected that led to the most profound learning experiences.

The teaching staff who coordinated and led this example of a short-term study abroad experience reflected that it had the potential to offer 'students meaningful experiences that can challenge their taken-for-granted understandings of culture and invite them to critically reflect on how their interpretations are often more cultural than analytic or logical' (VeLure Roholt and Fisher 2013: 63). But they equally acknowledged that it was essential that the learning method and pedagogy used was optimally suited to maximising the learning potential in a short time abroad with a focus on experiential education. This makes sense due to the claim by Lutterman-Aguilar and Gingerich (2002: 46) that 'study abroad and experiential education are natural partners because they share the common goal of empowering students and preparing them to become responsible global citizens'. But it is something that depends on the skills and experiences of those facilitating these programmes. Moreover, the short-term study abroad experience needs to be tightly embedded in a broader curriculum which integrates global perspectives and enables students to enhance their critical-thinking skills. As Jackson (2011: 92) emphasises, a 'short-term sojourn can have a significant impact on participants if critical reflection and experiential learning ... are embedded into the program ... [and if] individual and group reflection [are] promoted before, during, and after a sojourn'.

Innovations in global learning 89

Returning to elements that would be in a framework for cosmopolitan education, it certainly appears that the short-term study abroad programme discussed here appears to have met most of its elements. The learning experience enables students to gain an awareness of diversity, to consider alternative paradigms, to develop new knowledge that incorporates critical reflections on the assumptions involved and to draw on resources and understandings from around the world. Students are able to connect with those outside of their institution and who are unlike themselves and gain an understanding of global inequality, which is likely to prompt reflections of how humans define their moral communities. It also appears that teaching staff fostered a number of cosmopolitan values including an ethical position towards difference as well as openness, reciprocity, empathy, compassion, mindfulness and criticality. But this is one very small programme, with students who have self-selected and shown a prior interest in global knowledge. Moreover, it appears that the teaching staff that led this example had advanced skills in optimising the experience for students and applying appropriate pedagogy. It is hoped that this can equally be said of all short-term study abroad programmes but this is questionable. Moreover, there are a number of important issues that need to be considered, including the pressure that short-term study abroad programmes can place on host organisations (Chao 2014); the skills development required for educators to take students abroad (Mullens et al. 2012); the reciprocity and communication between partners in setting up programmes (Jackson and Nyoni 2012); how best to nurture student engagement with others (Smith et al. 2014); and how much language instruction is appropriate (Herbst 2011).

Conclusion

This chapter has focused on four very different examples of the implementation of international curricula. The question it asked was whether an international curriculum automatically gave students the opportunity to enhance or gain cosmopolitan assets. Foreign campuses and collaborative programmes were included as an example of common forms of international education in which students are given the opportunity to participate in an international curriculum. As the discussion suggests, care needs to be taken in making assumptions about what the 'international' in these curricula actually means. If it simply indicates that a curriculum from one country is implemented in another, then this will not necessarily lead to students gaining the opportunity to enhance their cosmopolitan attributes. Certainly, students may significantly enhance their language skills, gain an insight into alternative ways of looking at the world and be regarded by potential employers as international in some way. But if we look at aspects that constitute a cosmopolitan education framework then many of those characteristics are not automatically present.

Sciences Po is an example of an institution that has entirely structured its bachelor programmes around an international curriculum. This gives students

90 *Innovations in global learning*

incredible opportunities to not only gain an international education but to undertake activities, gain knowledge and practice values that will stand them in good stead to contribute to, and lead, diverse societies in the future. While the favourable status of Sciences Po allows it to deliver education to students in a fairly boutique manner, many lessons can be drawn from this example and used in other institutions with a desire to help students gain cosmopolitan assets. While often regarded as too insubstantial to make a difference, short-term study abroad programmes can offer students opportunities to have their perspectives challenged and to experience intercultural engagement. Their role in helping students whose ability to access international input in other ways should not be denied on the basis of their duration.

Ultimately, the ability of any of these expressions of international curricula to provide students with an opportunity to gain cosmopolitan attributes comes down to a common element – how they are implemented. Optimising international curricula relies on teaching staff having appropriate preparation, knowledge and skill sets to implement the curriculum in such a way as to optimise its cosmopolitan potential. It relies on the application of appropriate pedagogy: that which stimulates students in ways that challenge their assumptions and open their eyes to different realities. And it relies on assessment tasks that call on students to demonstrate the evolution in their thinking and understanding. These issues are explored in the following chapter.

7 Cosmopolitan classrooms

Introduction

It has been argued in previous chapters that it is essential that higher education students are adequately prepared to contribute to, and lead, heterogeneous societies in our globally connected world. Ensuring that students have opportunities to gain cosmopolitan attributes during their studies is therefore an important responsibility for contemporary and future educators. But this will not happen automatically. As we have seen, neither student mobility, nor the opportunity to interact with students from different cultural backgrounds, nor an international curriculum inevitably gives students appropriate cosmopolitan opportunities. While institutions may make claims about the global attributes that their graduates have gained as a consequence of their higher education, they are less good at demonstrating exactly what these are or what strategies they have in place to ensure that students gain them.

Transcending the rhetoric to ensure coherent outcomes requires careful decisions on the part of educators and their institutions. It is essential to consider *what* is taught – the curriculum, *how* it is taught – the pedagogy, and *who* it is taught by – the preparation, skills and knowledge of educators. Moreover, it cannot be assumed that students will gain what is hoped for from an educational experience. Thus, appropriate assessment needs to be implemented, both to inform and assess learning and also to inform improvements in teaching. This chapter considers each of these elements in turn. In doing so, it does not underestimate the importance of disciplinary learning and the need to ensure that students have appropriate subject-specific and generic skills to ensure their employability. Instead it suggests that the opportunity to gain cosmopolitan attributes should be interwoven into all other elements of a higher education. As such, these initiatives should be regarded as strengthening and reinforcing, rather than competing with, the many excellent activities already undertaken by educators around the world.

Cosmopolitan attributes

Before going further it is worth reminding ourselves of the attributes and skills that all higher education students should have the opportunity of gaining

92 *Cosmopolitan classrooms*

prior to the end of their degrees. First, the ability to engage with difference and gain an appreciation of multiple perspectives while recognising their own positioning. Second, a willingness to engage in critical reflection on the way in which humans define their moral obligations towards diverse groups, considering different paradigms and values and the subjectivity of knowledge creation. Third, an intellectual and emotional engagement with difference and a recognition of the value of cooperation and mutuality. Fourth, awareness of the interdependence of humans and a willingness to help others achieve their goals. Fifth, the willingness to critically assess preconceptions and to acknowledge how roles and actions are informed by context.

As has been suggested in the previous chapter, opportunities to gain cosmopolitan attributes will only emerge from a higher education if they are made explicit. This means going far beyond vague statements about global learning, or international elements that are haphazardly tagged on to the main focus of study. A cosmopolitan curriculum needs to specify exactly what cosmopolitan attributes students should be expected to gain from their degrees and how this is to be achieved. Learning outcomes need to be defined in a way that makes cosmopolitan attributes explicit, at the institutional level, the degree level and for each subject or course. Achieving this can be done by following the example of some of the most advanced approaches in internationalisation. For example Leeds Metropolitan University in the UK has developed generic international learning outcomes for adaptation to each disciplinary area (Jones and Killick 2013). Appropriate pedagogy and assessment then need to be put into place to ensure that intended outcomes are activated during teaching and that they are actually achieved. Such a 'constructive alignment' approach is highly student centred in that it 'makes the students themselves do the real work, the educator simply acts as "broker" between the student and a learning environment that supports the appropriate learning activities' (Biggs and Tang 2007: 54). Ensuring that this works requires a holistic approach. This should incorporate staff development, a clear explanation of the value to students and the identification of champions across an institution to push the cosmopolitan agenda forward. At the same time, innovations need to be aligned with pertinent agendas at the local, regional and international level (Jones and Killick 2013). Crucially, a serious attempt to provide students with a cosmopolitan education also requires pedagogy, assessment and the skills of educators to be in alignment. There also needs to be a thorough evaluative process specifically designed to reflect these aspirations.

Pedagogy

There is no language – yet – for cosmopolitan pedagogy. Thus in considering appropriate pedagogy to assist students to gain cosmopolitan assets, reference needs to be made to alternative constructs. There is an enormous range of pedagogical approaches to choose from, all of which have their merits and

Cosmopolitan classrooms 93

drawbacks. Some are well entrenched and have been developed over a long period of time. Others have been developed relatively recently in response to specific educational contexts. In this section a number will be considered for their potential to proffer opportunities for students to gain cosmopolitan attributes. It is not possible to consider all possible approaches and the discussion here is not meant to give a comprehensive overview of all pedagogies that might inform a cosmopolitan education. Overall, what we are looking for is pedagogy that is basically 'good teaching', teaching that helps students gain skills that enable them to tackle the many challenges faced in the contemporary world (Bowser et al. 2007).

One approach of relevance to a cosmopolitan education is worldly pedagogy (Fanghanel and Cousin 2012), which draws on Arendt's (1958) discussion of a diversity of humans sharing a common world. This pedagogy was developed from a scheme in which Palestinian and Israeli students came together to undertake degrees in the UK. It enabled the educators to harness the differences and tensions between their students as a basis for debate and dialogue, specifically aimed at helping the cohort to develop an appreciation of plurality. Critically, students began to understand their own situatedness and the competing narratives around their experience, something which Hill (2000: 35) terms a 'dialectics of distantiation and participation'. This attunes with Goulah's (2012: 1006) concept of value creative dialogue that is 'based primarily on a deep valuation and appreciation of the Other's humanity, and on the belief that engagement in dialogue with the Other is the best and, indeed, only means for developing both/all interlocutors' shared humanity'. The most important elements of worldly pedagogy are critical reflection and critical engagement with difference, followed by the interweaving of formal knowledge in the curriculum with the students' own lived experiences. As such this has echoes of the pedagogy of transformative learning (Mezirow and Associates 1990) in which reflection is used to deepen critical analysis of personal assumptions. When used in the context of an international curriculum, a transformative learning pedagogy helps students to question the assumptions that underlie how they interpret the world around them.

Critical to worldly pedagogy is learning to be reflective. It can be argued that there are three key forms of reflective inquiry (Reardon and Snauwaert 2011). The first, critical/analytical reflection, engages students in considerations of power and how it is mediated by social institutions with a resulting impact on human lives. The second, moral/ethical reflection, focuses students on issues around fairness and justice. The third, contemplative/ruminative reflection, guides students to consider broad interrelationships, both in the external world and within their own assumptions and desires. It can be argued that 'reflective inquiry is an ethical requirement, and thus a constitutive element, of cosmopolitanism' (Reardon and Snauwaert 2011: 4).

Beyond critical reflection, another important element of a cosmopolitan pedagogy is to ground learning in the lives of students. The pedagogy of experiential learning (Kolb 1984) centralises student experience and uses

94 *Cosmopolitan classrooms*

this to validate abstractions. Kolb uses Lewin's (1942) work to create a cyclical experiential learning model that moves from concrete experience, to observation and reflections, to the formation of abstract concepts and generalisation, to testing implications of concepts in new situations and back again to concrete experience. Kolb builds on the work of Dewey (1938) and Piaget (1970) to suggest that learning should be regarded as a process in which knowledge is 'formed and reformed through experience' (Kolb 1984: 26). While some view Kolb's insights as being too prescriptive and instrumental, they can provide a framework that is ripe for adaptation by knowledgeable educators. Experiential learning can leverage any form of experience in the lives of students and use structured reflection and critical analysis to stimulate learning. While this approach is often applied to activities such as short-term study abroad (Lutterman-Aguilar and Gingerich 2002), it does not require students to go anywhere or do anything in particular. References to experiential learning inevitably reflect the enlightened pedagogy advocated by Freire, as discussed at length in Chapter Two. Freire's focus on utilising the prior experience and knowledge of students, unpacking contradictions inherent in both the subject matter and their own subjectivities, and then facilitating a process in which all participants are active in co-creating knowledge through dialogue, is clearly echoed in the approach taken in experiential learning.

But Freire goes beyond this, demanding that students and educators interrogate their social and political positioning. This requires drawing on additional pedagogical approaches. One that is relevant for a cosmopolitan approach is decolonial pedagogy. De Lissovoy (2010) describes decolonial pedagogy as something that challenges the Eurocentrism inherent in many curricula and instead builds solidarity around shared human experience. The first step is taken in order to become aware of the historical conditions out of which the present world order has been constituted. It involves reframing the diverse forms of being and thinking to understand their roots and legacies, hence developing a cosmopolitan sense of the world and our knowledge of it, rather than one that is located in time and space. This highlights the interconnectedness of humans in creating the world around us and the importance of using multiple perspectives to investigate our reality. It also calls on students to critically engage with knowledge paradigms about the other in their curriculum and learning materials (Tallon 2011). It may involve a pedagogy of discomfort (Bender and Walker 2013; Boler 1999) in which unpacking long-held assumptions and beliefs about the world can be challenging to students and may generate emotional responses. These 'moments of disequilibrium' can either aid cognitive development or lead to resistance (Lee et al. 2012: 211). This highlights the need for skilled facilitation and the creation of safe spaces.

Decolonial pedagogy responds to Lingard's (2006) call for the de-parochialisation of education. It can be achieved through creating learning environments in which diverse perspectives are encouraged and in which

Cosmopolitan classrooms 95

contributions to disciplinary thinking from outside the traditional Anglo-European core are acknowledged. Cultural coexistence and interconnection are emphasised and nationalism interrogated with students encouraged to engage in an 'enlarged solidarity that reaches beyond the local and the nation to participate in the construction of a global community' (De Lissovoy 2010: 288). Ideally, educators draw on the diversity present in the classroom but this requires intercultural interaction that is designed in a careful and intentional manner, rather than left to chance (Lee et al. 2012; Marin 2000). Indeed, Marin emphasises the need for educators to recognise the educational value of diversity and then use it as a guide in a supportive and inclusive environment that enables active learning to take place. One example is an assignment in which first-year students described a physical object that reflected an aspect of their identity. This activity was found to have a prolonged impact on students, breaking down barriers, facilitating interaction, encouraging the questioning of assumptions and challenging students' preconceptions about difference (Lee et al. 2012).

While taking the lead from the diversity in the classroom is extremely valuable as a way for students to gain cosmopolitan attributes, so too are efforts to draw on the local community, or pedagogies of place (Morgan 2009). Most institutions of higher education are located in relatively close proximity to a community and it is unlikely that this is entirely homogeneous. Pedagogy that is rooted in the community may involve service-learning type activities. But it can also simply involve making explicit reference to how elements in the curriculum are playing out in the local, regional or national context, and the differentiated impact on various groups. This approach draws strongly on an active learning pedagogy. Active learning was first popularised by Bonwell and Eison (1991) and involves students engaging in actions and then using higher-order thinking to reflect on and evaluate those actions. Watkins et al. (2007) suggest that active learning incorporates behavioural, cognitive and social dimensions, all of which enhance learning. Drew and Mackie (2011) consider that it also contains an affective dimension, impacting on feelings, emotions and self-perceptions.

In cosmopolitan terms, the pedagogies outlined above are extremely valuable but do not go far enough. Learning about different ways of being, reflecting, engaging with the other, thinking critically, engaging in dialogue, unpacking contradictions, questioning assumptions, interrogating social positioning, valuing diverse perspectives, referencing context and engaging with alternative knowledge paradigms are, indeed, powerful pedagogical activities that can have an impact on students' moral reasoning (Hurtado et al. 2012). As Kahane (2009: 59) suggests, however, students also need to be given the opportunity to understand 'the habits of thought, judgment, and reaction that keep them trapped in the cocoon of their own privilege' through contemplative pedagogy. This means doing what Putnam (2007) refers to as defining a 'broader sense of we'. Contemplative pedagogy is a recent comer to the pedagogical suite but something that is gaining traction

96 *Cosmopolitan classrooms*

(Contemplative Mind 2014; Gravois 2005; Gunnlaugson et al. 2014; Zajonc 2014). Zajonc (2013) suggests that in addition to helping students develop compassion and empathy, contemplative pedagogy can also aid students to develop attention and emotional balance, while supporting creativity and learning. Activities include mindfulness, concentration, open awareness and sustaining contradictions (Zajonc 2013). Kahane (2009: 57) reports that the impact of contemplative pedagogy on students is significant, resulting in 'a willingness to experiment with their own tolerance for letting in others' suffering, and with what this might feel like in action'.

As this brief oversight has indicated there are a host of pedagogies which can be adapted and implemented to ensure that students have opportunities to gain cosmopolitan assets. There are undoubtedly many more than those discussed here which are also of relevance. Perhaps most important of all in pedagogical choice, however, is that it is authentic (Kreber 2010). This means that educators need to choose pedagogical approaches that reinforce their own theories of teaching and learning and that sit well with their values, experiences, skills and knowledge. It is certainly not recommended that contemplative pedagogy, for example, is attempted without – at the very least – relevant professional development. But equally, it is important that the values of educators and their views of students are reflected in the chosen pedagogy. Ultimately, each educator is responsible for choosing their own ways to bring cosmopolitan pedagogy into their teaching. But while there are already many practitioners putting many of the pedagogical approaches discussed above into action, it is likely that they remain in the minority. Changing this situation requires us to consider the skills and attributes required by cosmopolitan educators.

Educators

Educators in higher education institutions have a profound impact on their students, not only in what they teach and in how they teach it, but also in how they model behaviour. Thus when we consider a model for cosmopolitan education we cannot focus only on the curriculum and pedagogy. Instead, however imbued with cosmopolitan aspects these are, their expression depends on their interpretation, adaptation and application by the person allocated the task of teaching. Most of us have experienced the good and bad of teaching. Those memorable educators who, independent of their subject matter, inspired us, excited us, challenged us, demanded that we question our assumptions and opened up a new world of understanding. Unfortunately most of us have also been forced to endure the inverse. The dry, the disinterested, the slumber-inducing, the read-aloud-from-the-textbook, the person who would clearly prefer to be doing almost anything else in the world than spend any time in the presence of students.

We cannot demand that all higher education educators are cosmopolitans. This would be quite ridiculous, and indeed the great variety of diverse (and

Cosmopolitan classrooms 97

often eccentric) personalities, values, beliefs and behaviours that make up the body of educators of a higher education institution embodies immeasurable worth. But we can require all educators to be good educators. And, as has been consistently argued throughout this book, good education in the contemporary world means that students need to be given the opportunity to gain cosmopolitan attributes by the end of their degrees. The next obvious question is 'whose responsibility is it?' Much as for ensuring that students gain employability by the time they graduate, the answer is 'everybody's'. But while a sense of personal responsibility will encourage some educators to adapt best practice strategies for cosmopolitan learning, this will not be sufficient. So what can institutions do to support and guide educators towards cosmopolitan approaches? Responses to this question can be considered on a number of levels. First, a consideration of which educators are recruited by institutions and the basis on which they are promoted. Second, professional development and support given to educators to assist them gain relevant skills and attributes. Third, that institutional leaders model the attributes that they desire educators to impart to students. Each of these elements is addressed in turn.

Opportunities for students to gain cosmopolitan attributes will not come about unless educators have some insights into what it means to operate in a global space. If educators are to teach students about communication that embraces and values a diversity of perspectives, they need to not only model this themselves but also have a skill set that enables them to facilitate an appropriate learning environment. It is insufficient for educators to be trained in pedagogy – for it to be effective they need to believe in the need for it and value its importance. This calls on educators to have the 'attitudes and dispositions' (Lutterman-Aguilar and Gingerich 2002: 72) that support a cosmopolitan philosophy. In part this requires an 'ethics of care' in teaching in which educators view themselves as having an interdependent relationship with their students. Semetsky (2012: 54) defines this as 'self-becoming-other by means of entering into another person's frame of reference and taking upon oneself the other perspective'. This is extremely relevant to cosmopolitan education in that the notion of moral interdependence with others in our direct context can then be expanded to others who are further removed from us, and hence to incorporate all human beings, through what Noddings (2010: 394) terms 'modelling, dialogue, practice and confirmation'. Moreover, it is important that educators can draw on the rich resource inherent in their students' experiences and view this as an educational tool. Whether or not a cohort of students is culturally diverse, they are likely to have a broad range of life experiences. As Tran (2010) emphasises, this is a valuable component of knowledge and enabling students to build on knowledge they already have will help embed what they are learning during their higher education studies, as well as contribute to mutual learning between students and educators.

How can we ensure that educators have an appropriate background and skill set to embed these approaches in their teaching, and to practice the

98 *Cosmopolitan classrooms*

pedagogies discussed above? Transcending an intellectual appraisal of the international to engage in a visceral experience is vital if educators are to impart their insights to students. Thus recruitment of educators with appropriate backgrounds and the ongoing professional development of educators to enhance their international exposure are essential. As Brandenburg et al. (2009: 72) suggest, 'the internationality of lecturers and their commitment to and involvement in the process of internationalisation are of fundamental significance. Without an internationally oriented teaching body, it is difficult for other aspects ... to make any essential contribution to internationalisation'. Activities such as visiting lectureships and international study programmes are extremely valuable, and benefit educators in more ways than an enhancement of their international outlook alone. Research on the impact of the mobility of educators under the auspices of the Erasmus programme (Bracht et al. 2006) has found that mobile educators are viewed by their institutions as having better intercultural understanding and intercultural skills than their peers on their return, gained through contact with their foreign colleagues and students and their experience of life in another country. Moreover, their time abroad flows into an ongoing internationalisation of their research and teaching activities, with benefits for their career as a whole.

One way to ensure that educators have appropriate backgrounds to conduct cosmopolitan education is for institutions to hire educators from abroad, on either a short- or long-term basis. This is a policy that is already actively pursued by many institutions although Coryell et al. (2012) find that its implementation tends to be somewhat patchy across institutions. For example Yuan (2011) reports that Tsinghua University in China brings in approximately 800 international visiting educators each year, with a further 200 for a longer duration. This is not to say that coming from another country automatically means that someone has the appropriate skill set to ensure that students gain cosmopolitan skills. But being taught by educators from a range of backgrounds will help students to gain a consciousness of different perspectives. This is confirmed by a study undertaken in New York that finds that students appreciate the alternative cultural perspectives they gain from educators from other countries (Constantinou et al. 2011). This may be of particular importance if the student body is lacking in diversity. The research also found, however, that international educators are not always respected by students and other educators due to misconceptions that arise from accented or imperfect English. This indicates the need for support from academic leaders and colleagues to embrace the diversity among educators and to leverage this to enhance the experience of students, something that educators from minority groups feel that institutions do not currently do well (Eagan et al. 2014). Moreover, Constantinou et al. (2011: 268) suggest that 'incidents of negative attitude ... should be treated as "teachable moments" and be used as a springboard to educate students or faculty members about culturally responsible behaviours'.

Beyond hiring educators who have international experiences, it is also important that institutions include international elements in their criteria for the promotion of educators. For example Brustein (2007) indicates that some institutions such as Michigan State University have altered the requirements for promotion to make internationalisation one of the key metrics. This is essential. Promotion criteria speak volumes about the performance that institutions expect from educators. The move towards recognising the scholarship of teaching in some institutions (Vardi and Quin 2011) is a good demonstration of how the inclusion of new elements in promotion criteria can influence practice. Making explicit reference to international aspects through both reward and recognition will, at the very least, stimulate awareness among educators of the value of enhancing their international attributes. Moreover, the notion of academic citizenship can be broadened to incorporate international elements. As such, the 'service pyramid' for educators (Macfarlane 2007) should be expanded so that student and collegial service are focused on international student bodies and globally dispersed educators while institutional, discipline and public service should reference the international community and the need to prepare students to lead a globally interconnected and multicultural world. As such, the internationalisation of educators should be regarded as a crucial element of institutions that claim to be international.

Ensuring that educators with international experiences are both employed and promoted is important, not only in their own capacity to educate students in ways that provide them opportunities to gain cosmopolitan attributes. It can also influence the take up of international elements across campuses. In research with Australian educators Bell (2004) found a 'spectrum of acceptance' among educators with reference to internationalising the curriculum. Some educators expressed their support for internationalisation, considering it to be a fundamental element of their responsibility towards students. As Francois (2014) suggests, this is likely due to personal interest, the opportunity to enhance teaching and develop new ideas, the opportunity to improve satisfaction with teaching and the desire for an intellectual challenge. But this attitude is not found across the board and Bell (2004: 5) was confronted with educators who viewed internationalisation as irrelevant, inappropriate or unnecessary. One commented 'the material I teach is stateless' and another that 'it is not the discipline's responsibility to produce culturally aware and sensitive graduates'. I suspect we all have colleagues who would share those views. These findings match with Leask and Bridge (2013), almost a decade later, who find that many educators view internationalisation of the curriculum as having nothing to do with them, do not understand what it means or do not know how to make it work within their disciplinary context. Overcoming this requires what the authors term 'careful nurturing'. And it would be likely that careful nurturing falls on more fertile ground when educators are already primed by their own personal experiences of operating in different international environments.

100   *Cosmopolitan classrooms*

This also has implications for academic leadership in its broadest definition (Bolden et al. 2014), particularly with reference to moral and social responsibility. If institutions wish to have an agenda of cosmopolitan education then their leadership teams need to not only embody this but also to identify leaders within the community to take this further. Fostering cosmopolitan education at senior levels will lead to the development of partnerships with like-minded institutions and to the recruitment of staff who understand the value of working towards cosmopolitan outcomes. And a cosmopolitan ethos will ensure that cosmopolitan practices are recognised and valued. This can be done through nurturing an environment in which efforts to adopt cosmopolitan pedagogies are made visible and are rewarded, while making clear that it is the responsibility of all educators to provide students opportunities to gain cosmopolitan attributes (Bonwell and Eison 1991). This is important because the institutional context is one of the seven filters that Fanghanel (2007) identifies as impacting on an educator's professional practice. Moreover, it is a filter that is under the direct control of institutions, in contrast to external influences such as discipline and professional accreditation requirements. The importance of the institution in supporting educators to facilitate cosmopolitan practices is reinforced by Francois (2014), who finds that key extrinsic factors that influence educators to internationalise their curriculum include recognition, support and encouragement from institutional leaders, and the inclusion of internationalisation activities in evaluation for promotion and salary increases. Another factor is the provision of funds to support internationalisation activities, and determinations about expenditure are another area in which institutional leaders play an important role.

Beyond an appropriate institutional environment, diffusion of cosmopolitan practices throughout an institution requires appropriate professional development to be available to educators. Another filter identified by Fanghanel (2007) was pedagogical beliefs. This incorporates elements such as assumptions about the capacity of students, the role of the educator, personal experiences of learning and expectations of learning outcomes. While not as easily shaped as elements such as institutional mission, institutions can still do a great deal to influence the pedagogical beliefs of their educators, which Fanghanel (2007: 15) describes as 'highly agentic and ideologically rich'. Professional development for educators is essential if they are to possess the optimal skill set to utilise cosmopolitan pedagogies. Lee et al. (2012: 14) suggest that educators need 'occasions of cognitive disequilibrium' to help them develop an awareness of diversity and to ensure that students gain the same. This requires educators to critically reflect on the extent to which entrenched discourses in their disciplines are thought to be 'value-free' and to consider the relative positioning of 'objective' versus 'subjective' knowledge. Educators need to be prepared to do a number of things that they may not already have in their teaching arsenal. These include helping students deal with any anxiety which arises from cosmopolitan pedagogy, allowing students to assert their own identities, modelling ways to deal with ambiguity, challenging social segmentation in the classroom, responding to inappropriate behaviour or comments and facilitating an atmosphere in which open dialogue is welcomed. On the last point, Arkoudis et al. (2013) suggest a framework for conceptualising relevant teaching practices that includes designing interaction into teaching practices, using strategies to overcome student hesitation, setting expectations about interactions, explaining the benefits of interactions and encouraging students to engage in reflection and critical thinking.

Fanghanel (2007) suggests that the academic unit – school, department or faculty – is the right space to enhance teaching practices. This can be done in a number of ways including mentoring (Law et al. 2014), workshops (Lattuca et al. 2014), co-teaching (Devlin-Scherer and Sardone 2013) and the implementation of communities of practice (Green et al. 2013). Professional development needs to be undertaken with an understanding that change can be challenging. As Bonwell and Eison (1991: 68) suggest, 'for many faculty, then, things are the way they are today because that is the way they have always been'. Changing this requires concerted effort, something that is difficult to find time for when research is rewarded above teaching. Bonwell and Eison (1991) recommend that innovative practices are introduced to educators in terms of their advantages, their good fit with existing practices, their simplicity, their ready ability to be trialled and the ability to learn from their own attempts and the attempts of others. Moreover, educators need to have the opportunity for ongoing engagement in, and reflection on, new approaches to teaching (Green et al. 2013), and professional development should be tailored to the way in which it is likely to be implemented in the classroom (Penuel et al. 2007). Educators should be given the support and encouragement to proactively seek professional development which sits well with their own learning needs (Warhurst 2008). None of this can happen overnight but, as Bonwell and Eison (1991: 94) suggest (albeit in reference to active learning), 'if faculty, faculty developers, administrators and educational researchers join in a coordinated and consistent effort to understand and implement ... in the classroom, an educational revolution *will* occur in the next decade' (italics in original).

Assessment

Ensuring that assessment practices are imbued with cosmopolitan values is vital if cosmopolitan education is to be implemented successfully. Assessment is a major influence on how students learn and on how teaching is designed. Knight (1995: 13) suggests that 'what we choose to assess, and how, shows quite starkly what we value'. Thus decisions about assessment in a cosmopolitan education need to model the cosmopolitan values being espoused. The path to achieving cosmopolitan assessment starts with a clear understanding of the role of assessment in higher education, and a consideration of best practice in achieving cosmopolitan outcomes. Starting at the beginning, it is

102   *Cosmopolitan classrooms*

valuable to reflect on the purpose of assessment. As Astin and Antonio (2012) emphasise, assessment should help students move closer to their educational goals and add value to their educational experience. This suggests that good assessment is 'for' learning as well as 'of' learning. At the same time, assessment should be sustainable, that is, it should promote life-long learning, both formal and informal (Boud and Falchikov 2005). More broadly, assessment and evaluation should enable institutions to demonstrate that their efforts to produce globally literate graduates are bearing fruit, something that does not currently tend to happen in a systematic way (Coryell et al. 2012).

Good assessment practices rely on clarity of intent and should both reflect the values of an institution and advance the purposes of higher education more broadly. As such, cosmopolitan assessment practices need to be developed with a clear understanding of their purpose and should reflect and advance cosmopolitan values, enhancing the opportunities of students to gain cosmopolitan attributes. For example, if a learning goal is to enhance students' capacity to engage in cross-cultural interaction then this needs to be made explicit in assessment design (Arkoudis et al. 2013). In addition, assessment should give students feedback on their progress, identifying the gap between where they are now and where they want to be in a way that motivates further learning (Falchikov 2005). Students need assessment that gives them feedback on how to enhance their learning, that is innovative and interesting enough to engage them (perhaps involving students in the design of assessment tasks) and that incorporates formative aspects (enabling them to improve their performance) (Bols 2012). All of this should be achieved at the same time as giving educators information about the effectiveness of educational practices through providing information on where students start, where they finish and the environment in which they are learning (Astin and Antonio 2012).

When educators are asked to define the capacities that students need to transfer from higher education to inform effective professional performance and citizenship after graduation, they point to several key elements (Rogers and Mentkowski 2004). Three of these are extremely well correlated with cosmopolitan attributes. First, the ability to collaborate with others, including the conceptualisation of social processes and an ability to consider alternatives. This element incorporates consideration of the perspectives and values of others as well as acting in ways that demonstrate respect for others. Second, the ability to develop others and to be open to interrogating their own biases towards diverse perspectives. This includes demonstrating empathy and sensitivity to difference. Third, the ability to assess their own performance and abilities through reflection on conflicts between different perspectives and values. If these elements are deemed important by educators, then it is essential that they are reflected in specifications of learning outcomes, and hence in assessment practices. There are a number of ways in which this can be done.

Learner-centred assessment practices have much to offer to cosmopolitan assessment. This is an approach to assessment that focuses on fostering students' learning and can include activities such as students evaluating each other's work, presentations and team projects. This is a good starting place for cosmopolitan assessment as learner-centred practices are already widely used in the higher education sector (Webber 2011). 'Performance assessment' refers to ways of assessing, and enhancing, the ability of students to integrate theory and practice. This can be done through authentic assessment that calls on students to demonstrate considered action in addressing a situation in a specific context (Mentkowski and Sharkey 2011). The ability to integrate and apply learning is correlated with the ability to transfer learning to different contexts. As Mentkowski and Sharkey (2011: 98) explain, 'a strong transferer will adapt what he or she knows and has applied before to construct a new performance informed by prior experience, with enough flexibility to manage the ambiguities and approximations this process of refining and judgment entails'. It is enhanced when self-reflection is included as an element in the assessment, with students not only reflecting on their performance but also analysing it and seeking feedback from others. Overall, this sounds very much like a relevant skill for someone developing cosmopolitan attributes.

'Authentic assessment' is assessment that in some way reflects real world complexities. It tends to be formative assessment that involves performance-based tasks that are based on real-world situations, are cognitively complex, require students to work collaboratively and that have multiple scoring indicators (Frey et al. 2012). An authentic assessment task should be meaningful in its own right, not simply regarded as a means of measurement, and should engage students in a rewarding activity. A 'public defence' of the outcomes, in which students present and argue for their conclusions, is also regarded as being highly beneficial (Wiggins 1989). Action research is one form of authentic assessment that can be particularly valuable in calling on students to address the complexities they are likely to encounter as professionals (see, for example, Maxwell 2012). 'Self-assessment' and 'peer assessment' involve students applying criteria in order to make judgements (Falchikov and Goldfinch 2000). Both approaches have a number of benefits including that they support professional practice and life-long learning of students (Nulty 2011). Nulty (2011: 501) explains that 'they support the exchange of ideas, values and culture [and] provide multiple perspectives and insights'. They give students a degree of autonomy and responsibility for their learning and that of others and can deepen learning as a result (Falchikov 2005). They also challenge the 'ritualised routines' of educators and students and can prompt critical thinking about the learning process (McGarr and Clifford 2013).

It is difficult to measure cosmopolitan attributes. Undoubtedly criteria will be developed in the future, but for now it is necessary to rely on tangential measures. One is the global citizenship scale, with key components of social

104 *Cosmopolitan classrooms*

responsibility, global competence and global civic engagement (Morais and Ogden 2011). While social responsibility appears to be a rather vague term that is difficult to measure in a rigorous way, the other two components seem to incorporate reliable subscales. For global competence these are self-awareness, intercultural communication and global knowledge and for global civic engagement these are involvement in civic organisations, political voice and global civic activism. While initially appearing to be valuable this scale has only been tested with a relatively small number of students in the United States, which raises questions about its broader applicability. Moreover, many of the statements used appear to reflect only very weak notions of global citizenship and to be open to multiple interpretations, such as 'I am able to write an opinion letter to a local media source expressing my concerns over global inequalities and issues' or 'over the next 6 months, I plan to help international people who are in difficulty' (Morais and Ogden 2011: 453–454).

Much more rigorous work has been done around intercultural competence. While espoused learning outcomes of higher education institutions often mention, or at least make a vague reference to, intercultural competence, this is rarely actually measured. There appears to be agreement among higher education scholars and practitioners on a number of essential components, including flexibility, respect, empathy, mindfulness, curiosity, cultural knowledge and understanding, the ability to engage ambiguity and socio-linguistic competence (Deardorff 2006). But this list is so long, and the scope so broad, that it is not particularly helpful to educators who wish to assess their students' intercultural competence. Fortunately, greater advances have been made in the field of psychology, particularly driven by the need for professionals to perform well in the field of international business. A number of tests have been developed to measure cross-cultural competence (also known as 3C). In common, these posit that success in cross-cultural competence consists of two key constructs. First, that individuals are able to successfully adapt, that is alter their behaviour to respond to a given context in order to achieve their objectives. Second, that individuals are able to successfully adjust, that is experience adaptation in a way that is positive, with any negative elements minimised (Matsumoto and Hwang 2013).

Measures of cross-cultural competence look to assess the knowledge, skills and abilities that are believed to influence adaptation and adjustment. Some are culture specific while others are more general in scope. In an evaluation of ten tests of cross-cultural competence, three were found to be the most rigorous, including that they used valid and reliable variables, had concurrent and predictive validity and had been tested on cross-cultural groups (Matsumoto and Hwang 2013). The so-called CQ (Ang et al. 2006) measures how well individuals cope with cultural diversity and includes mental, motivational and behavioural elements. CQ indicates that individuals who are open to new experiences tend to have the best cross-cultural competence. The Intercultural Adjustment Potential Scale (ICAPS) (Matsumoto et al.

Cosmopolitan classrooms   105

2001, 2007) measures the social psychology of adjustment. ICAPS indicates that the ability to regulate emotions, alongside critical thinking and openness are essential ingredients of intercultural adaptation. The multicultural personality questionnaire (MPQ) (van der Zee and van Oudenhoven 2000) measures a number of factors including empathy, openness, curiosity and flexibility. The MPQ suggests that social initiative, in addition to flexibility, openness and emotional stability, is an important element of cross-cultural competence. While each of these three tests highlights different elements, it is interesting to consider the apparent commonalities with the overall importance of openness, flexibility, the ability to control emotions, empathy and critical thinking.

Although Matsumoto and Hwang (2013) are rather critical of the Intercultural Development Inventory (IDI) (Hammer et al. 2003), this is a measure of intercultural competence that has been successfully used with higher education students. It thus serves as an example of how a measure of cross-cultural competence might be used by educators. The IDI is based on the Developmental Model of Intercultural Sensitivity (Bennett 1986), which consists of a continuum from ethnocentrism to ethnorelativism that proceeds from denial, defence and minimisation to acceptance, adaptation and, ultimately, integration. The IDI consists of 50 items delivered online and was developed to measure constructions of cultural difference. While the instrument has been designed for multiple uses, it can be used in educational settings to determine an individual or group's stance towards cultural difference, for example prior to and after an educational intervention aimed at enhancing an appreciation of cultural difference. It can also be used to inform pedagogy. For example, if students are measured at the 'minimisation' stage then relevant pedagogy might include strategies that increase students' understanding of the notion of culture, the basis for cultural difference and a self-awareness of their own cultural orientation(s) (Wang 2013). Using a combination of self-reflective exercises and a repeat of the IDI would be a possible means of assessing learning in this context.

As has been discussed in this section, there are numerous forms of assessment that can be appropriately tailored to measure cosmopolitan attributes. Ensuring their uptake does require, however, a consideration of the structures in place which determine assessment practices in institutions. Norton et al. (2013) find that major constraints to the implementation of innovative assessment practices include a lack of incentive from institutions, factors such as cost and high student numbers and students' focus on grades. Overcoming these kinds of barriers requires support from institutional leaders to nudge the perspectives of students and educators on assessment. This incorporates opening both groups up to forms of assessment in which the power relations between educator and student are reconsidered (Bevitt 2015). The process of change will be aided by educators conducting research into the impact of different assessment styles and sharing the results with colleagues and students (Dickson and Treml 2013).

Conclusion

This chapter has discussed three vital elements for a cosmopolitan education. First, pedagogies that lend themselves to cosmopolitan outcomes, including worldly pedagogy, experiential learning, decolonial pedagogy, active learning and contemplative pedagogy. Second, ensuring that educators have appropriate skills and attributes through hiring educators with international experience, the inclusion of global engagement in promotion criteria, leaders modelling cosmopolitan practices and professional development for educators. Third, assessment practices that both assess and reinforce cosmopolitan learning, such as learner-centred and authentic models of assessment and the use of measures of interculturality. When combined with a cosmopolitan curriculum, these elements will give students the best possible opportunity of gaining cosmopolitan attributes during their higher education studies. While revolutionary in potential, none of the approaches discussed are eccentric in character. In fact their strength lies in the fact that they all represent excellence in higher education and have been proven to optimise students' learning across numerous contexts. The one element that has not yet been discussed is how to draw the potential represented by online methods into the mix. That is the focus of the next chapter.

8 Learning at a distance

Introduction

The previous two chapters have considered cosmopolitan curriculum, pedagogy, assessment and educators. In considering each of these it is common to imagine students learning together in a physical classroom. But this aspect of a higher education is now being turned on its head. Much as social interactions are increasingly conducted online, so too are online modes increasingly infiltrating educational practices. Unsurprisingly, tangible expressions of contemporary education are heavily influenced by the opportunities that innovations in information and communication technologies provide. In the same way that networked communications remove the need to reference geography, education is being 're-spatialised' to become a globally networked form of learning (Seddon 2014). While many students do still attend physical classrooms, it is now common for them to engage in learning activities using a blend of face-to-face and online modalities. At the same time, opportunities are opening up for students to gain a higher education without ever stepping foot in a higher education institution. This has profound implications for higher education sectors around the world and is challenging the increasingly outdated notion that distance learning is some kind of second-class education.

While some doomsayers believe online learning marks the beginning of the end for higher education institutions, for cosmopolitan educators the prospects are stimulating and exciting. When educators are able to tap into the powerful new world of networked learning environments, they have the capacity to transform students' understanding of global civil society, teaching them about how knowledge is shared across boundaries. In many ways this can be seen as 'renewing the cultural mission of higher education' (Starke-Meyerring and Wilson 2009: 2). Online modes enable educators and students to escape the confines of place-based classrooms, build connections with their peers around the world and experience real-time and truly authentic cosmopolitan pedagogies. For educators, they facilitate the diffusion of educational practices across cultures, opening up the space for professional development.

108 *Learning at a distance*

This chapter considers the development of online modes for teaching and learning in higher education. It looks at the way in which they are playing out around the world and their infiltration into higher education practices. It considers the opportunities that are on offer for cosmopolitan educators and the challenges that these opportunities present. It looks at a number of initiatives that are taking place around the world and evaluates their success and potential in terms of assisting students to gain cosmopolitan outcomes. And it concludes with some 'good practice' principles for leveraging online modalities to optimise cosmopolitan learning.

The evolution of online education

Computers have transformed education as much as they have transformed other elements of our lives. Online access has done the same. Harasim (2000) estimates that the first class offered entirely online was 'The Source' in 1981, suggesting that since then online learning has become a mainstream element of higher education. Inevitably distance education was the first to latch on to the potential of online modes in learning, building on the previous model of correspondence courses. For example the British Open University started using an online conferencing system in 1986, and this gradually began replacing some face-to-face tutoring, then expanding to group projects and to enabling global activities (Mason 2000). Change since that time has been rapid and profound. It is perhaps most valuable to view online education on a continuum rather than as an either/or proposition. In some 'traditional' classes all teaching is face to face and learning materials are all available to students in physical format. But, even then, it is very unlikely that students do not, at the very least, google key terms or refer to Wikipedia for some information. In other classes a blended approach is used. Allen and Seaman (2013) define 'blended or hybrid' instruction as when between 30 and 80 per cent of content is delivered online. This is increasingly common, with students viewing video recordings of classes online, accessing learning materials online, logging into library and reference systems to access resources, and submitting assignments by email. The furthest end of the continuum is fully online classes. Under the same definition, these are classified as ones in which more than 80 per cent of course content is delivered online.

Perhaps the ultimate expression of online learning is the 'virtually unlimited classrooms' of Massive Open Online Courses (MOOCs) (Toven-Lindsey et al. 2015). There is no denying that MOOCs have changed the higher education landscape in important ways. Their exponential growth in recent years has opened up new opportunities of access to education from some of the top institutions in the world. The *New York Times* called 2012 the 'Year of the MOOC' (Pappano 2012) and millions of students around the world are enrolled in them. The potential of MOOCs for transnational education is increasingly being recognised by multilateral organisations, with initiatives around the world, particularly aimed at reaching emerging economies. OpenupEd is a European Union initiative that began in 2013 (European Union 2015). Free courses are offered in 11 languages and are designed for self-study. Innovations are now underway to expand OpenupEd to other parts of the world, in partnership with UNESCO (UNESCO 2014). In addition the European Multiple MOOC Aggregator project will allow users to build their own courses using units from a large number of MOOCs (European Union 2014a). In another part of the world, MiriadaX is an Ibero-American platform to share knowledge freely and accommodates courses from 1,345 Latin American higher education institutions (MiriadaX 2015). In China, XuetangX has been created from a consortium of leading Chinese higher education institutions using the edX platform. In addition to making courses from Chinese institutions available, XuetangX will also translate courses from foreign institutions into Mandarin (Cavallario 2014).

MOOCs are clearly an important phenomenon in contemporary higher education. But in many ways the vast amount of attention paid to MOOCs has been a sideshow distracting from more important changes within higher education systems. And this is the slow but inexorable integration of online learning into everyday institutional activities. This is arguably more important than the MOOC phenomenon because it has the potential to impact the experience of many more students. A 2012 survey of more than 4,500 higher education institutions in the US found that 88 per cent of them neither currently offer, nor are planning to offer, a MOOC. Yet 86.5 per cent have online offerings for their students and 70 per cent of academic leaders view online education as an essential element of their institution's long term strategy (Allen and Seaman 2013). Despite the impressive statistics, caution is required in interpreting these figures. Although it might seem impressive that almost nine in ten institutions have 'online offerings', does this actually represent a paradigm shift? Research in the European Union suggests the contrary. A major study found what while there are 'pockets' of innovative activity around online education throughout higher education sectors, these are often regarded as 'optional extras' to mainstream practice. Indeed the report concludes that 'teachers and students alike are more comfortable and familiar with the lecture hall and more traditional teaching styles' (European Union 2014b: 24).

Thus it would appear that while online education is an increasingly valid option for higher education practice, and has the potential to influence the learning experience of higher education students around the world, its uptake has been less widespread than might be expected. This is important in optimising its strengths for cosmopolitan learning because it suggests that both educators and students need support in adapting to new modes of learning. Data from the US, for example, indicate that just 17.4 per cent of educators have taught a subject exclusively online and just 16.1 per cent of educators use online discussion boards on a regular basis (Eagan et al. 2014). This would

110 *Learning at a distance*

indicate that a great deal of support and professional development for educators is required if the opportunities offered by online learning are to infiltrate curricula in a systematic way. This is a particularly important issue when we consider that higher education leaders recognise that teaching online requires more resources and time than face-to-face teaching (Allen and Seaman 2013). Institutions frequently turn to workshops to help educators become more comfortable with new pedagogies. While these can be valuable, research indicates that forms of professional development such as one-on-one assistance, mentoring, collaborative teaching, access to 'how to' videos and training from instructional designers are of greater value (Lackey 2011). This finding concurs with McQuiggan (2012), who suggests that preparing educators for online learning requires not simply translation but instead transformation, including the opportunity to reflect on teaching per se, and to look at education through new eyes.

In the same way that many educators are not ready to integrate online learning into their pedagogy, neither can it be assumed that all students are fully fledged digital natives with the capacity to make the most of online learning. While most contemporary higher education students are familiar with using the internet, this does not necessarily translate to an ability to incorporate online practices into their learning. Research suggests that although most students are able to access online content, their ability to engage in other online educational practices such as navigating large bodies of content, extracting information from a variety of formats and working collaboratively with peers cannot be assumed (Parkes et al. 2015). Dray et al. (2011) point to the need to assess students' beliefs, values, confidence and comfort with online learning, while Dabbagh (2007) suggests that to succeed in online learning students also need to have good communication skills, skills in collaboration and the ability to self-direct their learning. The evidence appears to suggest that institutions need to take steps to ensure that their students are ready to optimise online learning activities.

Overall, online learning has grown in importance in the higher education space, and its promise to add value to learning has been recognised by both institutions and multilateral organisations. Despite its promise, we can assume neither that it is currently being used to its potential, nor that all educators and students yet have the wherewithal to optimise the opportunities it presents. Nevertheless, there is now a sufficient critical mass of experience in online education to enable an evaluation of what works and what does not. For cosmopolitan educators this opens up two crucial opportunities. First, to learn from a host of initiatives in online learning in order to determine which ingredients are most likely to help students gain cosmopolitan attributes through online learning. Second, to shed light on good educational practices in online learning and hence be able to inform the further roll-out of online learning across higher education sectors worldwide.

The cosmopolitan potential of online learning

Much of the value of online learning is that it can be experienced by students who are geographically dispersed, rendering access to place-based learning less important. In many ways this can be regarded as democratising access to higher education and rendering national boundaries less potent. As such online education could be viewed as the ultimate expression of international education, opening up cosmopolitan possibilities. But caution is required. As discussed in previous chapters, there is nothing about course content being delivered across national borders that means it will inevitably embody opportunities for students to gain cosmopolitan attributes. Done badly, online learning simply represents a new means of distributing information to students, putting a contemporary face on archaic educational practices (Carroll 2013). Indeed, there are numerous complaints about online education being impersonal and tending to utilise one-way communication (Prude 2013). As a review of pedagogy used in MOOCs concludes, they continue to rely on a model in which educators are producers of knowledge and students are recipients (Toven-Lindsey et al. 2015), hence undermining the transformative potential of online learning.

Done well, however, online learning has the revolutionary potential of removing both physical and mental boundaries between learners, opening them up to commonalities in the human experience and enabling them to draw on knowledge that is multi-perspectival in character. Globally networked learning environments are ones that should facilitate both the transcending of territorial barriers and new types of interactions in which educators and students cooperate to build new knowledge through a process of critical reflection and deep interaction. This potential was recognised more than 20 years ago when Riel (1993: 222) discussed the role of computers in global education, arguing that when students and educators engage in collaborative learning activities through the medium of computers 'the power and speed of human learning is extended by their collective knowledge and rich set of experiences'. This sentiment was further expanded by McLoughlin (2001: 15) who argued that virtual communities that come together in computer-mediated networks can enable learning in which 'cross-national dialogue leads to new forms of understanding'. As both point out, however, this will not occur automatically but requires educators to use appropriate pedagogies and to embody relevant values. While hopes for the transformatory potential of online learning are high, the greatest challenge is to move to higher forms of learning, in which knowledge is built and students gain a greater understanding of themselves (Wallace 2003).

In considering the potential for online learning to give students opportunities to gain cosmopolitan attributes, it is worth breaking down online learning into discrete pedagogical elements and then assessing current practices against each one. Perhaps the most well-known categorisation was developed

112 *Learning at a distance*

by Salmon (2000) who identifies five pedagogical stages in online learning (see also Salmon et al. 2010). First, 'access and motivation' in which students get used to an online environment and are welcomed and encouraged by educators. Second, 'online socialisation' in which students start sending and receiving messages and educators support students by familiarising them with the online environment and its potential in helping students learn from each other. Third, 'information exchange' in which students engage in tasks that call on them to send and receive relevant information to and from their peers, and educators facilitate communications and support the use of learning materials. Fourth, 'knowledge construction' in which students negotiate with each other to develop new knowledge and educators facilitate progress. Fifth, 'development' in which students gain new understanding through self-reflection and explore how they can integrate what they have gained from the online experience into other elements of their learning, with educators simply supporting.

A number of important themes arise from this staged model. First, that students need to be given a step-by-step introduction to online learning that enables them to take greater and greater control over their own learning. Second, that educators should start by taking an active role but, as students gain confidence, they need to move out of the spotlight towards supporting student-led activities. Third, that basic information exchange is required before students can start to build knowledge together. This step enables the development of trust between students and establishes collaborative norms. Finally, and of greatest relevance for cosmopolitan learning, the potential for students to transcend their own paradigms and to gain an awareness of, and appreciation for, different perspectives, comes in stages four and five. For this to happen, stages one to three need to be very carefully designed and facilitated. And as accounts of online learning make clear again and again, this tends to be where things go awry, undermining any cosmopolitan potential. Common issues that are highlighted in the literature, some of which are discussed at greater length below, include that students have inadequate internet access or poor internet speeds, educators do not know how to facilitate students' introduction to online learning, timelines are too limited for students to work through the five stages, tasks are not designed to stimulate peer-to-peer sharing, and the continued central role of educators prevents students from taking responsibility for their own learning and from building knowledge together.

Pitfalls of online learning

For obvious reasons, the discipline of geography is one of those more advanced in international collaborative online learning. The focus on space-based adaptations to global forces – both environmental and social – lends itself to engaging perspectives from around the world. In the United States, the Association of American Geographers has developed the Center for

Global Geography Education (CGGE). CGGE is a library of online resources that geography educators can use to support collaborative teaching and learning. This has been done in an explicit response to enhance student skills in international collaboration, spatial analysis of problems, intercultural communication and their ability to critically reflect on their place-based perspectives (Klein and Solem 2008). As these objectives suggest, the resources should stimulate students to engage in communication, learning and thinking that is cosmopolitan in nature. The online modules also lend themselves to a cosmopolitan pedagogy, with a focus on global themes such as migration, climate change, population and natural resources (Association of American Geographers 2015). Each module includes collaborative projects designed for online collaboration between geography students in different countries. They use wikis, blogs and discussion forums, in addition to freely available online resources, to facilitate students working together to research and evaluate issues within the modules. Again, this should enable deep interaction between students from different parts of the world.

An evaluation of the implementation of CGGE collaborative projects across ten countries found that by working collaboratively students were engaged in the perspectives of their peers from other countries, enhancing their understanding of the issues at hand. Examples include a collaboration between students in Texas and those in Papua New Guinea on a module on nationalism (Baiio and Ray 2011) and a collaboration between students in California and those in Chile on sustainable development (Conway-Gomez and Araya-Palacios 2011). Disappointingly, however, evaluations have shown extremely mixed results when it comes to the impact on students. And it certainly does not seem that students have gained much in the way of cosmopolitan attributes as a result. Indeed, the inverse could have occurred. While students found the experiences to be positive overall, and appeared to gain confidence in their geographic skills, in the California-Chile example, Chilean students reported that their concern for how people in other countries are affected by global issues actually *declined* after the collaboration and students in the USA reported that they thought it was *less* important to learn about how their peers think about global issues after the collaboration than before (Conway-Gomez and Araya-Palacios 2011). It was thought that the short (four-week) duration and lack of video conferencing could have led to these negative outcomes by depersonalising the experience. Similarly, while some groups engaged in deep dialogue and numerous personal interactions, others did not go beyond the task requirements and a review of nine different collaborations concluded that 'true international collaboration and problem-solving was limited' (Klein and Solem 2008: 253). Again it was felt that the lack of synchronous communication could have led to this outcome. In the Texas-Papua New Guinea example, which was rendered logistically complex by poor infrastructure in the latter location, the overall conclusion was that 'more prolonged and in-depth interaction would be preferred' (Baiio and Ray 2011: 295).

114 *Learning at a distance*

These issues highlight the need for extremely careful design and facilitation of online learning collaborations. As Nichol et al. (2012) suggest, a culture shift is required to optimise the learning potential from online technologies, incorporating an increase in the support that institutions provide to educators to design learning activities. It is all too easy for students to fall back into familiar patterns, as evidence from an online learning experience aimed at teaching educators in China and the UK about intercultural online learning demonstrated. Despite the subject matter of the course, and the expectation that participants would be intrinsically motivated to go out of their way to interact across cultures, there was significantly more interaction between participants from the same background than between participants from different backgrounds (Stepanyan et al. 2014). This speaks volumes about the need to carefully consider a number of elements in designing online learning to achieve cosmopolitan outcomes. In a review of online learning activities aimed at enhancing intercultural sensitivity, Bégin-Caouette (2013) suggests that student outcomes are particularly influenced by collaboration, intensity and mutuality. He argues that intense collaboration, characterised by a significant level of interaction and deeply meaningful tasks, is of special importance in helping transform the way in which students think about each other.

Making online learning cosmopolitan

Much of the research into cross-cultural online education is bogged down in assumptions about how students from different cultures interact online. This needs to be problematised and transcended in order to optimise the cosmopolitan potential of online learning. The current approach reinforces stagnant beliefs about clear demarcations between uniform cultures, something that is not only inaccurate but that also acts as a barrier to cosmopolitan understandings. Many educators suggest that students from one culture (e.g. 'Westerners') tend to approach online education in a different way to students from another culture (e.g. 'Asians') (see, for example, Kim and Bonk 2002; Popov et al. 2014; Wresch et al. 2005). Indeed a review of 27 experiences found that facilitators agreed that 'culture is inseparable from distance learning and teaching' and made assumptions about how students from different backgrounds were expected to behave (Uzuner 2009). Most studies rely on Hofstede's (2001) identification of five cultural dimensions – power distance, individualism/collectivism, masculinity/femininity, uncertainty avoidance and long-/short-term orientation. This has had a profound impact on the way in which cultural difference is regarded and conceptualised, not only in education but also in many other fields, including management. Fortunately, their applicability is beginning to be questioned. Taras et al. (2010: 428) examined 598 studies on these dimensions and suggest that at the individual level of analysis there is little statistical evidence to support the predictive power of any of them. They argue that a much wider array of

Learning at a distance 115

cultural values need to be considered and ask 'are cultural values too broad and the approach to studying them too deterministic to be useful in future research?'.

Thus, the first step in a cosmopolitan agenda for online education is to get away from overly simplistic categorisations in order to develop a more sophisticated understanding of cross-cultural interactions. This does not mean assuming that all students will interact online in the same way. Instead, it is important to acknowledge that a number of dimensions influence how students engage in learning. For educators this means that no assumptions can be made about how students will approach online collaborations with their peers around the world. No uniformity in expectations should be assumed. Students may have experienced different norms and be familiar with different styles of communication in an educational environment. This may encompass perceptions of turn taking, time management and task distribution, as well as the interpretation of social cues (Popov et al. 2013). As Wang (2007) suggests, educators need to ensure that learning activities are designed to ensure that all learners – regardless of their differences – can experience optimal learning. Indeed, the same could be said for any educational activity. Tapanes et al. (2009) take this further, suggesting that providing a learning environment in which all students – regardless of their preconceptions about interaction – feel safe to participate is important for success in online learning. This is important because the quality of group interactions has a strong influence on student learning outcomes (Lim and Liu 2006). This awareness is particularly important in ameliorating potential problems. If, for example, some teams of students are more reluctant to build solidarity with each other than others, there is evidence that this can be improved through educator-facilitated interaction (Lim and Liu 2006). An awareness of different perceptions among students towards content, technology, collaboration is essential in informing pedagogy for online learning. In addition to ensuring that all participants have access to sufficient infrastructure to facilitate their online interaction, the considerations discussed here are an essential element in Salmon's (2000) stage one pedagogy of access and motivation.

Stage two in Salmon's (2000) model refers to online socialisation in which students begin to interact with each other. This is followed by stage three in which students exchange information with each other. Many online learning experiences fall down in these stages with numerous reports of imbalances in interaction, disagreements about who should do what, delays in responding, miscommunications and some students withdrawing from interacting altogether. The prevalence of such occurrences across years of online learning has led to significant advances in how interaction can be facilitated. In optimising online learning for cosmopolitan outcomes, students need to be encouraged to engage in interactions that are most likely to stimulate cosmopolitan attributes. Thus the methods that have been developed to stimulate online interaction more broadly can usefully be applied.

116 *Learning at a distance*

Perhaps the most powerful approach is to use collaboration scripts, which are 'scaffolds' that stimulate students by making explicit the goal of collaborative tasks, outlining useful methodologies, and assigning roles (Fischer et al. 2013). They can be developed by students or provided by educators, and they can be fixed or dynamic. Their aim is to support students to go beyond what they are familiar with in order to engage in a more advanced and complex level of collaboration than may naturally occur, and to guide students towards particular learning outcomes. If online collaboration involves students in different locations it is not easy to determine how team members are progressing with their tasks. One solution is to use a group awareness tool incorporating both cognitive and social awareness (Janssen and Bodemer 2013). Examples include having group members construct concept maps of the learning issue so they can compare their knowledge and identify gaps (Engelmann and Hesse 2010), or asking students to rate the contributions of their peers (Buder and Bodemer 2008). Scripts such as these have been found to particularly enhance interaction among groups of students from different cultural backgrounds, leading to more questions, more requests for both feedback and information and greater checking of understanding (Popov et al. 2013).

Implementing this kind of engagement can be challenging for educators, particularly if they are expected to cede control of learning to students. It is essential that educators feel confident to facilitate online international collaborations among students. And the hardest part of teaching can be knowing when to let go. It would be inadvisable to throw educators into the 'deep end' and expect them to know what to do. One possibility is that they begin with a 'low-risk' project in which student interactions are relatively limited but in which educators gain experience in collaborating in teaching with colleagues in other countries. The '6 Continents Project' is an example of a collaborative online learning exercise in the field of social work, with participation from students in the USA, Sweden, Trinidad and Tobago, Australia and Hong Kong (the participation of students in Lesotho was initially included but was unable to occur) (Rowan et al. 2014). The project utilised asynchronous video sharing in which educators uploaded videos of their students discussing social work problems in their contexts. Educators reported gaining confidence in their own cultural competence and a greater understanding of the international context that resulted in changes in the curriculum. The technology used was relatively simple and it is likely this gave educators confidence to take more risks in the future. While students did not participate in synchronous interactions with each other, they reported that they had gained insights into international social work issues. There are clear opportunities to deepen the interactions of students, and to engage them in group work, in order to enhance opportunities for cross-cultural learning. But as a first step a project of this kind is valuable in connecting educators and facilitating an initiation into the possibilities for online learning across cultures, learning that has great potential for cosmopolitan outcomes.

More sophisticated approaches are required if online learning is to move to the fourth and fifth stages of Salmon's (2000) model. In a cosmopolitan model, students should be able to build a cosmopolitan understanding as they construct knowledge with their peers and reflect on their perspectives. For educators these are the most 'hands-off' stages of online learning, but that does not mean that they can be left to chance. Instead, design of online learning becomes ever more important. It is well known that diverse teams have value in the range of experiences and perspectives that they can bring to a situation, but this can only be an advantage if dialogue is able to bring forth implicit knowledge (Berg 2012). The 'Cross-Cultural Rhetoric Project' at Stanford University developed protocols and best practices for learning across cultures through online collaboration (Stanford University undated). Its focus was rhetoric, viewed as 'texts that embody cultural values' (O'Brien and Eriksson 2009: 2). In the project students worked in cross-cultural teams through online technologies to consider multiple perspectives on examples of rhetoric, with the objective of enhancing intercultural competency in communication. Students at Stanford connected via webcam with small teams of peers in Sweden, Singapore, Australia and Egypt. Students were assessed through group assignments such as joint projects, speech writing and blogs. Research indicates that students learned to engage in cross-cultural communication with a greater degree of sensitivity, awareness and understanding (O'Brien and Eriksson 2009).

This is an example of a carefully designed project that focuses on deep interaction between students and has an explicit objective of improving the ability of students to question their own perspectives. Other studies have utilised a range of approaches to stimulate deep levels of cultural understanding in students through intensive interactions. In a study of online synchronous communication between the USA and Azerbaijan, Osman and Herring (2007) found that equal participation, collaborative negotiation and cognitive activity all increase across synchronous interactions, leading to dynamic exchanges despite significant language difficulties. This points to the value in real-time interactions between students. Although video discussions are often regarded as essential in synchronous communication, this example effectively utilised online chatting between students, something that was found to stimulate spontaneous communication and deep learning. Other studies have also emphasised the value of synchronous chat in stimulating critical thinking (Levin et al. 2006). Another study brought together students from the USA, UK, Russia, South Korea and Sweden on a five-week shared wiki-development project. Despite the relatively short duration, the project was found to have had a significant impact on the cultural competencies of participants (Ertmer et al. 2011). Students were shown to have become more open and accepting of different cultures based on a pre- and post-survey. A different approach was utilised in Norway to overcome the self-imposed segmentation of a multicultural group of students. In online interaction in team activities, identities were anonymised so that students did

118 *Learning at a distance*

not know who they were interacting with. This was found to enhance collaboration, including when identities were revealed and teams continued to work together (Berg 2012).

These are just a small number of examples of many online learning exercises. Their diversity illustrates that there is no 'best' way to design online learning to encourage students to engage in deep learning, but that facilitating authentic learning activities that engage students in intensive communication with each other are essential in achieving positive outcomes. While all of the examples here had a goal of enhancing communications across cultures, none explicitly aimed to ensure that students gained cosmopolitan attributes. But other examples of online learning activities have much more explicit goals in mind – aiming to enhance students' engagement with global issues in order to alter their knowledge and assumptions. One example is a peace education initiative from the European Middle East Virtual University that brought together Christian, Jewish and Muslim students (Firer 2008). This was developed to give students access to up-to-date and factual knowledge and to enhance attributes including empathy, tolerance and respect. This was shown to enable students to create connections around their mutual challenges and a desire to disrupt assumptions held by members of their communities. Firer (2008) contends that online education is particularly well suited to active and latent conflict situations, giving students access to information beyond the rhetoric of opposing groups, enabling low-risk interactions in a relatively neutral environment, providing ample time for reflection and opening up windows on former conflict zones where tensions have been largely resolved.

Taking a different approach, the Global Solidarity Network Study e-Broad Program is an initiative of Catholic Relief Services. It links students at Catholic institutions such as Seattle University with aid workers in the field around the world through live video sessions in order to give students an insight into global justice issues (Pozniak 2015). Evaluation has suggested that the programme advances students' understanding of global justice issues and enhances their compassion towards those affected by difficult circumstances (Harrison et al. 2010). A further example is the International Online Race Conference that brought together social work and criminology students from the USA, UK and South Africa to address racism. The conference took place through online discussion boards over a four-week period, with students encouraged to think critically about the social, cultural and personal nature of racism (Buchanan et al. 2008: 681). Student evaluations indicate an increase in knowledge about racism as well as an enhanced ability to view issues from the perspectives of others and the authors conclude that 'this medium could lend itself to exposing students to multi-identity discussions across differences in ways they otherwise would not be exposed to in their respective university settings'.

As has been illustrated in this section, there is an array of approaches to online education that lend themselves to cosmopolitan learning. The basic advantage of online education is that it enables students to learn with peers from other parts of the world. But simply giving students the opportunity to interact with each other is insufficient to achieve cosmopolitan outcomes. Instead, attention needs to be paid to all elements of online learning. Of greatest importance is how students interact – stimulating deep learning, critical thinking and an awareness of, and valuing of, multiple perspectives will not come about unless interactions are carefully designed and well structured. Increasing attention is now being paid to the technology underlying online learning. As social media becomes omnipresent in modern lives, educators are finding more and more ways to optimise it for educational outcomes. But moving far beyond this, educators are also starting to realise the potential that lies in games and simulations, placing students in a virtual world and having them respond to authentic situations.

Leveraging advances in online interaction

Beyond purpose, design, support for interaction and educator preparedness, another element of online learning relates to the choice of technology to use. A myriad of forms of social media are used in higher education, both by students and educators. Twitter to Tumblr, Facebook to Flickr and many more forms of social media have been woven into contemporary higher education practice enabling interactions, the transfer of knowledge and the fostering and reinforcement of relationships. As Johnson et al. (2014: 8) suggest, social media 'augments already-established relationships while providing spaces for people who are separated by physical distance or other barriers to connect with each other'. It responds to the call for graduates who are both proficient in communication and also engaged with the global community (Helfand 2013). As such they have much to offer cosmopolitan communities of practice. A whole range of web conferencing platforms are available to facilitate collaborative learning. A review of 15 different platforms found that Adobe Connect and Google Hangouts were particularly well suited to enable collaboration between students (McDaniel et al. 2013)

A study of educators at higher education institutions in the US found that 59 per cent believe that learning environments can be enhanced by online and mobile technologies (Seaman and Tinti-Kane 2013). The greatest impact reported is that technologies have massively increased the contact between educators and students. In terms of usage, more than 70 per cent of educators use social media at least monthly, 55 per cent use it for work and 41 per cent use it in their teaching. Blogs, wikis and podcasts are most commonly used for teaching, with educators asking students to create, as well as consume, them. Concerns remain, however, about how to verify student achievement and also how to protect the integrity of both students and educators. While some educators are already actively using online and social media platforms in their teaching, many are not. Digital literacy cannot be assumed among all educators and thus it falls on institutions to ensure that educators can

120   *Learning at a distance*

access professional development where needed. As Johnson et al. (2014) suggest, such professional development requires more than superficial engagement and needs to enable experiential learning.

Games and simulation are relatively new to the higher education arena but are growing in uptake. Both have the potential to provide students with learning experiences that are highly engaging and that also generate effective learning outcomes. As with other forms of internet-facilitated learning, they have particular potential for collaborative learning across distances, making them of interest to cosmopolitan educators. Both approaches can place students in virtual environments that mimic the real world and in which students are called on to find solutions to problems (Buck 2013). In the case of gaming, they use entertainment to achieve educational goals (Greitzer et al. 2007). Both can be designed to call on students to engage in collaborative action and can stimulate deep levels of communication in achieving goals (Webb and Sims 2006). Where collaboration is required, individuals are called on to value the diversity of each other's perspectives and to negotiate outcomes, bringing players together in a 'collective dynamic'. In many cases experiential learning and reflection are embedded and this strengthens their potential to be effective in education (Webb and Sims 2006). Instant feedback that students receive can enhance student engagement (Charles et al. 2011). Much remains to determine how games and simulation can be used in higher education to generate effective learning outcomes, however (Tsekleves et al. 2014). And the use of games in cosmopolitan learning has not yet come under serious consideration.

Both games and simulation tend to involve role playing. This involves students taking on personas and addressing challenges in their assumed role in a complex social learning environment (Russell and Shepherd 2010). Role playing can provide students with authentic learning environments that call on them to engage in a particular role, communicate with other players, engage in reflective activities and collaborate to solve problems. An example is the International Communication and Negotiation Simulations (ICONS), which is run by the Center for International Development and Conflict Management in the Department of Government and Politics at the University of Maryland in the United States (University of Maryland 2015). This provides the opportunity for educators to use online role-play simulations in their teaching. The simulations address complex issues and require students to take on the roles of stakeholders in a given situation and negotiate solutions. Simulations include a border dispute between Thailand and Cambodia, multi-country responses to globalisation, a crisis between India and Pakistan, debates at the International Whaling Commission, responding to international crime, global food security and waste management. The platform enables students to communicate with each other, collaboratively edit documents and vote on decisions, and it has been used by higher education institutions in 53 countries.

Another form of role playing is a 3-D virtual environment such as Second Life (Linden Research Inc. 2015) or ActiveWorlds (ActiveWorlds Inc. 2015).

These differ from more commonly used online environments by utilising a shared virtual environment and allowing students to create, and interact as, avatars. Arguably, this provides students with a sense of real-world interaction, supporting communication and information processes and enhancing team collaboration (van der Land et al. 2011). The ability to design their own avatars (animated figures) enables students to present themselves as they wish, and the interaction of avatars enables the use of a greater range of cues than in standard online interaction, increasing cooperation. Salmon has updated her five stage pedagogy of online education to address education in 3-D environments (Salmon et al. 2010). This considers the creation of avatars as 'access and motivation', connecting through artefacts and activities as 'online socialisation', helping others to achieve goals as 'information exchange', collaborating in the construction and manipulation of artefacts as 'knowledge construction' and the reflection on experiences in the 3-D environment and links to real life as 'development'. The authors suggest that, much as for other forms of online learning, the 'online socialisation' stage 'provides the building blocks in the scaffold for much more group learning later on' (2010: 181). Initiatives such as the Second World Immersive Future Teaching at the University of Leicester in the United Kingdom are developing 'immersive learning' activities for students, currently in the discipline of biomedical sciences but with the intention of broader applications in the future (University of Leicester 2015).

Virtual worlds tend to be used in educational contexts to give students a sense of contextualised learning and to engage students by enabling them to explore, develop and alter virtual objects (Dalgarno and Lee 2010). They enable synchronous interaction and communication by multiple parties (Kim et al. 2012). There are examples from a range of disciplines in which simulations are used to enhance student learning. For example medical students can interview and diagnose virtual patients (Danforth et al. 2009), law students can deal with probate (Serby 2011), language learners can immerse themselves in a foreign environment (Peterson 2010), religion students can visit a Buddhist temple (Prude 2013) and science students can undertake virtual laboratory experiments (Bainbridge 2007). In some cases virtual campuses are created to enable students in a range of disciplines to engage in simulated experiential learning (Herold 2012; Hong Kong Polytechnic University 2011).

One example is Monash Chinese Island, created by the Chinese Studies Programme at Monash University in Australia. Using Second Life, Chinese Island provides an immersive Chinese environment to learn about Chinese language and culture. While primarily designed for language students at the university, it is also available to external users (Monash University 2015). Users can engage in both synchronous and asynchronous task-based activities and access a range of multimedia learning materials. It is designed to be learner centred and incorporates elements such as chatting with characters and communicating with educators at the National Taiwan Normal University.

122 *Learning at a distance*

Tasks become increasingly complex as students' language skills develop. For example early learners may need to purchase a train ticket, medium learners visit a doctor, while more advanced learners interview guests on a television chat show.

Virtual learning environments enable the creation of 'pedagogical agents' in the form of animated characters who can help guide student learning (Haake and Gulz 2009). Such agents can take on the role of educators or can embody a character designed to challenge student perspectives and prompt critical thinking. This requires careful design to both optimise authenticity and to allow for flexibility in responses. For example the system needs to select scenarios that are appropriate for the needs of a given student or group of students at a moment in time and then adapt the simulation in response to student interaction (Wray et al. 2009). Agents can also stimulate student interaction through, for example, directed interventions. This has been shown to increase the level of reasoning among students, leading to more sophisticated dialogue (Tegos et al. 2014). The type and frequency of student interactions can also be recorded and correlated with learning outcomes to indicate how design can be improved to enhance learning (Yoo and Kim 2014).

Many of the characteristics of simulation lend themselves to assisting students to gain cosmopolitan attributes, and there are a number of examples where this has been attempted. A number of virtual learning environments have been created to enable students to gain cultural knowledge and communication skills, including Adaptive Thinking and Leadership System (Raybourn et al. 2005), Bilateral Negotiation Trainer (Institute for Creative Technologies 2015), Tactical Language and Culture Training System (Johnson and Valente 2009) and Virtual Environment Cultural Training for Operational Readiness (ChiSystems 2015). These tend to position 'culture' as a uniform construct and this reduces their potential for cosmopolitan learning. This is partly due to their purpose – all were created for use by the United States military, for example teaching soldiers how to interact with Iraqis. Nevertheless, they demonstrate the potential that simulation has for enabling cosmopolitan outcomes, if designed appropriately, and it is thus worth considering their stronger points, particularly their attempts to prompt students to question their assumptions. All use scenarios that place students in virtual real world contexts and ask them to respond to authentic situations. Several involve a perspective-taking approach in which students are called on to adopt the interests, needs and attitudes of a character. All incorporate the need to communicate and interact with people from different backgrounds and with a range of motivations, and some use communication simulations that assess the effectiveness of a chosen strategy in achieving certain outcomes (Lane et al. 2013). Some include peer rating in which students assess each other's effectiveness in playing roles. Others incorporate guided reflection in which the pedagogical agent reviews the role plays and encourages students to reflect on their choices, behaviours and assumptions (Ogan and Lane 2010).

Learning at a distance 123

While these simulations contain promising features they do not incorporate elements that are designed to stimulate cosmopolitan attributes such as empathy and openness, and further development and research is required to see if this is possible to achieve. Ogan and Lane (2010) suggest that using narrative to evoke these responses could be done by building on elements built in to commercial video games, and by incorporating intercultural competence assessment to learn about the mechanisms that lead to specific outcomes in students. The ability to use 'adaptive tailoring' to target certain behaviours (Wray et al. 2009) offers particular potential for cosmopolitan learning. For example, simulations can be scaffolded to assist the development of particular attributes through altering the environment in response to student contributions. As student responses show development, the scaffolds can be removed so that students can demonstrate higher levels of learning. At the same time, challenges or situations can be adapted to suit different levels of student awareness and to target particular behaviours. All of these enable the manipulation of the virtual environment to optimise student outcomes (Wray et al. 2009). Wiggins (2012) suggests that a combination of socially situated contexts, experiential learning, situated decision making, reflexivity and reflection are essential elements in encouraging students to move beyond their familiar paradigms to acknowledge different cultural constructs. It is evident that the development of games or simulations that stimulate cosmopolitan attributes would be a significant contribution to contemporary higher education.

Conclusion

This chapter has considered the possibilities offered by online learning in assisting students to gain cosmopolitan outcomes during their higher education studies. It has considered a range of approaches, from those already commonly utilised in contemporary higher education to those that are very much at the cutting edge of higher education practice (and which many educators may regard as a step too far). The myriad of examples of online practices included in this chapter are but a small sample of those which have been developed in practice. But as some of the discussion in this chapter has indicated, too many attempts to utilise online learning to achieve particular outcomes fail to achieve their objectives. It could be said that this is equally true of many offline forms of education. But when online learning is specifically designed to bring students from different backgrounds together to enhance some form of cross-cultural understanding, the disappointment when it does not achieve its goals is somehow all the more cutting. Fortunately, there is now a sufficiently large wealth of experience to begin to be able to discern what differentiates a successful online educational activity from one that fails to optimise the online space. This chapter concludes with some indications of what these might be.

If online learning is to help students gain cosmopolitan attributes it needs to start with a clear purpose in mind. Many activities reflect the face-to-face

124 *Learning at a distance*

assumption that if students interact with those different to themselves they will somehow be transformed by the experience. We know that this is not the case, so a very careful design of online learning activities is essential. Cosmopolitan elements should imbue the entire process, from design, to learning activities, to evaluation. When educators from more than one institution are to be involved then it is critical that design is genuinely collaborative, modelling the behaviour that educators wish to stimulate in students. Students themselves need to be properly prepared for the experience. This includes giving them a clear idea of expectations and an opportunity to think about how to solve problems they may encounter. Explicit reference to the dangerous assumptions that can be made when collaborating online with peers in other countries could usefully be addressed in advance, at the very least ensuring that students become self-reflective if they experience frustration. Learning activities need to ensure that students are given a gradual introduction to online learning and are allowed to engage in relatively low-risk information-transfer type activities before they are called on to engage with peers on a deeper basis. This is essential in building trust between students and establishing good relationships to enable more sophisticated activities to take place.

Learning tasks themselves, including those which will be assessed, need to be designed in a way that ensures that they call on students to draw on each other's perspectives and value their diverse range of experiences. They should give students the opportunity to create new forms of knowledge, giving them a large degree of freedom in how they reach desired objectives. Deep levels of interaction have been shown to have great importance in online learning, and using scaffolds to ensure that these take place is an excellent approach for educators to use. At the same time, educators must be prepared to stand on the sidelines and facilitate, rather than lead, learning. As interactions deepen and students begin to drive the creation of knowledge, educators must be prepared to stand aside and let learning evolve. A wide range of technologies available to students may mean that they choose to interact in an entirely different way to that specified by the design of the activity. These choices should be supported and be allowed to evolve as they are an important factor in students taking control over their own learning.

Reflection should be integrated throughout, not just as a summative activity. Self-reflection and peer reflection can consider elements such as how students engage with each other, how they take responsibility for creating knowledge, how their assumptions and perspectives are challenged, and any changes in their understanding of the world. If claims are to be made about the impact that a learning activity has on student beliefs then a rigorous pre-/post-test assessment needs to be used to establish the extent of change and to identify which mechanisms have had the greatest impact. Finally, student and educator experiences should be thoroughly evaluated in order to learn from the experience and to inform future activities. None of these elements is revolutionary, indeed all of them would be considered fairly standard aspects of good pedagogical practice in any higher education subject or course.

9 Theory to practice and back again

Educational responses to global contexts

At the time of writing, the news is full of hatred and conflict. Suicide bombers have killed 137 and injured 345 at mosques in Yemen. Gang violence has erupted among marginalised immigrant communities in Sweden. Ancient Christian and Shia Muslim shrines have been destroyed in Iraq. The dead bodies of would-be asylum seekers have been retrieved from the Mediterranean Sea. The European Union has determined that Jerusalem is on the verge of descending into violence. Boko Haram has seized towns in Nigeria and kidnapped or killed their inhabitants. China, Japan and South Korea are embroiled in territorial disputes. And these are just a small selection of news items on one given day. Higher education institutions around the world have arisen from local contexts. But in the twenty-first century they are increasingly defined by the international. With scholarly networks stretching like a web around the world, they cannot be immune to the problems the world is facing. In a recent article, two giants of international education – Altbach and de Wit (2015: 9) – suggest that the cross-border cooperation and exchange enabled by international education plays a fundamentally important role in 'keeping communication open and dialogue active'. More than this, it is essential that higher education institutions graduate students who actively promote mutual understanding with all those they encounter. As future leaders of what is increasingly one global society, they need to be equipped with a set of skills that enable them to facilitate goodwill and positive cooperation.

This poses a profound challenge for contemporary institutions, one that they cannot choose to ignore. When Al Qarawiyyin was established more than 1,100 years ago its focus, along with those of its peers, was on social containment (Talbani 1996). All these years later, what is needed is a focus on social *expansion*. Certainly, there continues to be a need for graduates to gain skills and knowledge with functional value (Halstead 2004) but the value can no longer be measured on local needs alone. Indeed, it is increasingly difficult to conceive of local needs that are in isolation from global needs. And thus institutions cannot maintain a *uni* focus but need to instead

126 *Theory to practice and back again*

focus on the *multi*. For too long student mobility has been regarded by institutions as a proxy for their global engagement. Those that admit large numbers of students from other countries are quick to point to the global environment on campus, as if close proximity will lead to a form of osmosis in which cultural practices are exchanged in an atmosphere of mutual understanding and respect. As we have seen, this is an inadequate response to the demands for global graduates, one that may lead to divisions being entrenched rather than overcome. In the absence of an explicit effort to help students engage with those different from themselves and to develop practices that open them up to absorbing and learning from the influences around them, they take nothing away other than fleeting observations and ill-informed assumptions. The reluctance of higher education institutions to interrogate whether there is added value in the learning that students accrue from a higher education experience, one that takes place in a space tinged with international influences, indicates a derogation of duty, one that can no longer be countenanced. Instead, it is imperative that higher education institutions unpack the assumptions on which their claims of offering students an international experience are based. Institutions need to expand their practice to ensure that students who will be exposed to global spheres of activity are equipped with the cosmopolitan habitus demanded of them as future leaders of a diverse and increasingly interdependent world.

Thus, the discussion in this book has focused on an alternative approach to increasing the likelihood that graduates have an appropriate set of skills for the contemporary world. Instead of students relying on having the financial and social means to engage in mobility, the approaches discussed in the book are democratic in nature, giving all students the opportunity to gain cosmopolitan attributes while they are studying. For too long the presence of students from diverse backgrounds has been taken as code for giving students opportunities to gain global attributes, with institutions making much of the range of food outlets on campus and the 'cultural' celebrations they foster. Instead, this is exactly what theorists mean by a pseudo-cosmopolitan experience. Students may eat food from around the world, travel to other countries in their breaks, share classes with students who are different to them in any number of ways and feel that they are in some way 'worldly'. But unless education explicitly addresses what it means to be a member of the family of human beings, and unless curricula and pedagogy provide students with meaningful opportunities to gain cosmopolitan assets, the 'multicultural campus' is nothing more than window dressing that obscures a failure to adequately educate students to lead in a global era.

The book started with Frijhoff's (1996) suggestion that three elements – learning, utility and virtue – guide the development of higher education institutions. It has been consistently posited throughout this book that weaving insights from the cosmopolitan literature into higher education practice is an optimal response to contemporary challenges. Cosmopolitan learning is crucial in leading to cosmopolitan utility and cosmopolitan virtue

Theory to practice and back again 127

in a world in which the alternative to a cosmopolitan way of being is frighteningly apparent in the news headlines. This is arguably the obvious next step in the continuing evolution of the higher education sector. Changes to the shape and practice of institutions over time have both reflected and influenced social practices. In a world where the social is global, whether we engage with those on the other side of the world directly or are simply drawn into the international sphere of influence, the global demands appropriate responses. Applying cosmopolitan theory to higher education practice starts from the understanding that human interactions are the ultimate expression of globalisation, and that it is not necessary to be globally mobile in order to engage with those who are different from ourselves. A cosmopolitan approach to education is a response to the need for higher education institutions to help students gain a set of skills and attributes that will stand them in good stead as they become leaders of tomorrow's world, a world in which there is an urgent need to view diversity as an asset rather than a challenge and to find ways to expand definitions of 'we'.

Emerging challenges for educators

The prevalent models and discourses in higher education have always been, and continue to be, prescribed by those in nations that dominate the political and economic spheres of activity. But we are living in an era in which new forms of power are emerging, new not only in their geographic locus but also new in their directionality. Traditional forms of power, in which nation states and financial markets shape the contours within which we live our lives, are shifting inexorably from North America and Europe to Asia and the 'South'. At the same time, new forms of power are arising, characterised by bottom-up forms of civic participation and action, connected by information and communication technologies, drawing together actors around the globe to leverage their collective power on issues of importance (Biccum 2015). Both of these dynamics – North–West to South–East and top-down to bottom-up – are likely to pose a set of new challenges for those tasked with leading higher education sectors and institutions around the world. As Gramsci (1971) argues, education has long been a force of compliance producing subjects that can reinforce the prevailing hegemony. As that prevailing hegemony alters, so too does education need to, and it will. At the same time, we need to ensure that education challenges prevailing assumptions to promote what Freire terms 'emancipatory change' (Freire and Torres 1994).

This context calls for a forward-looking approach to education policy and practice. As new hegemonies and disparate forces converge, the education space will undoubtedly respond. A key element in how this response will be formulated is the cadre of key actors in global educational policy making. Recent research illustrates the commonalities of those who currently hold these positions. Lingard et al. (2015: 36) identify their middle-class cultural capital, 'high-modernist disposition' and understanding of education in

128   *Theory to practice and back again*

global terms. Most pertinently the authors note an emphasis on 'the homogenising force of "globalisation" as both discourse and practice . . . tends to minimise the importance of cultural specificity at national/local scales'. It is likely that this approach will come under increasing pressure from the forces noted above. And the strength of the cosmopolitan approach in dealing with such forces is an important consideration. Hansen et al. (2009: 605) suggest that the value of a cosmopolitan approach to education is that it provides an opportunity for students to learn about:

> the concrete consequences of their ways of enacting values ... [creating] a dynamic platform for reconstructing creatively culture and values such that they can survive and endure while also contributing humanely to a cosmos in which every person's actions, and every community's actions, increasingly affect others both near and far.

This means that through practicing dialogue, engagement and self-reflexivity, students can learn to imagine a common future that is no longer fractured by distrust of those who seem to be different. Achieving this outcome requires approaches to education that start with the perspective and experience of students and facilitate students working together to construct knowledge through the interrogation of their reality.

A cosmopolitan approach enables us to see how life can be transformed in a way that does not require people to pick sides, but instead to understand that we are all on the same side. In looking back through history there are numerous examples of conflict arising from perceptions of difference. But there are also examples of people transcending difference in order to reach out to those in need. Learning from moments in which humans throughout history have come together rather than focusing on entrenched difference, and gaining an appreciation of the dynamic nature of human life, can help us learn how to navigate the complexities we will inevitably encounter. Hansen (2010: 164) suggests that a cosmopolitan approach starts from viewing ourselves as human first, and entertaining novelty in people, ideas and values through an understanding of the multiplicity that characterises our humanity. Through education infused with cosmopolitan notions, students can learn about themselves and about how to interact with others. As Hansen (2008: 308) argues, 'ultimately, a cosmopolitan sensibility may be a crucial outlook for persons everywhere who aspire, in a rapidly changing world, to realize the fullness of experience rather than merely suffer it'.

An important consideration for cosmopolitan educators is the need to remain open to a diversity of perspectives, some of which may be resolutely ambivalent to, or even at odds with, a cosmopolitan ethos. 'Cosmopolitan' cannot be imposed on those who resist it and thus educators have to remain cognisant of the need to ensure that a cosmopolitan approach to education simply provides students with the opportunity to gain cosmopolitan attributes. It cannot become a prescriptive notion to which all students must abide

Theory to practice and back again 129

without contradicting its own ethos of openness to difference. Accepting this reality can be unsettling but educators must resist the temptation to judge by what Todd (2007: 36) terms "'thinking cosmopolitan", as opposed to "thinking according to cosmopolitanism"'. Instead, educators need to leave themselves open to an infinite number of interpretations of reality and ways of thinking. As higher education students become increasingly diverse in age, background and geographic location, the need to stay open to a range of views is becoming ever-more crucial. As higher education practice increasingly inhabits a space not bound by geographical constraints, the range of experiences of students becomes almost infinite. Optimising the opportunities provided by ever-evolving technology to connect students in Papua New Guinea with their peers in Panama and those in Paris inevitably raises tensions for educators. The process of gaining a cosmopolitan disposition requires us to have unsettling encounters, to critically reflect on our discomfort, to challenge our preconceptions and to nurture an emerging sense of the global. But in shepherding students through this process, educators need to be equipped to steer what may be a leaky boat through potentially stormy waters in order to find a safe harbour at the other side. This is not a voyage for the faint-hearted and requires the confidence (and sense of trust in, and from, institutional leaders) to take risks in curriculum design, pedagogy and assessment.

Moreover, if educators are to model a cosmopolitan ethos to students then it is incumbent upon us to be prepared to critically interrogate our own assumptions, including those we make about what it means to be a cosmopolitan in a rapidly changing world. This includes avoiding rendering groups as victims as we emphasise the need for empathy. The danger of doing so was conveyed by a letter addressed to the producer of CBS' *60 Minutes* and signed by numerous scholars and journalists from around the world (French 2015). As the letter made clear, the signatories were concerned about the misrepresentation of Africa in reporting by *60 Minutes*, in which Africans 'are typically limited to the role of passive victims, or occasionally brutal or corrupt villains and incompetents; they are not otherwise shown to have any agency or even the normal range of human thoughts and emotions'. Such representation is important for education because, as Hansen (2008) emphasises, the media can be regarded as a mode of cosmopolitan education. This example is also important as it illustrates how, even with the best will in the world, it is easy to fall back on simplistic characterisations of 'the other'. As such, Papastephanou (2011: 609) highlights the need for 'doing one's homework critically' in order to avoid making assumptions about our positioning relative to others. This means accepting the profound limitations of our ability to understand the world from the perspective of those who do not share our relative wealth and mobility. As such, we need to acknowledge the inherent character of our ignorance and our reliance on subaltern knowledge to fill out our world view. Papastephanou (2013: 192–193) suggests that education should 'focus on the cultivation of the self whose desire for an as yet

130 *Theory to practice and back again*

unreached (and perhaps unreachable) wisdom and goodness dis-places self-hood and moves it toward an ec-centric citizenship of an as-yet no place'.

Against the challenges involved lie the possibilities. Current and future generations of students are increasingly primed to be open to multiple perspectives. Their life experience is different to that of their parents, as is the case for each generation. They can be described as 'intellectually invested global citizens ready for curriculum that encourages them to cultivate cosmopolitan habits of mind such as cooperation and hospitality, dialogue and curiosity' (DeJaynes and Curmi 2015: 75). In response, educators need to leverage diversity to help students unpack preconceptions, engage in meaningful encounters, become proficient in critical thinking. This is not currently being done well. As Lee et al. (2012: 1) suggest:

> Current demographic, social, and economic contexts underscore the need for colleges and universities to comprehensively utilize diversity in ways that foster excellence and inclusion on behalf of students' intellectual and social development. In light of the pressing need to effectively support educational outcomes for an increasingly heterogeneous population, and to prepare graduates for the cognitive and intercultural complexity of the twenty-first century, higher education practitioners and scholars need a deeper understanding of how to effectively engage diversity.

To achieve this, educators need to nurture students' curiosity, help them build alliances, work with students to co-construct new concepts of belonging and to create knowledge that is inclusive and that represents the multiple experiences of all involved. There remain few countries on earth that are so entirely unaffected by the circulation of human beings around the globe for thousands of years that they do not contain a multitude of forms of cultural expression. Long histories of immigration in many nations ensure that encounters with difference, which student mobility is considered to give access to, are in fact available in the adjacent suburb. As communities around the world become progressively diverse, opportunities to expose students to diverse expressions of humanity are more and more available. But simply exposing students to difference is, as we have seen, insufficient. Instead, educators are required to be skilled in 'the art of translation and bridge-building' (Beck 2006: 89).

From educational practice to reinvigorated theory

This book has focused on how to leverage insights from cosmopolitan thought to help inform contemporary higher education practice. As the book comes to an end it is important to consider the opposite dynamic, how insights from educational practice can be leveraged to inform, and reinvigorate, cosmopolitan thought. As Hansen (2013: 38) suggests, 'one of the tasks of the scholar has always been to reclaim concepts, to reconstruct them, to retrieve and rehabilitate them, to chip off encrusted associations and release them to go to work for us'. At the same time, one of the responsibilities of the practitioner is to use the mirror lens of practice to bounce beams of light back on to theory, to highlight its limitations, to pinpoint opportunities for forward motion and to illuminate new considerations. The social cosmopolitan project has considerable worth in informing educational practice, but the promise that it embodies to help humans to find solutions to social challenges is undermined by a shortage of rigorous empirical investigations and a lack of methodological tools. In particular, the notion of a cosmopolitan disposition is well developed but there is little hint of the process involved in its development. Theory appears to suggest that proximity and opportunities for interaction are sufficient. Anderson (2004) points to the need for a 'cosmopolitan canopy' where distrust and wariness are diminished and those from different backgrounds can build trust. But evidence collected from higher education students shows that even when the conditions appear to be optimal, patterns of interaction can ensure that negative assumptions are reinforced and any move to the development of cosmopolitan dispositions is made less, rather than more, likely.

What more, then, is required for the formation of cosmopolitan sensibilities? This book has examined this question in the context of higher education institutions, looking at curricula, pedagogy, assessment and the skills and backgrounds of educators. The consistent story has been one of intent – designing educational interventions with a cosmopolitan intent. This does not mean an education system that brainwashes all students into becoming proto-cosmopolitans. Instead, inherent in a cosmopolitan approach is openness. This not only means taking the prior experience of students into account, but also requires educators to design a context in which students have the opportunity to gain cosmopolitan attributes and then be given space to do so, or not. And this opens up yet another question for theory: what are the preconditions that predispose one person to be open to cosmopolitan learning and others to reject it outright? Is it simply a matter of the exposure they have to diversity? This cannot be true as we see the entrenchment of anti-cosmopolitan social expressions in diverse societies around the world. So, what is the 'tip-off point' (Phillips and Smith 2008) at which the path towards gaining a cosmopolitan disposition begins? Extensive social research is needed to determine what the trigger is, and the educational space presents a rich laboratory in which to do this. But educational practice cannot wait for the findings to come in. Instead institutional leaders and educators are duty-bound to establish learning spaces where students can learn to understand and critically assess situations they encounter on a daily basis as well as how to engage with their peers as members of a shared global humanity.

One of the pejorative claims made about cosmopolitan theory is that it is prescriptive and every effort has been made in this book to stay away from

132 *Theory to practice and back again*

any suggestion that there is only one perfect approach to contemporary higher education. At the same time, the book has started from the position that students need to be equipped to grapple with contemporary realities that demand of them the ability to regard the globe and its people holistically. Thus it has been suggested that cosmopolitan thought can provide educators with an intellectual prism that has both deep historical roots and contemporary intellectual vigour. Taking educational practice and experience as a starting point to interrogate cosmopolitan thought can also help overcome some of its inherent flaws. Looking back to the origins of cosmopolitan thought, it is clear that its foundations are not without significant defects. It is certain that the application of cosmopolitan thought to politics and philosophy and the social has resulted in unevenness and contradictions. Thus it has been opened up to claims of elitism, paternalism, a justification for colonialism and discordance with social reality. Nevertheless, the substance of cosmopolitan thought relates to two key elements: the coexistence of multiple ways of being and hospitality towards our fellow humans.

From Hierocles onwards, the notion of belonging to our local community as well as to the global one has much pertinence in today's increasingly complex world. The growing attraction of 'border thinking' (Mignolo 2000) is simply because it is a good fit with contemporary needs. If students can learn to value multiple perspectives and to critically evaluate their own assumptions then their ability to deal with modern challenges will be enhanced. Equally, the way in which students around the world apply a multi-perspectival approach to addressing immediate situations can shed light on what it means to be a border thinker. This in itself may provide theorists with valuable new insights into the philosophical underpinnings of cosmopolitan thought. And it is critical that empirical investigations are undertaken with students and others both within and outside of Western countries, for an incontrovertible limitation of cosmopolitan thought is that it evolved from narrow geographic roots. Overcoming this is only going to be possible if theorists practice the openness they so stridently proclaim, absorbing a multitude of ways of doing and being from around the globe.

While Kant is arguably the grandfather of cosmopolitan thinking, he is also the target of much critique, and deservedly so. Some of his writing is indeed highly problematic. But he was inevitably a product of his time. And while there is almost no limit to the arguments that could be made against many of his declarations, it is worth acknowledging his achievement in foregrounding 'universal hospitality'. This is something that remains apposite in a world characterised by increasing movement, both chosen and imposed, creating ever-growing ranks of displaced people, those groups who could be considered the rootless and the uprooted. Many higher education students will lead lives characterised by movement, something that has become a mark of the global elite. Investigating the malleability of their views about individual achievement versus social responsibility is something that could

Theory to practice and back again 133

shed light on the currency of the notion of universal hospitality. Do they see double standards in the right of the elite to move freely around the globe while persecuting those who dare to claim international passage as a means of overcoming their disenfranchisement? Do the trajectories of graduates illustrate tensions between the acceptance of otherness in different contexts? Does entrance to the global elite mean that they will come to look down on the 'uncosmopolitans' (Fardon 2008) and become aesthetic cosmopolitans alone? Or do their identities become increasingly inclusive? Longitudinal research that follows higher education students through an education in which they are exposed to the opportunity to gain cosmopolitan attributes, and then charts their evolving identity and assumptions as they progress through their careers, would go a long way to shedding light on the contemporary expression of allegiance and hospitality. It would help illuminate the process in which 'translation and bridge-building' (Beck 2006) are constructed, or not.

The future of education

Educating the future leaders of our world is a huge responsibility. The context in which we live changing so quickly that graduates will need to be fleet-footed in their responses. This highlights the need for them to be equipped with a toolbox that helps them thrive in a world of complexity, contradiction and growing challenges. Higher education should leverage the fact that many students already have a highly developed cognitive grasp of the need to develop skills that will enable them to skilfully navigate global contexts, and hence of the advantages of engagement with those different to themselves. But educators also need to acknowledge that this is not true of all students and that remaining open to a diversity of perspectives is a fundamental obligation of their profession. Any attempt to force reluctant students in the direction of cosmopolitan approaches would not only cause immense resentment but also lead them to see cosmopolitan aspects as malign. With this in mind, higher education institutions that are serious about educating students in a way that ensures that planetary conviviality (Mignolo 2000) emerges from their future leadership need to adopt 'proactive and interventionist strategies' (Smart et al. 2000) that reimagine the content of curricula, and the ways in which they are taught. This is an approach that needs to leverage the diversity of students as a valuable resource.

In doing so they would fulfil their responsibility in contributing to the good of all humanity (Rizvi 2004), helping prepare students to be members and leaders of the diverse communities they will inherit. This incorporates gaining the interpersonal reflexivity to succeed in a world in which social relations are becoming increasingly fluid (Field 2003). This book has suggested a number of extant approaches that may be applicable to embedding opportunities to gain cosmopolitan attributes in the practice of higher education institutions around the world. But further work is needed to investigate how their application plays out and the outcomes that result. Until there is evidence of successful educational outcomes from practices of cosmopolitan education, there will be no basis on which to advance their expansion into the broad curricula. And in improving the ways in which students are prepared for a global world through ensuring they are given the opportunity to gain cosmopolitan attributes, there is no time to lose.

References

Abubakar, B., Shanka, T. and Nkombo Muuka, G. (2010) Tertiary education: An investigation of location selection criteria and preferences by international students – The case of two Australian universities, *Journal of Marketing for Higher Education* 20(1): 49–68.

ActiveWorlds Inc. (2015) *ActiveWorlds*. Accessed 21 March 2015 from www.activeworlds.com/web/index.php

Ahmed, M. (1987) Islamic education prior to the establishment of madrassa, *Journal of Islamic Studies* 26(4): 321–348.

Alesina, A. and La Ferrara, E. (2002) Who trusts others? *Journal of Public Economics* 85: 207–234.

Allen, I. E. and Seaman, J. (2013) *Changing Course: Ten years of tracking online education in the United States*. Babson Park, MA: Babson Survey Research Group.

Altbach, P. and de Wit, H. (2015) Internationalization and global tension: Lessons from history, *Journal of Studies in International Education* 19(1): 4–10.

Altbach, P. and Teichler, U. (2001) Internationalization and exchanges in a globalized university, *Journal of Studies in International Education* 5(1): 5–25.

Anderson, A. (1996) Cosmopolitanism, universalism and the divided legacies of modernity, in Cheah, P. and Robbins, B. (Eds.) *Cosmopolitics: Thinking and Feeling beyond the Nation*. Minneapolis: University of Minnesota Press, 265–289.

Anderson, E. (2004) The cosmopolitan canopy, *Annals of the American Academy of Political and Social Science* 565: 14–31.

Ang, S., Van Dyne, L. and Koh, C. (2006) Personality correlates of the four-factor model of cultural intelligence, *Group and Organization Management* 31(1): 100–123.

Anthias, G. (2006) Belongings in a globalising and unequal world: Rethinking translocations, in Yuval-Davis, N., Kannabiran, K. and Vieten, U. (Eds.) *The Situated Politics of Belonging*. London: SAGE Publications, 17–31.

Anzar, U. (2003) *Islamic Education – A Brief History of Madrassas With Comments on Curricula and Current Pedagogical Practices*. Washington, DC: World Bank.

Appiah, K. (1998) Cosmopolitan patriots, in Cheah, P. and Robbins, B. (Eds.) *Cosmopolitics: Thinking and Feeling Beyond the Nation*. Minneapolis: University of Minnesota Press, 91–114.

Appiah, K. (2006) *Cosmopolitanism – Ethics in a World of Strangers*. New York: Norton.

Archer, W. and Davison, J. (2007) *Graduate Employability: What do employers think and want?* London: Council for Industry and Higher Education.

Areden, A., De Decker, F., Divis, J., Frederiks, M. and de Wit, H. (2013) Assessing the internationalisation of degree programmes: Experiences from a Dutch-Flemish

136 *References*

pilot certifying internationalisation, *Compare: A Journal of Comparative and International Education* 43(1): 56–78.

Arendt, H. (1958) *The Human Condition.* Chicago: University of Chicago Press.

Arkoudis, S., Watty, K., Baik, C., Yua, X., Borland, H., Chang, S., Lang, I., Lang, J. and Pearce, A. (2013) Finding common ground: Enhancing interaction between domestic and international students in higher education, *Teaching in Higher Education* 18(3): 222–235.

Association of American Geographers (2015) *Center for Global Geography Education.* Accessed 20 January 2015 from www.aag.org/cgge

Astin, A. and Antonio, A. (2012) *Assessment for Excellence. The Philosophy and Practice of Assessment and Evaluation in Higher Education.* Second Edition. Plymouth: Rowman and Littlefield.

Australian Bureau of Statistics (2012) *Cultural Diversity in Australia: Reflecting a Nation – Stories from the 2011 Census.* Canberra: Commonwealth of Australia.

Australian Bureau of Statistics (2013a) International migration, *Year Book Australia 2012.* Canberra: Commonwealth of Australia.

Australian Bureau of Statistics (2013b) Country of birth, *Year Book Australia 2012.* Canberra: Commonwealth of Australia.

Australian Curriculum, Assessment and Reporting Authority (2014) *Australian Curriculum.* Accessed 17 November 2014 from www.australiancurriculum.edu.au/

Autio, T. (2014) The internationalisation of curriculum research, in Pinar, W. (Ed.) *International Handbook of Curriculum Research.* Second Edition. New York and London: Routledge, 17–31.

Baiio, W. and Ray, W. (2011) The challenges and rewards of an international undergraduate student learning interaction in geography, *International Research in Geographical and Environmental Education* 20(4): 287–296.

Bainbridge, W. (2007) The scientific research potential of virtual worlds, *Science* 317(5837): 472–476.

Bamgbose, A. (2001) World Englishes and globalisation, *World Englishes* 20(3): 357–363.

Bauman, Z. (1998) *Globalisation: The Human Consequences.* Cambridge: Polity Press.

Bauman, Z. (1999) *In Search of Politics.* Cambridge: Polity Press.

Bauman, Z. (2000) *Liquid Modernity.* Cambridge: Polity Press.

Becher, A. and Trowler, P. (2001) *Academic Tribes and Territories.* Second Edition. Buckingham: SHRE and Open University Press.

Beck, U. (2002) The cosmopolitan perspective: Sociology in the second age of modernity, in Vertovec, S. and Cohen, R. (Eds.) *Conceiving Cosmopolitanism. Theory, Context and Practice.* Oxford: Oxford University Press, 61–85.

Beck, U. (2006) *The Cosmopolitan Vision.* Cambridge: Polity Press.

Beck, U. (2008) Mobility and the cosmopolitan perspective, in Canzler, W., Kaufmann, V. and Kesselring, S. (Eds.) *Tracing Mobilities: Towards a Cosmopolitan Perspective.* Aldershot: Ashgate Publishing, 25–35.

Beck, U. and Grande, E. (2007) *Cosmopolitan Europe.* Translated by Ciaran Cronin. Cambridge: Polity Press.

Beck, U. and Sznaider, N. (2006) Unpacking cosmopolitanism for the social sciences: A research agenda, *The British Journal of Sociology*, 57(1): 1–23.

Beck, U., Levy, D. and Sznaider, N. (2009) Cosmopolitanization of memory: The politics of forgiveness and restitution, in Nowicka, M. and Rovisco, M. (Eds.) *Cosmopolitanism in Practice.* Farnham: Ashgate Publishing, 111–127.

Bégin-Caouette, O. (2013) Globally networked learning environments as eduscapes for mutual understanding. Critical intersections in education, *An OISE/UT Student's Journal* 1(2): 54–70.

Bell, M. (2004) Internationalising the higher education curriculum – Do academics agree? *HERDSA Conference Paper.* Accessed 10 January 2015 from www.herdsa.org.au/wp-content/uploads/conference/2004/PDF/P036-jt.pdf

Belliveau, M. (2005) Blind ambition? The effects of social networks and institutional sex composition on the job search outcomes of elite coeducational and women's college graduates, *Organization Science* 16(2): 134–150.

Belyavina, R., Li, J. and Bhandari, R. (2013) *New Frontiers: U.S. Students Pursuing Degrees Abroad – A 2-year analysis of key destinations and fields of study.* New York: Institute of International Education.

Bender, A. and Walker, P. (2013) The obligation of debriefing in global health education, *Medical Teacher* 35: 1027–1034.

Benhabib, S. (2006) *Another Cosmopolitanism.* New York: Oxford University Press.

Bennett, M. (1986) A developmental approach to training for intercultural sensitivity, *International Journal of Intercultural Relations* 10(2): 179–196.

Bennett, R. and Ali-Choudhury, R. (2009) Prospective students' perceptions of university brands: An empirical study, *Journal of Marketing for Higher Education* 19(1): 85–107.

Berg, M. (2009) Between cosmopolitanism and the national slot: Cuba's diasporic children of the revolution, *Identities: Global Studies in Culture and Power* 16(2): 129–156.

Berg, R. (2012) The anonymity factor in making multicultural teams work: Virtual and real teams, *Business Communication Quarterly* 75(4): 404–424.

Berry, W. (1987) *The Loss of the University.* Republished 2013. McLean, VA: The Trinity Forum.

Bevitt, S. (2015) Assessment innovation and student experience: A new assessment challenge and call for a multi-perspective approach to assessment research, *Assessment and Evaluation in Higher Education* 40(1): 103–119.

Biccum, A. (2015) The politics of education for globalisation: Managed activism in a time of crisis, *Australian Journal of International Affairs* 69(3): 321–338.

Biggs, J. and Tang, C. (2007) *Teaching for Quality Learning at University.* Maidenhead, UK: Open University Press.

Boateng, A. and Thompson, A. (2013) Study abroad Ghana: An international experiential learning, *Journal of Social Work Education* 49(70): 701–715.

Bochner, S., McLeod, B. and Lin, A. (1977) Friendship patterns of overseas students: A functional model, *International Journal of Psychology* 12(4): 277–294.

Bochner, S., Hutnik, N. and Furnham, A. (1985) The friendship patterns of overseas and host students in an Oxford student residence, *Journal of Social Psychology* 125(6): 689–694.

Boix Mansilla, V. and Jackson, A. (2011) *Educating for Global Competence: Preparing Our Youth to Engage the World.* New York: Asia Society.

Bolden, R., Gosling, J. and O'Brien, A. (2014) Citizens of the academic community? A societal perspective on leadership in UK higher education, *Studies in Higher Education* 39(5): 754–770.

Boler, M. (1999) *Feeling Power: Emotions and Education.* New York: Routledge.

Boli, J., Ramirez, F. and Meyer, J. (1985) Explaining the origins and expansion of mass education, *Comparative Education Review* 29(2): 145–170.

138 *References*

Bols, A. (2012) Student views on assessment, in Clouder, L., Broughan, C., Jewell, S. and Steventon, G. (Eds.) *Improving Student Engagement and Development Through Assessment: Theory and Practice in Higher Education.* Abingdon: Routledge, 4–18.

Bonwell, C. and Eison, J. (1991) Active learning; creating excitement in the classroom, *ASHE-ERIC Higher Education Report No. 1.* Washington, DC: The George Washington University, School of Education and Human Development.

Boon, V. and Delanty, G. (2007) Cosmopolitanism and Europe: Historical considerations and contemporary applications, in Rumford, C. (Ed.) *Cosmopolitanism and Europe.* Liverpool: Liverpool University Press, 19–38.

Boud, D. and Falchikov, N. (2005) Redesigning assessment for learning beyond higher education, *Higher Education Research and Development Society of Australasia Conference.* Accessed 16 January 2015 from http://conference.herdsa.org.au/2005/pdf/refereed/paper_398.pdf

Bourdieu, P. (1977) *Outline of a Theory of Practice.* Cambridge: Cambridge University Press.

Bowser, D., Danaher, P. and Somasundaram, J. (2007) Indigenous, pre-undergraduate and international students at Central Queensland University, Australia: Three cases of the dynamic tension between diversity and commonality, *Teaching in Higher Education* 12(5): 669–681.

Boyatzis, R. and McKee, A. (2005) *Renewing Yourself and Connecting with Others Through Mindfulness, Hope and Compassion.* Boston, MA: Harvard Business School Press.

Bracht, O., Engel, C., Janson, K., Over, A., Schomburg, H. and Teichler, U. (2006) *The Professional Value of ERASMUS Mobility.* Brussels: European Commission.

Brandenburg, U., Ermel, H., Federkeil, G., Fuchs, S., Groos, M. and Menn, A. (2009) How to measure the internationality and internationalisation of higher education institutions: indicators and key figures, in De Wit, H. (Ed.) *Measuring Success in the Internationalisation of Higher Education.* EAIE Occasional Paper 22. Amsterdam: European Association for International Education, 65–76.

Brock, G. and Brighouse, H. (2005) Introduction, in Brock, G. and Brighouse, H. (Eds.) *The Political Philosophy of Cosmopolitanism.* Cambridge: Cambridge University Press, 1–9.

Brock-Utne, B. (1999) African universities and the African heritage, *International Review of Education* 45(1): 87–104.

Brooks, R. and Waters, J. (2009) A second chance at success, *Sociology* 43(6): 1085–1102.

Brooks, R., Waters, J. and Pimlott-Wilson, H. (2012) International education and the employability of UK students, *British Educational Research Journal* 38(2): 281–298.

Brustein, W. (2007) The global campus: Challenges and opportunities for higher education in North America, *Journal of Studies in International Education* 11(3/4): 382–391.

Buchanan, J., Wilson, S. and Gopal, N. (2008) A cross cultural virtual learning environment for students to explore the issue of racism: A case study involving the UK, USA and SA, *Social Work Education* 27(6): 671–682.

Buck, T. (2013) The Awesome Power of Gaming in Higher Education. *EdTech Magazine.* Accessed 19 January 2015 from www.edtechmagazine.com/higher/article/2013/10/awesome-power-gaming-higher-education

Buder, J. and Bodemer, D. (2008) Supporting controversial CSCL discussions with augmented group awareness tools, *International Journal of Computer-Supported Collaborative Learning* 3(2): 123–139.

References   139

Byrne, D. (2005) *Social Exclusion.* Second Edition. Maidenhead, UK: Open University Press.

Calcutt, L., Woodward, I. and Skrbis, Z. (2009) Conceptualizing otherness: An exploration of the cosmopolitan schema, *Journal of Sociology* 45(2): 169–186.

Calhoun, C. (2002) The class consciousness of frequent travellers: Toward a critique of actually existing cosmopolitanism, *The South Atlantic Quarterly* 101(4): 869–897.

Carroll, N. (2013) E-learning – the McDonaldization of education, *European Journal of Higher Education* 3(4): 342–356.

Carroll, W. and Ratner, R. (1994) Between Leninism and radical pluralism: Gramscian reflections on counter-hegemony and the new social movements, *Critical Sociology* 20(3): 3–26.

Cavallar, G. (2014) Sources of Kant's cosmopolitanism: Basedow, Rousseau, and cosmopolitan education, *Studies in Philosophy and Education* 33(4): 369–389.

Cavallario, P. (2014) *A Deeper Partnership with XuetangX to Increase Quality Education for Chinese Students.* Accessed 21 January 2015 from www.edx.org/blog/deeper-partnership-xuetangx-increase#.VL8QiS58u1Q

Center for Internationalization and Global Engagement (2012) *Mapping Internationalization on U.S. Campuses.* Washington, DC: American Council on Education.

Chan, K. (2002) Both sides, now: Culture contact, hybridization, and cosmopolitanism, in Vertovec, S. and Cohen, R. (Eds.) *Conceiving Cosmopolitanism – Theory, Context and Practice.* Oxford: Oxford University Press, 191–208.

Chao, F. (2014) International medical electives: Time for a rethink? *Australian Medical Student Journal* 4(2): 5–6.

Charles, D., Charles, T., McNeill, M., Bustard, D. and Black, M. (2011) Game-based feedback for educational multi-user virtual environments, *British Journal of Educational Technology* 42(4): 638–654.

Cheah, P. (1998) Introduction Part II: The cosmopolitical – today, in Cheah, P. and Robbins, B. (Eds.) *Cosmopolitics – Thinking and Feeling Beyond the Nation.* Minneapolis: University of Minnesota Press, 20–41.

Cheah, P. (2006) Cosmopolitanism, *Theory, Culture and Society* 23(2–3): 486–496.

Chen, L. (2008) Internationalization or international marketing? Two frameworks for understanding international students' choice of Canadian universities, *Journal of Marketing for Higher Education* 18(1): 1–33.

Cheng, C. (2006). Education for morality in global and cosmic contexts: The Confucian model, *Journal of Chinese Philosophy* 33(4): 557–570.

ChiSystems (2015) *Virtual Environment Cultural Training for Operational Readiness.* Accessed 31 January 2015 from http://vector.chisystems.com/index.htm

Choi, M. (1997) Korean students in Australian universities: Intercultural issues, *Higher Education Research and Development* 16(3): 263–282.

Christie, H. (2007) Higher education and spatial (im)mobility, *Environment and Planning* 39(10): 2445–2463.

Clayton, M., Cavanagh, K. and Hettche, M. (2012) Institutional branding: A content analysis of public service announcements from American universities, *Journal of Marketing for Higher Education* 22(2): 182–205.

Clegg, S. (2011) Cultural capital and agency: Connecting critique and curriculum in higher education, *British Journal of Sociology of Education* 32(1): 93–108.

Collins, M., Kim, S., Clay, C. and Perlstein, J. (2009) Addressing issues of globalization in the training of public child welfare workers: Lessons from a training program in the USA, *International Social Work* 52: 72–83.

140 References

Constantinou, P., Bajracharya, S. and Baldwin, S. (2011) Perceptions of international faculty in the United States, *The International Journal of Science in Society* 2(3): 253–271.

Contemplative Mind (2014) *Association for the Contemplative Mind in Higher Education.* Accessed 9 January 2015 from www.contemplativemind.org/programs/acmhe

Conway-Gomez, K. and Araya-Palacios, F. (2011) Discussing the geography of sustainable development through an international online collaboration with students in Chile and the USA, *Journal of Geography in Higher Education* 35(2): 265–279.

Coryell, J., Durodoye, B., Wright, R., Pate, E. and Nguyen, S. (2012) Case studies of internationalization in adult and higher education: Inside the processes of four universities in the United States and the United Kingdom, *Journal of Studies in International Education* 16(1): 75–98.

Coryell, J., Spencer, B. and Sehin, O. (2014) Cosmopolitan adult education and global citizenship: Perceptions from a European itinerant graduate professional study abroad program, *Adult Education Quarterly* 64(2): 145–164.

Crystal, D. (2003) *English as a Global Language.* Cambridge: Cambridge University Press.

Culver, S., Puril, I., Spinelli, G., DePauw, K. and Dooley, J. (2012) Collaborative dual-degree programs and value added for students: Lessons learned through the Evaluate-E Project, *Journal of Studies in International Education* 16(1): 40–61.

Dabbagh, N. (2007) The online learner: Characteristics and pedagogical implications, *Contemporary Issues in Technology and Teacher Education* 7(3): 217– 226.

Dalgarno, B. and Lee, M. (2010) What are the learning affordances of 3-D virtual environments? *British Journal of Educational Technology* 41(1): 10–32.

Danforth, D., Procter, M., Heller, R., Chen, R. and Johnson, M. (2009) Development of virtual patient simulations for medical education, *Journal of Virtual Worlds Research* 2(2): 3–11.

Dapous, R. (2012) *The Role of English-medium Teaching in European Higher Education.* London: British Council.

Datta, A. (2009) Places of everyday cosmopolitanism: East European construction workers in London, *Environment and Planning* 41: 353–370.

De Lissovoy, N. (2010) Decolonial pedagogy and the ethics of the global, *Discourse: Studies in the Cultural Politics of Education* 31(3): 279–293.

Deardorff, D. (2006) Identification and assessment of intercultural competence as a student outcome of internationalization, *Journal of Studies in International Education* 10(3): 241–266.

Deardorff, D. (2011) Assessing intercultural competence, *New Directions for Institutional Research* 149: 65–79.

Deardorff, D., Thorndike Pysarchik, D. and Yun, S. (2009) Towards effective international learning assessment: Principles, design and implementation, in De Wit, H. (Ed.) *Measuring Success in the Internationalisation of Higher Education.* EAIE Occasional Paper 22. Amsterdam: European Association for International Education, 23–37.

Deem, R., Mok, K. and Lucas, L. (2008) Transforming higher education in whose image? Exploring the concept of the world class university in Europe and Asia, *Higher Education Policy* 21(1): 83–97.

DeJaynes, T. and Curmi, C. (2015) Youth as cosmopolitan intellectuals, *English Journal* 104(3): 75–80.

References   141

Delanty, G. (2006) The cosmopolitan imagination: Critical cosmopolitanism and social theory, *The British Journal of Sociology* 57(1): 25–47.

Delanty, G. and He, B. (2008) Cosmopolitan perspectives on European and Asian transnationalism, *International Sociology* 23(3): 323–344.

Delhey, J. and Newton, K. (2003) Who trusts? The origins of social trust in seven societies, *European Societies* 5(2): 93–137.

Department for Education (2014) *National Curriculum.* Accessed 17 November 2014 from www.gov.uk/government/collections/national-curriculum

Department of Education, Employment and Workplace Relations (2011) *Finance 2010: Financial Reports of Higher Education Providers.* Canberra: Department of Education, Employment and Workplace Relations.

Department of Education and Training (2014) *2013 All Students.* Accessed 1 January 2015 from http://docs.education.gov.au/node/35961

Devlin-Scherer, R. and Sardone, N. (2013) Collaboration as a form of professional development: Improving learning for faculty and students, *College Teaching* 61(1): 30–37.

Dewey, J. (1938) *Experience and Education.* New York: Kappa Delta Pi.

Dickson, K. and Treml, M. (2013) Using assessment and SoTL to enhance student learning, *New Directions for Teaching and Learning* 136: 7–16.

Dinesen, P. (2012) Does generalized (dis)trust travel? Examining the impact of cultural heritage and destination-country environment on trust of immigrants, *Political Psychology* 33(4): 495–511.

Donald, J. (2007) Internationalisation, diversity and the humanities curriculum: Cosmopolitanism and multiculturalism revisited, *Journal of Philosophy of Education* 41(3): 289–308.

Donnelly-Smith, L. (2009) Global learning through short term study abroad, *Peer Review* 11(4): 12–15.

Dray, B., Lowenthal, P., Miszkiewicz, M., Ruiz-Primo, M. and Marczynski, K. (2011) Developing an instrument to assess student readiness for online learning: A validation study, *Distance Education* 32(1): 29–47.

Drew, V. and Mackie, L. (2011) Extending the constructs of active learning: Implications for teachers' pedagogy and practice, *The Curriculum Journal* 22(4): 451–467.

Eagan, K., Bara Stolzenberg, E., Berdan Lozano, J., Aragon, M., Ramirez Suchard, M. and Hurtado, S. (2014) *Undergraduate Teaching Faculty: The 2013–2014 HERI Faculty Survey.* Los Angeles: Higher Education Research Institute, Graduate School of Education and Information Studies, University of California.

Egron-Polak, E. and Hudson, R. (2014) *Internationalisation of Higher Education: Growing Expectations, Fundamental Values.* Paris: IAU.

Engelmann, T. and Hesse, F. (2010) How digital concept maps about the collaborators' knowledge and information influence computer supported collaborative problem solving, *International Journal of Computer-Supported Collaborative Learning* 5(3): 299–319.

Ennew, C. and Fujia, Y. (2009) Foreign universities in China: A case study, *European Journal of Education* 44(1): 21–36.

Ertmer, P., Newby, T., Yu, J-H., Liu, W., Tomory, A., Lee, Y-M., Sendurur, E. and Sendurur, P. (2011) Facilitating students' global perspectives: Collaborating with international partners using Web 2.0 technologies, *Internet and Higher Education* 14: 251–261.

142   *References*

European Commission (2013a) *Joint International Master Programmes: The first generation. Lessons learnt from Erasmus Mundus.* Brussels: European Commission.

European Commission (2013b) *Table: Outgoing Erasmus student mobility for studies from 1987/88–2010/11.* Accessed 13 October 2013 from http://ec.europa.eu/education/erasmus/statistics_en.htm#1

European Commission (2013c) *Outgoing and incoming Erasmus student mobility for studies in 2010/2011.* Accessed 16 November 2013 from http://ec.europa.eu/education/erasmus/doc/stat/1011/studies.pdf

European Commission (2014) *Erasmus Mundus Programme.* Accessed 6 January 2015 from http://eacea.ec.europa.eu/erasmus_mundus/index_en.php

European Union (2012) *Erasmus – Changing Lives, Opening Minds for 25 Years.* Luxembourg: European Union.

European Union (2014a) *European Multiple MOOC Aggregator.* Accessed 21 January 2015 from http://europeanmoocs.eu/

European Union (2014b) *New Modes of Learning and Teaching in Higher Education. High Level Group on the Modernisation of Higher Education.* Accessed 14 November 2014 from http://ec.europa.eu/education/library/reports/modernisation-universities_en.pdf

European Union (2015) *OpenupEd.* Accessed 21 January 2015 from www.openuped.eu/

European University Association (2013) *EUA Membership.* Accessed 18 May 2013 from www.eua.be/eua-membership-and-services/Home.aspx

Falchikov, N. (2005) *Improving Assessment Through Student Involvement – Practical Solutions for Aiding Learning in Higher and Further Education.* Abingdon: RoutledgeFalmer.

Falchikov, N. and Goldfinch, J. (2000) Student peer assessment in higher education: A meta-analysis comparing peer and teacher marks, *Review of Educational Research* 70(3): 287–322.

Falk, R. (1996) Revisioning cosmopolitanism, in Nussbaum, M. and Cohen, J. (Eds.) *For Love of Country?* Boston, MA: Beacon Press, 53–60.

Falzon, M. (2009) Ethnic groups unbound: A case study of the social organisation of cosmopolitanism, in Nowicka, M. and Rovisco, M. (Eds.) *Cosmopolitanism in Practice.* Aldershot: Ashgate Publishing, 37–50.

Fanghanel, J. (2007) *Investigating University Lecturers' Pedagogical Constructs in the Working Context.* York: The Higher Education Academy.

Fanghanel, J. and Cousin, G. (2012) 'Worldly' pedagogy: A way of conceptualising teaching towards global citizenship, *Teaching in Higher Education* 17(1): 39–50.

Fardon, R. (2008) Cosmopolitan nations, national cosmopolitans, in Werbner, P. (Ed.) *Anthropology and the New Cosmopolitanism: Rooted, Feminist and Vernacular Perspectives.* Oxford: Berg, 233–259.

Farhang, A., Siadat, S., Arbabisarjou, A., Farhang, M. and Shirazi, M. (2012) Education in ancient Iran, *Interdisciplinary Journal of Contemporary Research in Business* 4(2): 1005–1015.

Field, J. (2003) *Social Capital.* London: Routledge.

Fielden, J., Middlehurst, R. and Woodfield, S. (2007) *Global Horizons for UK Students – A Guide for Universities.* London: Council for Industry and Higher Education.

Findlay, A. (2011) An assessment of supply and demand-side theorizations of international student mobility, *International Migration* 49(2): 162–190.

References 143

Findlay, A., King, R., Smith, F., Geddes, A. and Skeldon, R. (2012) World class? An investigation of globalisation, difference and international student mobility, *Transactions of the Institute of British Geographers* 37: 118–131.

Fine, R. (2003) Kant's theory of cosmopolitanism and Hegel's critique, *Philosophy and Social Criticism* 29(6): 609–630.

Fine, R. (2007) *Cosmopolitanism.* Oxford: Routledge.

Firer, R. (2008) Virtual peace education, *Journal of Peace Education* 5(2): 193–207.

Fischer, F., Kollar, I., Stegmann, K. and Wecker, C. (2013) Toward a script theory of guidance in computer-supported collaborative learning, *Educational Psychologist* 48(1): 56–66.

Foucault, M. (1984) *Michel Foucault.* Cousins, M. and Hussain, A. (Eds.) London: Macmillan.

Francois, E. (2014) Development of a scale to assess faculty motivation for internationalising their curriculum, *Journal of Further and Higher Education* 38(5): 641–655.

Franzen, A. and Hangartner, D. (2005) Social networks and occupational success – An analysis of the labor market entrance of college graduates, *Kölner Zeitschrift für Soziologie und Sozialpsychologie* 57(3): 443–465.

Freire, P. (1970) *Pedagogy of the Oppressed.* Translated by Myra Bergman Ramon. London: Penguin Books.

Freire, P. and Torres, C. (1994) Twenty years after 'Pedagogy of the Oppressed'. Paulo Freire in Conversation with Carlos Alberto Torres, in McLaren, P. and Lankshear, C. (Eds.) *Politics of Liberation. Paths from Freire.* London: Routledge, 100–107.

French, H. (2015) *How Does Africa Get Reported? A letter of concern to 60 Minutes.* Accessed 28 March 2015 from www.howardwfrench.com/2015/03/how–does-africa-get-reported-a-letter-of-concern-to-60-minutes/

Frey, B., Schmitt, V. and Allen, J. (2012) Defining authentic classroom assessment, *Practical Assessment Research and Evaluation* 17(2): 1–18.

Frijhoff, W. (1996) Patterns, in Ridder-Symoens, R. de (Ed.) *A History of the University in Europe. Volume II – Universities in Early Modern Europe (1500–1800).* Cambridge: Cambridge University Press, 43–84.

Furnham, A. and Alibhai, N. (1985) The friendship networks of foreign students: A replication and extension of the functional model, *International Journal of Psychology* 20(6): 709–722.

Garam, I. (2005) *Study on the Relevance of International Student Mobility to Work and Employment.* Helsinki: Centre for International Mobility.

Giddens, A. (1990) *The Consequences of Modernity.* Stanford, CA: Stanford University Press.

Gill, S. and Kirkpatrick, A. (2013) English in Asian and European higher education, in Chapelle, C. (Ed.) *The Encyclopaedia of Applied Linguistics.* London: Wiley Blackwell, 1–4.

Glaeser, E., Laibson, D., Scheinkman, J. and Soutter, C. (2000) Measuring trust, *The Quarterly Journal of Economics* 115(3): 811–846.

Global Higher Education (2014) *Branch Campus Listing.* Accessed 3 January 2015 from www.globalhighered.org/branchcampuses.php

Global Leadership Excellence (2013) *Global Competence Aptitude Assessment.* Accessed 16 November 2013 from www.globalcompetence.org/

144 References

Goleman, D. (1998) *Working with Emotional Intelligence.* New York: Bantam.

Goleman, D., Boyatzis, R. and McKee, A. (2002) *Primal Leadership: Realising the Power of Emotional Intelligence.* Boston, MA: Harvard Business School Press.

Goulah, J. (2012) Daisaku Ikeda and Value-Creative Dialogue: A new current in interculturalism and educational philosophy, *Educational Philosophy and Theory* 44(9): 997–1009.

Gramsci, A. (1971) *Selections from the Prison Notebooks of Antonio Gramsci.* Hoare, Q. and Smith, G. (Eds.) New York: International Publishers.

Gravois, J. (2005) Meditate on it – Can adding contemplation to the classroom lead students to more eureka moments? *Chronicle of Higher Education,* 21 October.

Grayson, P. (2004) Social dynamics, university experiences and graduates' job outcomes, *British Journal of Sociology of Education* 25(5): 609–627.

Green, W., Hibbins, R., Houghton, L. and Ruutz, A. (2013) Reviving praxis: Stories of continual professional learning and practice architectures in a faculty-based teaching community of practice, *Oxford Review of Education* 39(2): 247–266.

Greenfield, E., Davis, R. and Fedor, J. (2012) The effect of international social work education: Study abroad versus on-campus courses, *Journal of Social Work Education* 48(4): 739–761.

Greitzer, F., Kuchar, O. and Huston, K. (2007) Cognitive science implications for enhancing training effectiveness in a serious gaming context, *Journal on Educational Resources in Computing* 7(3): 1–16.

Grewal, D. (2008) *Network Power: The Social Dynamics of Globalisation.* New Haven, CT: Yale University Press.

Group of Eight Australia (2014) *Policy Note: International students in higher education and their role in the Australian economy.* Accessed 1 January 2015 from https://go8.edu.au/ sites/default/files/docs/publications/international_students_in_higher_education_ and_their_role_in_the_australian_economy.pdf

Gunnlaugson, O., Sarath, E., Scott, C. and Bai, H. (Eds.) (2014) *Contemplative Learning and Enquiry Across Disciplines.* Albany: State University of New York Press.

Gurin, P. (1999) *Export Report of Patricia Gurin.* Accessed 5 April 2009 from http:// vpcomm.umich.edu/admissions/legal/expert/summ.html.

Gürüz, K. (2008) *Higher Education and International Student Mobility in the Global Knowledge Economy.* Albany: State University of New York Press.

Haake, M. and Gulz, A. (2009) A look at the roles of look and roles in embodied pedagogical agents: A user preference perspective, *International Journal of Artificial Intelligence in Education* 19(1): 39–71.

Habermas, J. (1998) *The Inclusion of the Other.* Cambridge, MA: The MIT Press.

Haigh, M. (2013) From internationalisation to education for global citizenship: A multi-layered history, *Higher Education Quarterly* 68(1): 6–27.

Hall, S. (2008) Cosmopolitanism, globalisation and diaspora: Stuart Hall in conversation with Pnina Werbner, in Werbner, P. (Ed.) *Anthropology and the New Cosmopolitanism: Rooted, Feminist and Vernacular Perspectives.* Oxford: Berg, 345–360.

Halstead, J. (2004) An Islamic concept of education, *Comparative Education* 40(4): 517–529.

Hammer, M., Bennett, M. and Wiseman, R. (2003) Measuring intercultural sensitivity: The intercultural development inventory, *International Journal of Intercultural Relations* 27(4): 421–443.

Hannerz, U. (1990) Cosmopolitans and locals in world culture, *Theory, Culture and Society* 7: 237–251.

Hanoi University (2014) *About HANU.* Accessed 3 January 2015 from http://english. hanu.vn/index.php?option=com_contentandtask=viewandid=26andItemid=101

Hansen, D. (2008) Curriculum and the idea of a cosmopolitan inheritance, *Journal of Curriculum Studies* 40(3): 289–312.

Hansen, D. (2010) Chasing butterflies without a net: Interpreting cosmopolitanism, *Studies in Philosophy and Education* 29(2): 151–166.

Hansen, D. (2013) Cosmopolitanism as a philosophy for life in our time, *Encounters/ Encuentros/Rencontres on Education* 14: 35–47.

Hansen, D., Burdick-Shepherd, S., Cammarano, C. and Obelleiro, G. (2009) Education, values, and valuing in cosmopolitan perspective, *Curriculum Inquiry* 39(5): 587–612.

Harasim, L. (2000) Shift happens: Online education as a new paradigm in learning, *Internet and Higher Education* 3(1–2): 41–61.

Hardaker, Glenn and Sabki A'ishah Ahmad (2012) An insight into Islamic pedagogy at the University of al-Qarawiyyin, *Multicultural Education and Technology Journal,* 6(2): 106–110.

Harrison, Y., Kostic, K., Toton, S. and Zurek, J. (2010) Globalizing social justice education: The case of The Global Solidarity Network Study e-Broad Program, *Internet and Higher Education,* 13: 115–126.

Harvey, D. (2009) *Cosmopolitanism and the Geographies of Freedom.* New York: Columbia University Press.

Hegel, G. (1952) *Philosophy of Right.* Translated by T. Knox. London: Oxford University Press.

Held, D. (2002) Culture and political community: National, global and cosmopolitan, in Vertovec, S. and Cohen, R. (Eds.) *Conceiving Cosmopolitanism. Theory, Context and Practice.* Oxford: Oxford University Press, 48–58.

Held, D. (2005) Principles of cosmopolitan order, in Brock, G. and Brighouse, H. (Eds.) *The Political Philosophy of Cosmopolitanism.* Cambridge: Cambridge University Press, 10–27.

Held, D., McGrew, A., Goldblatt, D. and Perraton, J. (1999) *Global Transformations: Politics, Economics and Culture.* Stanford, CA: Stanford University Press.

Helfand, D. (2013) Watering the roots of knowledge through collaborative learning, *The Chronicle of Higher Education,* 8 July.

Hemsley-Brown, J. (2012) 'The best education in the world': Reality, repetition or cliché? International students' reasons for choosing an English university, *Studies in Higher Education* 37(8): 1005–1022.

Herbst, M. (2011) Building a faculty-led study abroad program: From development to history – pedagogy in Istanbul, *The History Teacher* 44(2): 209–226.

Herold, D. (2012) Second Life and academia – reframing the debate between support-ers and critics, *Journal of Virtual Worlds Research* 5(1): 1–20.

Higher Education Academy (2014) *Internationalising Higher Education.* York: Higher Education Academy.

Hill, J. (2000) *Becoming a Cosmopolitan: What it means to be a human being in the new millennium.* Oxford: Rowman and Littlefield.

Himmelfarb, G. (1996) The illusions of cosmopolitanism, in Nussbaum, M. and Cohen, J. (Eds.) *For Love of Country?* Boston, MA: Beacon Press, 72–77.

Ho, D. (2006) I'm not west. I'm not east. So how leh? *English Today* 22(3): 17–24.

Hodgson, D. (2008) Cosmopolitics, neo-liberalism and the state: The indigenous rights movement in Africa, in Werbner, P. (Ed.) *Anthropology and the New Cosmopolitanism: Rooted, Feminist and Vernacular Perspectives.* Oxford: Berg, 215–230.

146 *References*

Hofstede, G. (2001) *Culture's Consequences: Comparing Values, Behaviors, Institutions, and Organizations across Nations.* Second edition. Thousand Oaks, CA: SAGE Publications.

Hollinger, D. (2006) *Cosmopolitanism and Solidarity: Studies in Ethnoracial, Religious and Professional Affiliation in the United States.* Madison: The University of Wisconsin Press.

Hong Kong Polytechnic University (2011) *Virtual Campus.* Accessed 30 January 2015 from http://coresl.edc.polyu.edu.hk/

Hopper, P. (2006) *Living with Globalisation.* Oxford: Berg.

Hopper, P. (2007) *Understanding Cultural Globalization.* Cambridge: Polity Press.

House of Lords (2011) *Higher Education: ERASMUS.* Oral Question 27 April. London: House of Lords.

Hudzik, J. (2011) *Comprehensive Internationalization – From Concept to Action.* Washington, DC: NAFSA Association of International Educators.

Hurtado, S., Dey, E. and Trevino, J. (1994) Exclusion or self-segregation? Interactions across racial/ethnic groups on college campuses. Paper presented at the Annual Meeting of the American Educational Research Association, New Orleans.

Hurtado, S., Mayhew, M. and Engberg, M. (2012) Diversity courses and students' moral reasoning: A model of predispositions and change, *Journal of Moral Education* 41(2): 201–224.

Institute for Creative Technologies (2015) *Bilateral Negotiation Trainer.* Accessed 31 January 2015 from http://ict.usc.edu/prototypes/bilat/

Institute of International Education (2014) Duration of U.S. Study Abroad, 2000/01–2012/13. *Open Doors Report on International Educational Exchange.* Accessed 5 January 2015 from www.iie.org/opendoors

IAACS (International Association for the Advancement of Curriculum Studies) (2014) *Preamble.* Accessed 2 January 2015 from www.iaacs.ca/about/

Internet World Stats (2014a) *World internet users and 2014 population stats.* Accessed 5 February 2015 from www.internetworldstats.com/stats.htm

Internet World Stats (2014b) *Internet Users by Language.* Accessed 7 February 2015 from www.internetworldstats.com/stats7.htm

Jackson, D. and Nyoni, F. (2012) Reflections on study abroad education: Guidelines on study abroad preparation and process, *Journal of Human Behavior in the Social Environment* 22: 201–212.

Jackson, J. (2011) Cultivating cosmopolitan, intercultural citizenship through critical reflection and international, experiential learning, *Language and Intercultural Communication* 11(2): 80–96.

James, E. (2000) Race related differences in promotions and support: Underlying effects of human and social capital, *Organization Science* 11(5): 493–508.

James, R., Bexley, E., Devlin, M. and Marginson, S. (2007) *Australian University Student Finances 2006: Final Report of a National Survey of Students in Public Universities.* Canberra: Universities Australia.

Janssen, J. and Bodemer, D. (2013) Coordinated computer-supported collaborative learning: Awareness and awareness tools, *Educational Psychologist* 48(1): 40–55.

Johnson, L., Adams Becker, S., Estrada, V. and Freeman, A. (2014) *NMC Horizon Report: 2014 Higher Education Edition.* Austin, TX: The New Media Consortium.

Johnson, W. and Valente, A. (2009) Tactical language and culture training systems: Using AI to teach foreign languages and cultures, *AI Magazine* 30(2): 72–83.

Johnston, R., Trlin, A., Henderson, A. and North, N. (2006) Sustaining and creating migration chains among skilled immigrant groups: Chinese, Indians and South Africans in New Zealand, *Journal of Ethnic and Migration Studies* 32(7): 1227–1250.

Jones, E. and Killick, D. (2013) Graduate attributes and the internationalized curriculum: Embedding a global outlook in disciplinary learning outcomes, *Journal of Studies in International Education* 17(2): 165–182.

Kahane, D. (2009) Learning about obligation, compassion, and global justice: The place of contemplative pedagogy, *New Directions for Teaching and Learning* 118: 49–60.

Kahn, J. (2008) Other cosmopolitans in the making of the modern Malay world, in Werbner, P. (Ed.) *Anthropology and the New Cosmopolitanism: Rooted, Feminist and Vernacular Perspectives.* Oxford: Berg, 261–280.

Kant, I. (1781) *Critique of Pure Reason.* Translated in Beck, U. (2002). The cosmopolitan society and its enemies, *Theory, Culture and Society* 19(1–2): 17–44.

Kant, I. (1891a) Perpetual peace, a philosophical essay, in Kant, I., *Principles of Politics.* Translated by Hastie, W. Edinburgh: Clark, 77–148.

Kant, I. (1891b) The principle of progress, in Kant, I., *Principles of Politics.* Translated by Hastie, W. Edinburgh: Clark, 63–76.

Kant, I. (1963) Idea for a universal history from a cosmopolitan point of view, in Kant, I., *On History.* Translated by Beck, L., Anchor, R. and Fackenheim, E. Indianapolis: Bobbs-Marrill, 11–26.

Kant, I. (1970) *Kant's Political Writings.* Reiss, H. (Ed.) Cambridge: Cambridge University Press.

Kant, I. (1996a) The doctrine of right, in Kant, I., *The Metaphysics of Morals.* Translated by Gregor, M. Cambridge: Cambridge University Press.

Kant, I. (1996b) On the common saying: That may be correct in theory, but is of no use in practice, in Kant, I., *Practical Philosophy.* Translated by Gregor, M. Cambridge: Cambridge University Press, 273–309.

Kennedy, P. (2009) The middle class cosmopolitan journey: The life trajectories and transnational affiliations of skilled EU migrants in Manchester, in Nowicka, M. and Rovisco, M. (Eds.) *Cosmopolitanism in Practice.* Farnham: Ashgate Publishing, 19–36.

Kern, D., Thomas, P. and Hughes, M. (2009) *Curriculum Development for Medical Education – A Six Step Approach.* Second Edition. Baltimore, MD: The Johns Hopkins University Press.

Kim, K. and Bonk, J. (2002) Cross-cultural comparisons of online collaboration, *Journal of Computer-Mediated Communication* 8(1): 1–12.

Kim, S., Lee, J. and Thomas, M. (2012) Between purpose and method: A review of educational research on 3D virtual worlds, *Journal of Virtual Worlds Research* 5(1): 1–18.

King, R., Findlay, A. and Ahrens, J. (2010) *International Student Mobility Literature Review.* Bristol: Higher Education Funding Council for England.

Kinser, K. and Lane, J. (2012) Foreign outposts of colleges and universities, *International Higher Education* 66(Winter): 2–3.

Kivinen, O. and Ahola, S. (1999) Higher education as human risk capital, *Higher Education* 38(2): 191–208.

Klein, P. and Solem, M. (2008) Evaluating the impact of international collaboration on geography learning, *Journal of Geography in Higher Education* 32(2): 245–267.

Knight, J. (2008) *Joint and Double Degree Programmes: Vexing Questions and Issues.* London: The Observatory on Borderless Higher Education.

148 *References*

Knight, P. (1995) Introduction, in Knight, P. (Ed.) *Assessment for Learning in Higher Education.* Abingdon: RoutledgeFalmer, 13–24.

Kofman, E. (2007) Figures of the cosmopolitan: Privileged nationals and national outsiders, in Rumford, C. (Ed.) *Cosmopolitanism and Europe.* Liverpool: Liverpool University Press, 239–256.

Kolb, D. (1984) *Experiential Learning: Experience as the Source of Learning and Development.* Englewood Cliffs, NJ: Prentice Hall.

Kreber, C. (2010) Teacher identities, authenticity and pedagogy, *Studies in Higher Education* 35(2): 171–194.

Kuder, M. and Obst, O. (2009) *Joint and Double Degree Programs in the Transatlantic Context: A Survey Report.* New York: Institute of International Education.

Kuhling, C. and Keohane, K. (2007) *Cosmopolitan Ireland: Globalisation and the Quality of Life.* London: Pluto Press.

Kumlin, S. and Rothstein, B. (2007) Minorities and Mistrust: The Cushioning Impact of Informal Social Contacts and Political-Institutional Fairness. Paper presented at the European Consortium for Political Research Joint Session of Workshops, Helsinki, 7–12 May.

La Trobe University (2014a) *Study at La Trobe in your Home Country.* Accessed 3 January 2015 from www.latrobe.edu.au/study/how-to-apply/international/your-country

La Trobe University (2014b) *International Activities.* Accessed 3 January 2015 from www.latrobe.edu.au/about/international

Lackey, K. (2011) Faculty development: An analysis of current and effective training strategies for preparing faculty to teach online, *Online Journal of Distance Learning Administration.* Accessed 21 December 2014 from www.westga.edu/~distance/ojdla/winter144/lackey144.html

Lamont, M. and Aksartova, S. (2002) Ordinary cosmopolitanisms: Strategies for bridging boundaries among working class men, *Theory, Culture and Society* 19(4): 1–25.

Lane, H., Hays, M., Core, M. and Auerbach, D. (2013) Learning intercultural communication skills with virtual humans: Feedback and fidelity, *Journal of Educational Psychology* 105(4): 1026–1035.

Langholm, S. (1995) The new nationalism and the new universities – the case of Norway in the early nineteenth century, *Scandinavian Journal of History* 20(1): 51–60.

Lattuca, L., Bergom, I. and Knight, D. (2014) Professional development, departmental contexts, and use of instructional strategies, *Journal of Engineering Education* 103(4): 549–572.

Law, A., Bottenberg, M., Brozick, A., Currie, J., DiVall, M., Haines, S., Jolowsky, C., Koh-Knox, C., Leonard, G., Phelps, S., Rao, D., Webster, A. and Yablonskim, E. (2014) A checklist for the development of faculty mentorship programs, *American Journal of Pharmaceutical Education* 78(5): 1–10.

Leask, B. and Bridge, C. (2013) Comparing internationalisation of the curriculum in action across disciplines: Theoretical and practical perspectives, *Compare: A Journal of Comparative and International Education* 43(1): 79–101.

Lee, A., Poch, R., Shaw, M., and Williams, R. (2012) Engaging diversity in undergraduate classrooms: A pedagogy for developing intercultural competence, *ASHE Higher Education Report* 38(2): 1–132.

Lee, A., Williams, R., and Kilaberia, R. (2012) Engaging diversity in first year college classrooms. *Innovative Higher Education* 37: 199–213

Lee, J. (2008) Beyond borders: International student pathways to the United States, *Journal of Studies in International Education* 12(3): 308–327.

References 149

Lee, T. (2000) *Education in Traditional China, A History*. Leiden: Koninklijke Brill.

Levin, B., He, Y. and Robbins, H. (2006) Comparative analysis of preservice teachers' reflective thinking in synchronous versus asynchronous online case discussions, *Journal of Technology and Teacher Education* 14(3): 439–460.

Lewin, K. (1942) Field theory and learning, in Cartwright, D. (Ed.) *Field Theory in Social Science: Selected theoretical papers.* London: Social Science Paperback.

Lewis, M., Simons, G. and Fennig, C. (Eds.) (2013) *Ethnologue: Languages of the World*, Seventeenth edition. Dallas, TX: SIL International.

Li, L., Findlay, A., Jowett, A. and Skeldon, R. (1996) Migrating to learn and learning to migrate, *International Journal of Population Geography* 2(1): 51–67.

Liberman, K. (1994) Asian student perspectives on American university instruction, *International Journal of Intercultural Relations* 18(2): 173–192.

Lim, J. and Liu, Y. (2006) The role of cultural diversity and leadership in computer-supported collaborative learning: A content analysis, *Information and Software Technology*, 48: 142–153.

Lin, N. (2001) *Social Capital: A Theory of Social Structure and Action.* Cambridge: Cambridge University Press.

Lincoln Commission (2005) *Global Competence and National Needs – One Million Americans Studying Abroad.* Washington, DC: Commission on the Abraham Lincoln Study Abroad Fellowship Program.

Linden Research Inc. (2015) *Second Life.* Accessed 21 March 2015 from http://secondlife.com/

Lingard, B. (2006) Globalisation, the research imagination and deparochialising the study of education, *Globalisation, Societies and Education* 4(2): 287–302.

Lingard, B., Sellar, S. and Baroutsis, A. (2015) Researching the habitus of global policy actors in education, *Cambridge Journal of Education* 45(1): 25–42.

Linklater, A. (2006) Cosmopolitanism, in Dobson, A. and Eckersley, R. (Eds.) *Political Theory and the Ecological Challenge.* Cambridge: Cambridge University Press, 109–127.

Liu, J. (2007) The expansion of higher education and uneven access to opportunities for participation in it, 1978–2003, *Chinese Education and Society* 40(1): 36–59.

Lulat, Y. (2005) *A History of African Higher Education: From Antiquity to the Present. A Critical Synthesis.* Westport, CT: Praeger.

Lutterman-Aguilar, A. and Gingerich, O. (2002) Experiential pedagogy for study abroad: Educating for global citizenship, *Frontiers: The Interdisciplinary Journal of Study Abroad*, 8: 41–82.

McCarthy, C., Bulut, E. and Patel, R. (2014) Race and education in the age of digital capitalism, in Pinar, W. (Ed.) *International Handbook of Curriculum Research.* Second Edition. New York and London: Routledge, 32–44.

McDaniel, J. (2008) *Gathering Leaves and Lifting Words. History of Buddhist Monastic Education in Laos and Thailand.* Seattle: University of Washington Press.

McDaniel, J., Metcalf, S., Sours, J., Janke, T., Newbrough, R., Shuck, L. and Varma-Nelson, P. (2013) *Supporting Student Collaboration in Cyberspace: A cPLTL Study of Web Conferencing Platforms.* Accessed 19 January 2015 from www.educause.edu/ero/article/supporting-student-collaboration-cyberspace-cpltl-study-web-conferencing-platforms

Macfarlane, B. (2007) Defining and rewarding academic citizenship: The implications for university promotions policy, *Journal of Higher Education Policy and Management* 29(3): 261–273.

150   *References*

McGarr, O. and Clifford, A. (2013) 'Just enough to make you take it seriously': Exploring students' attitudes towards peer assessment, *Higher Education* 65(4): 677–693.

McKenna, A. (2011) *The History of Western Africa.* New York: Encyclopaedia Britannica.

McLoughlin, C. (2001) Inclusivity and alignment: Principles of pedagogy, task and assessment design for effective cross-cultural online learning, *Distance Education* 22(1): 7–29.

McQuiggan, C. (2012) Faculty development for online teaching as a catalyst for change, *Journal of Asynchronous Learning Networks* 16(2): 27–61.

Maiworm, F. (2001) Continuity and change in the 1990s, *European Journal of Education* 36(4): 459–472.

Malcomson, S. (1998) The varieties of cosmopolitan experience, in Cheah, P. and Robbins, B. (Eds.) *Cosmopolitics. Thinking and Feeling Beyond the Nation.* Minneapolis: University of Minnesota Press, 233–245.

Marginson, S. (2008) Sojourning students and creative cosmopolitans, in Peters, M., Marginson, S. and Murphy, P. (Eds.) *Creativity and the Global Knowledge Economy.* New York: Peter Lang, 217–255.

Marginson, S. (2014) Student self-formation in international education, *Journal of Studies in International Education* 18(1): 6–22.

Marginson, S. and van der Wende, M. (2007) *Globalisation and Higher Education.* Education Working Group Paper 8. Paris: OECD.

Marin, P. (2000) The educational possibility of multi-racial/multi-ethnic college classrooms, in Maruyama, G., Moreno, J., Gudeman, R. and Marin, P. (Eds.) *Does Diversity Make a Difference? Three research studies on diversity in college classrooms.* Washington, DC: American Council on Education and American Association of University Professors, 61–84.

Maringe, F., Foskett, N. and Woodfield, S. (2013) Emerging internationalisation models in an uneven global terrain: findings from a global survey, *Compare: A Journal of Comparative and International Education* 43(1): 9–36.

Mason, R. (2000) From distance education to online education, *Internet and Higher Education* 3(1–2): 63–74.

Matsumoto, D. and Hwang, H. (2013) Assessing cross-cultural competence: A review of available tests, *Journal of Cross-Cultural Psychology* 44(6): 849–873.

Matsumoto, D., LeRoux, J. A., Ratzlaff, C., Tatani, H., Uchida, H., Kim, C. and Araki, S. (2001) Development and validation of a measure of intercultural adjustment potential in Japanese sojourners: The Intercultural Adjustment Potential Scale (ICAPS), *International Journal of Intercultural Relations* 25(5): 483–510.

Matsumoto, D., LeRoux, J. A., Robles, Y. and Campos, G. (2007) The Intercultural Adjustment Potential Scale (ICAPS) predicts adjustment above and beyond personality and general intelligence, *International Journal of Intercultural Relations* 31(6): 747–759.

Matthews, J. and Sidhu, R. (2005) Desperately seeking the global subject: International education, citizenship and cosmopolitanism, *Globalisation, Societies and Education* 3(1): 49–66.

Maxwell, T. (2012) Assessment in higher education in the professions: Action research as an authentic assessment task, *Teaching in Higher Education* 17(6): 686–696.

References 151

Maylath, B., Vandepitte, S., Minacori, P., Isohella, S., Mousten, B. and Humbley, J. (2013) Managing complexity: A technical communication translation case study in multilateral international collaboration, *Technical Communication Quarterly* 22(1):67–84.

Mentkowski, M. and Sharkey, S. (2011) How we know it when we see it: Conceptualizing and assessing integrative and applied learning-in-use, *New Directions for Institutional Research* 149: 93–107.

Meyer, J., Ramirez, F. and Soysal, Y. (1992) World expansion of mass education, 1870–1980, *Sociology of Education* 65(2): 128–149.

Mezirow, J. and Associates (1990) *Fostering Critical Reflection in Adulthood: A Guide to Transformative and Emancipatory Learning.* San Francisco, CA: Jossey-Bass.

Mignolo, W. (2000) The many faces of cosmo-polis: Border thinking and critical cosmopolitanism, *Public Culture* 12(3): 721–748.

MiriadaX (2015) *Nuestra filosofía.* Accessed 21 January 2015 from www.miriadax.net/nuestra-filosofia

Mitchell, K. (2007) Geographies of identity: The intimate cosmopolitan, *Progress in Human Geography* 31(5): 706–720.

Monash University (2015) *Monash Chinese Island.* Accessed 31 January 2015 from www.virtualhanyu.com/?page_id=87

Morais, D and Ogden, A. (2011) Initial development and validation of the Global Citizenship Scale, *Journal of Studies in International Education* 15(5): 445–466.

Morgan, A. (2009) Learning communities, cities and regions for sustainable development and global citizenship, *Local Environment* 14(5): 443–459.

Mullens, J., Bristow, R. and Cuper, P. (2012) Examining trends in international study: A survey of faculty-led field courses within American departments of geography, *Journal of Geography in Higher Education* 36(2): 223–237.

Nava, M. (2006) Domestic cosmopolitanism and the structures of feeling: The specificity of London, in Yuval-Davis, N., Kannabiran, K. and Vieten, U. (Eds.) *The Situated Politics of Belonging.* London: SAGE Publications, 42–53.

Nava, M. (2007) *Visceral Cosmopolitanism: Gender Culture and the Normalisation of Difference.* Oxford: Berg.

Nederveen-Pieterse, J. (2004) *Globalisation and Culture: Global Melange.* Lanham, MD: Rowman and Littlefield.

Nichol, D., Hunter, J., Yaseen, J. and Prescott-Clements, L. (2012) A simple guide to enhancing learning through web 2.0 technologies, *European Journal of Higher Education* 2(4): 436–446.

Nidiffer, J. and Cain, T. (2004) Elder brothers of the university: Early vice presidents in late nineteenth-century universities, *History of Education Quarterly* 44(4): 487–523.

Noddings, N. (2010) Moral education in an age of globalization, *Educational Philosophy and Theory* 42(4): 390–396.

Norton, L., Norton, W. and Shannon, L. (2013) Revitalising assessment design: What is holding new lecturers back? *Higher Education* 66(2): 233–251.

Nowicka, M. and Kaweh, R. (2009) Looking at the practice of UN professionals: strategies for managing differences and the emergence of a cosmopolitan identity, in Nowicka, M. and Rovisco, M. (Eds.) *Cosmopolitanism in Practice.* Farnham: Ashgate Publishing, 51–71.

Nowicka, M. and Rovisco, M. (2009) Making sense of cosmopolitanism, in Nowicka, M. and Rovisco, M. (Eds.) *Cosmopolitanism in Practice.* Farnham: Ashgate Publishing, 1–16.

152   References

Nulty, D. (2011) Peer and self-assessment in the first year of university, *Assessment and Evaluation in Higher Education* 36(5): 493–507.

Nussbaum, M. (1996) Patriotism and cosmopolitanism, in Nussbaum, M. and Cohen, J. (Eds.) *For Love of Country?* Boston, MA: Beacon Press, 2–17.

Nussbaum, M. (1997) Kant and Stoic cosmopolitanism, *The Journal of Political Philosophy* 5(1): 1–25.

Oakman, D. (2004) *Facing Asia: A History of the Colombo Plan.* Canberra: Pandanus Books.

O'Brien, A. and Eriksson, A. (2009) *Cross-Cultural Connections: Intercultural Learning for Global Citizenship.* Accessed 30 January 2015 from http://web.stanford.edu/group/ccr/archive/articles/Cross_cultural_connections.pdf

Obst, D. and Kuder, M. (2012) International joint- and double-degree programs, *International Higher Education* 66: 1–5.

Ogan, A. and Lane, H. (2010) Virtual environments for culture and intercultural competence, in Blanchard, E. and Allard, D. (Eds.) *Handbook of Research on Culturally Aware Information Technology: Perspectives and Models.* Hershey, PA: IGI Global, 501–519.

Omelaniuk, I. (2005) Best practices to manage migration: China, *International Migration* 43(5): 189–206.

OECD (Organisation for Economic Co-operation and Development) (2013) *Education at a Glance. Indicator C4: Who studies abroad and where?* Accessed 1 October 2013 from www.oecd.org/edu/educationataglance2013-indicatorsandannexes.htm

OECD (2014a) How many students study abroad and where do they go?, in *Education at a Glance 2014: Highlights.* Paris: OECD Publishing. Accessed 4 February 2015 from http://dx.doi.org/10.1787/eag_highlights-2014-11-en

OECD (2014b) *Foreign/International Students Enrolled.* Accessed 4 February 2015 from http://stats.oecd.org

Osman, G. and Herring, S. (2007) Interaction, facilitation, and deep learning in cross-cultural chat: A case study, *Internet and Higher Education* 10: 125–141.

Ossman, S. (2007) Linked comparisons for life and research, in Ossman, S. (Ed.) *Places We Share: Migration, Subjectivity and Global Mobility.* Lanham, MD: Lexington Books, 201–218.

Paige, R., Fry, G., Stallman, E., Josić, J. and Jon, J. (2009) Study abroad for global engagement: The long-term impact of mobility experiences, *Intercultural Education* 20(sup1): S29–S44.

Paige, R., Fry, G., Stallman, E., Jon, J. and Josić, J. (2010) *Beyond Immediate Impact: Study Abroad for Global Engagement.* Report Submitted to the US Department of Education. Accessed 5 January 2015 from www.calstate.edu/engage/documents/study-abroad-for-global-engagement.pdf

Pampaloni, A. (2010) The influence of organizational image on college selection: What students seek in institutions of higher education, *Journal of Marketing for Higher Education* 20(1): 19–48.

Papastephanou, M. (2011) The 'cosmopolitan' self does her homework, *Journal of Philosophy of Education* 45(4) 597–612.

Papastephanou, M. (2013) Being and becoming cosmopolitan: Higher education and the cosmopolitan self, *International Journal of Higher Education* 2(2): 184–194.

Papatsiba, V. (2005) Political and individual rationales of student mobility: A case-study of ERASMUS and a French regional scheme for studies abroad, *European Journal of Education* 40(2): 173–188.

References 153

Pappano, L. (2012) The year of the MOOC. *New York Times.* Accessed 21 January 2015 from www.nytimes.com/2012/11/04/education/edlife/massive-open-onlinecourses-are-multiplying-at-a-rapid-pace.html

Paquet, G. (2008) *Deep Cultural Diversity: A Governance Challenge.* Ottawa: University of Ottawa Press.

Parkes, M., Stein, S. and Reading, C. (2015) Student preparedness for university e-learning environments, *Internet and Higher Education* 25: 1–10.

Parry, J. (2008) Cosmopolitan values in a central Indian steel town, in Werbner, P. (Ed.) *Anthropology and the New Cosmopolitanism: Rooted, Feminist and Vernacular Perspectives.* Oxford: Berg, 325–343.

Penuel, W., Fishman, B., Yamaguchi, R. and Gallagher, L. (2007) What makes professional development effective? Strategies that foster curriculum implementation, *American Educational Research Journal* 44(4) 921–958.

Perry, L. and Southwell, L. (2011) Developing intercultural understanding and skills: Models and approaches, *Intercultural Education* 22(6): 453–446.

Persianis, P. (2003) British colonial higher education policy-making in the 1930s: The case of a plan to establish a university in Cyprus, *Compare: A Journal of Comparative and International Education* 33(3): 351–368.

Peterson, M. (2010) Computerized games and simulations in computer-assisted language learning: A meta-analysis of research, *Simulation and Gaming* 41(1): 72–93.

Phillips, T. and Smith, P. (2008) Cosmopolitan beliefs and cosmopolitan practices: An empirical investigation, *Journal of Sociology* 44(4): 391–399.

Piaget, J. (1970) *Genetic Epistemology.* New York: W.W. Norton and Company.

Pinar, W. (2014) Introduction, in Pinar, W. (Ed.) *International Handbook of Curriculum Research.* Second edition. New York and London: Routledge, 1–33.

Pollock, S., Bhabha, H., Breckenridge, C. and Chakrabarty, D. (2000) Cosmopolitanisms, *Public Culture* 12(3): 577–589.

Popov, V., Biemans, H., Brinkman, D., Kuznetsov, A. and Mulder, M. (2013) Facilitation of computer-supported collaborative learning in mixed-versus same-culture dyads: Does a collaboration script help? *Internet and Higher Education* 19: 36–48.

Popov, V., Noroozi, O., Barrett, J., Biemans, H., Teasley, S., Slof, B. and Mulder, M. (2014) Perceptions and experiences of, and outcomes for, university students in culturally diversified dyads in a computer-supported collaborative learning environment, *Computers in Human Behavior* 32: 186–200.

Post, R. (2006) Introduction, in Benhabib, S. *Another Cosmopolitanism.* New York: Oxford University Press, 1–9.

Postiglione, G. (2011) Global recession and higher education in eastern Asia: China, Mongolia and Vietnam, *Higher Education* 62(6): 789–814.

Pozniak, K. (2015) *Study Ebroad Connects Students to the World.* Accessed 30 January 2015 from www.crs.org/united-states/study-ebroad/

Prude, M. (2013) A classroom of bunnies, blimps, and werewolves: Teaching Asian religions online in Second Life, *ASIANetwork Exchange* 20(2): 1–12.

Pruneri, F. and Bianchi, A. (2010) School reforms and university transformations and their function in Italy from the eighteenth to the nineteenth centuries, *History of Education* 39(1): 115–136.

Putnam, R. (2004) *Education, Diversity, Social Cohesion and 'Social Capital'. Note for Discussion.* Meeting of OECD Education Ministers, Dublin, OECD.

154 References

Putnam, R. (2007) *E pluribus unum*: Diversity and community in the twenty-first century. The 2006 Johan Skytte Prize lecture. *Scandinavian Political Studies* 30(2): 137–174.

Puwar, N. (2006) Im/possible inhabitations, in Yuval-Davis, N., Kannabiran, K. and Vieten, U. (Eds.) *The Situated Politics of Belonging*. London: SAGE Publications, 75–83.

Ram, K. (2008) A new consciousness must come: Affectivity and movement in Tamil Dalit women's activist engagement with cosmopolitan modernity, in Werbner, P. (Ed.) *Anthropology and the New Cosmopolitanism: Rooted, Feminist and Vernacular Perspectives*. Oxford: Berg, 135–155.

Rapport, N. and Stade, R. (2007) A cosmopolitan turn or return? *Social Anthropology* 15(2): 223–229.

Raybourn, E., Deagle, E., Mendini, K. and Heneghan, J. (2005) *Adaptive Thinking and Leadership Simulation Game Training for Special Forces Officers*. I/ITSEC 2005 Proceedings, Interservice/Industry Training, Simulation and Education Conference Proceedings, 28 November–1 December, Orlando, Florida, USA. Accessed 31 January 2015 from www.sandia.gov/adaptive-training-systems/Raybourn%20 et.%20al.%20ITSEC%202370b.pdf

Readings, B. (1996) *The University in Ruins*. Cambridge, MA: Harvard University Press.

Reardon, E. and Snauwaert, D. (2011) Reflective pedagogy, cosmopolitanism, and critical peace education for political efficacy: A discussion of Betty A. Reardon's assessment of the field, *Journal of Peace Education and Social Justice* 5(1): 1–14.

Rebick, M. (2000) The importance of networks in the market for university graduates in Japan: A longitudinal analysis of hiring patterns, *Oxford Economic Papers* 52: 471–496.

Richardson, S. (2010) Through Students' Eyes: First Steps Towards a Cosmopolitan Higher Education. PhD Thesis, The University of Melbourne (unpublished).

Richardson, S. (2015) *Enhancing Cross-Border Higher Education Institution Mobility in the APEC Region – Research Report*. Singapore: APEC Secretariat.

Richardson, S. and Radloff, A. (2014) *Promoting Regional Education Services Integration: APEC University Associations Cross-Border Education Cooperation*. Workshop Discussion Paper, 20–22 May, Kuala Lumpur, Malaysia. Singapore: APEC Secretariat.

Richey, S. (2007) Manufacturing trust: Community currencies and the creation of social capital, *Political Behaviour* 29(1): 69–88.

Riel, M. (1993) Global education through learning circles, in Harasim, L. (Ed.) *Global Networks – Computers and International Communication*. Cambridge, MA: MIT Press, 221–236.

Rizvi, F. (2004) Globalisation and the dilemmas of Australian higher education. Critical perspectives on communication, *Cultural and Policy Studies* 23(2): 33–42.

Rizvi, F. (2005) International education and the production of cosmopolitan identities, *Research in Higher Education International Publication Series* 9: 1–11.

Rizvi, F. and Lingard, R. (2006) Edward Said and the cultural politics of education, *Discourse: Studies in the Cultural Politics of Education* 27(3): 293–308.

Rizvi, F., Lingard, R. and Lavia, J. (2006) Postcolonialism and education: Negotiating a contested terrain, *Pedagogy, Culture and Society* 14(3): 249–262.

Robbins, B. (1998) Comparative cosmopolitanisms, in Cheah, P. and Robbins, B. (Eds.) *Cosmopolitics. Thinking and Feeling Beyond the Nation*. Minneapolis: University of Minnesota Press, 246–264.

References 155

Roberts, J., Cruz, A. and Herbst, J. (1996) Exporting models, in Ridder-Symoens, H. (Ed.) *A History of the University in Europe: Volume II – Universities in Early Modern Europe (1500–1800)*. Cambridge: Cambridge University Press, 256 –282.

Robertson, R. (1992) *Globalization. Social Theory and Global Culture*. London: SAGE Publications.

Robinson, K. (2008) Islamic cosmopolitics, human rights and anti-violence strategies in Indonesia, in Werbner, P. (Ed.) *Anthropology and the New Cosmopolitanism: Rooted, Feminist and Vernacular Perspectives*. Oxford: Berg, 111–133.

Rodríguez González, C., Bustillo Mesanza, R. and Mariel, P. (2011) The determinants of international student mobility flows: An empirical study on the Erasmus programme, *Higher Education* 62: 413–430.

Rogers, G. and Mentkowski, M. (2004) Abilities that distinguish the effectiveness of five-year alumna performance across work, family and civic roles: A higher education validation, *Higher Education Research and Development* 23(3): 347–374.

Rohstock, A. (2011) The history of higher education, in Tröhler, D. and Barbu, R. (Eds.) *Education Systems in Historical, Cultural and Sociological Perspectives. The Future of Education Research*. Volume 1. Rotterdam: Sense, 91–104.

Rosenthal, D., Russell, J. and Thompson, G. (2006) *A Growing Experience: The Health and Well-Being of International Students at The University of Melbourne*. Melbourne: The University of Melbourne.

Rowan, D., Järkestig-Berggren, U., Cambridge, I., McAuliffe, D., Fung, A. and Moore, M. (2014) The 6 Continents Project: A method for linking social work classrooms for intercultural exchange through asynchronous video sharing, *International Social Work* doi: 10.1177/0020872813497384.

Rüegg, W. (1992) Themes, in Ridder-Symoens, R. de (Ed.) *A History of the University in Europe. Volume I – Universities in the Middle Ages*. Cambridge: Cambridge University Press, 3–34.

Rüegg, W. (1996) Themes, in Ridder-Symoens, R. de (Ed.) *A History of the University in Europe. Volume II – Universities in Early Modern Europe (1500–1800)*. Cambridge: Cambridge University Press, 3–42.

Rüegg, W. (2004) Themes, in Rüegg, W. (Ed.) *A History of the University in Europe. Volume III – Universities in the Nineteenth and Early Twentieth Centuries (1800–1945)*. Cambridge: Cambridge University Press, 3–32.

Rumford, C. (2007) Introduction: Cosmopolitanism and Europe, in Rumford, C. (Ed.) *Cosmopolitanism and Europe*. Liverpool: Liverpool University Press, 1–15.

Russell, C. and Shepherd, J. (2010) Online role-play environments for higher education, *British Journal of Educational Technology* 41(6): 992–1002.

Said, E. (1995) *Orientalism*. London: Penguin.

Salmon, G. (2000) *E-moderating: The Key to Teaching and Learning Online*. London: Kogan Page.

Salmon, G., Nie, M. and Edirisingha, P. (2010) Developing a five-stage model of learning in Second Life, *Educational Research* 52(2): 169–182.

Sawir, E., Marginson, S., Deumert, A., Nyland, C. and Ramia, G. (2008) Loneliness and international students: An Australian study, *Journal of Studies in International Education* 12(2): 148–180.

Schofer, E. and Meyer, J. (2005) The worldwide expansion of higher education in the twentieth century, *American Sociological Review* 70: 898–920.

Scholte, J. (2000) *Globalisation. A Critical Introduction*. London: Macmillan Press.

156   *References*

Sciences Po (2014a) *About Us – A Selective and Diverse French University.* Accessed 3 January 2015 from www.sciencespo.fr/en/content/3/who-are-we

Sciences Po (2014b) *An International University – Competitiveness and an International Focus.* Accessed 3 January 2015 www.sciencespo.fr/en/content/9/international-university

Sciences Po (2014c) *Le Grand Syllabus 2013–2014.* Accessed 4 January 2015 from http://asp.zone_secure.net/v2/index.jsp?id=1737/2223/45810andlng=en

Sciences Po (2014d) *1360 Students Going Abroad.* Accessed 4 January 2015 from www.international.sciences_po.fr/en/1360-students-going-abroad

Sciences Po (2014e) *Partner Universities.* Accessed 4 January 2015 from http://international.sciences-po.fr/en/partner-universities

Scott, J. (2006) The mission of the university: Medieval to postmodern transformations, *The Journal of Higher Education* 77(1): 1–39.

Seaman, J. and Tinti-Kane, H. (2013) *Social Media for Teaching and Learning.* Boston, MA: Pearson Learning Solutions.

Seddon, T. (2014) Making educational spaces through boundary work: Territorialisation and 'boundarying', *Globalisation, Societies and Education* 12(1): 10–31.

Semetsky, I. (2012) Living, learning, loving: Constructing a new ethics of integration in education, *Discourse: Studies in the Cultural Politics of Education* 33(1): 47–59.

Serby, T. (2011) Willing suspension of disbelief: A study in online learning through simulation, and its potential for deeper learning in higher education, *Liverpool Law Review* 32: 181–195.

Shanka, T., Quintal, V. and Taylor, R. (2005) Factors influencing international students' choice of an education destination – A correspondence analysis, *Journal of Marketing for Higher Education* 15(2): 31–46.

Shi, J. (2011) The foundation and trends of undergraduate education reform in China's research universities, *Chinese Education and Society* 44(5): 67–83.

Sichone, O. (2008) Xenophobia and xenophilia in South Africa: African migrants in Cape Town, in Werbner, P. (Ed.) *Anthropology and the New Cosmopolitanism: Rooted, Feminist and Vernacular Perspectives.* Oxford: Berg, 309–324.

Singh, M., Rizvi, F. and Shrestha, M. (2007) Student mobility and the spatial production of cosmopolitan identities, in Gulson, K. and Symes, C. (Eds.) *Spatial Theories of Education: Policy and Geography Matters.* New York: Routledge, 195–214.

Skrbis, Z. and Woodward, I. (2007) The ambivalence of ordinary cosmopolitanism: Investigating the limits of cosmopolitan openness, *The Sociological Review* 55(4): 730–747.

Skrbis, Z., Kendall, G. and Woodward, I. (2004) Locating cosmopolitanism: Between humanist ideal and grounded social category, *Theory, Culture and Society* 21(6): 115–136.

Slattery, P. (2013) *Curriculum Development in the Post-Modern Era. Teaching and Learning in an Age of Accountability.* Third Edition. New York and London: Routledge.

Smart, D., Volet, S. and Ang, G. (2000) *Fostering Social Cohesion in Universities: Bridging the Cultural Divide.* Canberra: Australian Education International and Department of Education, Training and Youth Affairs.

Smith, J., McAuliffe, G. and Rippard, K. (2014) Counseling students' transformative learning through a study abroad curriculum, *Counselor Education and Supervision* 53: 306–319.

Souto Otero, M. and McCoshan, A. (2006) *Survey of the Socio-Economic Background of Erasmus Students.* DG EAC 01/05. Final Report to the European Commission, Birmingham.

Spinelli, G. (2009) Measuring the success of internationalisation: The case for joint and double degrees, in De Wit, H. (Ed.) *Measuring Success in the Internationalisation of Higher Education.* EAIE Occasional Paper 22. Amsterdam: European Association for International Education, 49–55.

Spybey, T. (1996) *Globalisation and World Society.* Cambridge: Polity Press.

Stanford University (undated) *The Cross-Cultural Rhetoric Project.* Accessed 30 January 2015 from http://ccr.stanford.edu/project.html

Starke-Meyerring, D. and Wilson, M. (2009) Learning environments for a globally networked world: Emerging visions, in Starke-Meyerring, D. and Wilson, M. (Eds.) *Designing Globally Networked Learning Environments. Visionary Partnerships, Policies and Pedagogies.* Rotterdam: Sense Publishers, 1–17.

Statista (2015) *Frequency with which children in the United States used the internet as of March 2014, by gender.* Accessed 5 February 2015 from www.statista.com/statistics/297982/internet-usage-frequency-of-us-children-by-gender/

Stepanyan, K., Mather, R. and Dalrymple, R. (2014) Culture, role and group work: A social network analysis perspective on an online collaborative course, *British Journal of Educational Technology* 45(4): 676–693.

Stephenson, J. and Yorke, M. (2012) Foreword, in Stephenson, J. and Yorke, M. (Eds.) *Capability and Quality in Higher Education.* Abingdon: Routledge, vii–viii.

Stivens, M. (2008) Gender, rights and cosmopolitanisms, in Werbner, P. (Ed.) *Anthropology and the New Cosmopolitanism: Rooted, Feminist and Vernacular Perspectives.* Oxford: Berg, 87–109.

Stoner, K., Tarrant, M., Perry, L., Stoner, L., Wearing, S. and Lyons, K. (2014) Global citizenship as a learning outcome of educational travel, *Journal of Teaching in Travel and Tourism* 14(2): 149–163.

Strathdee, R. (2005) *Social Exclusion and the Remaking of Social Networks.* Aldershot: Ashgate Publishing.

Strydom, P. (2012) Toward a global cosmopolis? On the formation of a cosmopolitan cultural model, *Irish Journal of Sociology* 20(2): 28–50.

Sypnowich, C. (2005) Cosmopolitans, cosmopolitanism and human flourishing, in Brock, G. and Brighouse, H. (Eds.) *The Political Philosophy of Cosmopolitanism.* Cambridge: Cambridge University Press, 55–74.

Szerszynski, B. and J. Urry (2002) Cultures of cosmopolitanism, *The Sociological Review* 50(4): 461–481.

Tajfel, H. and Dawson, J. (Eds.) (1965) *Disappointed Guests: Essays by African, Asian and West Indian Students.* London: Institute of Race Relations.

Talbani, A. (1996) Pedagogy, power, and discourse: Transformation of Islamic education, *Comparative Education Review* 40(1): 66–82.

Tallon, R. (2011) Creating 'little sultans' in the social sciences: Learning about the other through benevolent eyes, *International Research in Geographical and Environmental Education* 20(4): 281–286.

Tapanes, M., Smith, G. and White, J. (2009) Cultural diversity in online learning: A study of the perceived effects of dissonance in levels of individualism/collectivism and tolerance of ambiguity, *Internet and Higher Education* 12: 26–34.

Taras, V., Kirkman, B. and Steel, P. (2010) Examining the impact of culture's consequences: A three-decade, multilevel, meta-analytic review of Hofstede's cultural value dimensions, *Journal of Applied Psychology* 95(3): 405–439.

Tegos, S., Demetriadis, S. and Tsiatsos, T. (2014) A configurable conversational agent to trigger students' productive dialogue: A pilot study in the CALL domain, *International Journal of Artificial Intelligence in Education* 24(1): 62–91.

158 References

Teichler, U. (2005) Temporary study abroad: The life of ERASMUS students, *European Journal of Education* 39(4): 395–408.

Tekin, U. and Hiç Gencer, A. (2013) Effects of the Erasmus programme on Turkish universities and university students, *Trakya Üniversitesi Sosyal Bilimler Dergisi Haziran* 15(1): 109–122.

Thelin, J. (2011) *A History of American Higher Education.* Second edition. Baltimore, MD: The Johns Hopkins University Press.

Todd, S. (2007) Teachers judging without scripts, or thinking cosmopolitan, *Ethics and Education* 2(1): 25–38.

Toven-Lindsey, B., Rhoads, R. and Berdan Lozano, J. (2015) Virtually unlimited classrooms: Pedagogical practices in massive open online courses, *Internet and Higher Education* 24: 1–12.

Tran, L. (2010) Embracing prior professional experience in meaning making: Views from international students and academics, *Educational Review* 62(2): 157–173.

Trice, A. and Elliott, J. (1993) Japanese students in America: II College friendship patterns, *Journal of Instructional Psychology* 20(3): 262–264.

Try, S. (2005) The use of job search strategies among university graduates, *The Journal of Socio-Economics* 34: 223–243.

Tsekleves, E., Cosmas, J. and Aggoun, A. (2014) Benefits, barriers and guideline recommendations for the implementation of serious games in education for stakeholders and policymakers, *British Journal of Educational Technology* doi: 10.1111/bjet.12223

UNESCO (United Nations Educational, Scientific and Cultural Organization) (2013) *Table 26: Historical Data, Tertiary Education. Education Statistics.* Accessed 25 May 2013 from http://stats.uis.unesco.org/unesco/TableViewer/tableView.aspx

UNESCO (2014) *High Level Workshop on OpenupEd OER and MOOCs for the National Open University of Nigeria.* Accessed 21 January 2015 from http://en.unesco.org/events/high-level-workshop-openuped-oer-and-moocs-national-open-university-nigeria

UNESCO Institute for Statistics (2015a) *Enrolment by Level of Education.* Accessed 3 February 2015 from http://data.uis.unesco.org/

UNESCO Institute for Statistics (2015b) *Gross Enrolment Ratio by Level of Education.* Accessed 5 February 2015 from http://data.uis.unesco.org/

University of Leicester (2015) *Second World Immersive Future Teaching.* Accessed 1 February 2015 from www2.le.ac.uk/projects/swift

University of Maryland (2015) *ICONS project.* Accessed 20 January 2015 from www.icons.umd.edu/education/home

University of Nottingham (2014) *A Global University.* Accessed 3 January 2015 from www.nottingham.ac.uk/aglobaluniversity/index.aspx

University of Oviedo (2014) *Erasmus Mundus Masters Course in Emergency and Critical Care Nursing.* Accessed 6 January 2015 from www.masternursing.eu/partnership

Uzuner, S. (2009) Questions of culture in distance learning: A research review, *The International Review of Research in Open and Distance Learning* 10(3): 1–19.

van der Land, S., Schouten, A., van den Hooff, B. and Feldberg, F. (2011) Modelling the metaverse: A theoretical model of effective team collaboration in 3D virtual environments, *Journal of Virtual Worlds* 4(3): 1–16.

van der Wende, M. (1997) Internationalizing the curriculum in higher education: An international comparative perspective, *Journal of Studies in International Education* 1(2): 53–72.

References 159

van der Wende, M. (2001) The international dimension in national higher education policies: What has changed in Europe in the last five years? *European Journal of Education* 36(4): 431–441.

van der Zee, K. I., and van Oudenhoven, J. P. (2000) The multicultural personality questionnaire: A multidimensional instrument of multicultural effectiveness, *European Journal of Personality* 14(4): 291–309.

Vardi, I. and Quin, R. (2011) Promotion and the scholarship of teaching and learning, *Higher Education Research and Development* 30(1): 39–49.

Varghese, N. (2008) *Globalization of Higher Education and Cross-border Student Mobility.* Paris: International Institute for Education Planning.

VeLure Roholt, R. and Fisher, C. (2013) Expect the unexpected: International short-term study course pedagogies and practices, *Journal of Social Work Education* 49: 48–65.

Vertovec, S. and Cohen, R. (2002) Introduction: Conceiving cosmopolitanism, in Vertovec, S. and Cohen, R. (Eds.) *Conceiving Cosmopolitanism. Theory, Context and Practice.* Oxford: Oxford University Press, 1–22.

Waks, L. (2009) Cosmopolitan education and its discontents, *Philosophy of Education Yearbook* 253–262.

Wallace, R. (2003) Online learning in higher education: A review of research on interactions among teachers and students, *Education, Communication and Information* 3(2): 241–280.

Walsh, J. (2009) The university movement in the north of England at the end of the nineteenth century, *Northern History* 46(1): 113–131.

Wang, J. (2013) Moving towards ethnorelativism: A framework for measuring and meeting students' needs in cross-cultural business and technical communication, *Journal of Technical Writing and Communication* 43(2): 201–218.

Wang, M. (2007) Designing online courses that effectively engage learners from diverse cultural backgrounds, *British Journal of Educational Technology* 38(2): 294–311.

Wang, X and Liu, J. (2011) China's higher education expansion and the task of economic revitalization, *Higher Education* 62(2): 213–229.

Warhurst, R. (2008) 'Cigars on the flight deck': New lecturers' participatory learning within workplace communities of practice, *Studies in Higher Education* 33(4): 453–467.

Warwick, P. and Moogan, Y. (2013) A comparative study of perceptions of internationalisation strategies in UK universities, *Compare: A Journal of Comparative and International Education* 43(1): 102–123.

Waters, J. (2012) Geographies of international education: Mobilities and the reproduction of social (dis)advantage, *Geography Compass* 6(3): 123–136.

Waters, M. (2001) *Globalization.* Second edition. London: Routledge.

Watkins, C., Carnell, E. and Lodge, C. (2007) *Effective Learning in Classrooms.* London: SAGE Publications.

Webb, R. and Sims, R. (2006) *Online Gaming and Online Gaming Communities: Ten Reasons Why They Matter.* Presented at the 12th Australasian World Wide Web Conference, Southern Cross University, East Lismore, Australia. Accessed 20 January 2015 from http://ausweb.scu.edu.au/aw06/papers/refereed/webb/paper.html

Webber, K. (2011) The use of learner-centered assessment in US colleges and universities, *Research in Higher Education* 53: 201–228.

Weenink, D. (2007) Cosmopolitan and established resources of power in the education arena, *International Sociology* 22(4): 1089–1106.

160 *References*

Werbner, P. (2008) Introduction: Towards a new cosmopolitan anthropology, in Werbner, P. (Ed.) *Anthropology and the New Cosmopolitanism: Rooted, Feminist and Vernacular Perspectives.* Oxford: Berg, 1–29.

Wiggins, B. (2012) Toward a model for intercultural communication in simulations, *Simulation and Gaming* 43(4): 550–572.

Wiggins, G. (1989) Teaching to the (authentic) test, *Educational Leadership* 46(7): 41–47.

Williams, A. and Balaz, M. (2009) *International Migration and Knowledge.* London: Routledge.

Woodward, I., Skrbis, Z. and Bean, C. (2008) Attitudes towards globalization and cosmopolitanism: cultural diversity, personal consumption and the national economy, *The British Journal of Sociology*, 59(2): 207–226.

Woolcock, M. and Narayan, D. (2000) Social capital: Implications for development theory, research and policy, *The World Bank Research Observer* 15(2): 225–249.

Woolf, M. (2009) Measuring success in education abroad: Who are we trying to impress?, in De Wit, H. (Ed.) *Measuring Success in the Internationalisation of Higher Education.* EAIE Occasional Paper 22. Amsterdam: European Association for International Education, 57–64.

Wray, R., Lane, H., Stensrud, B., Core, M., Hamel, L. and Forbell, E. (2009) *Pedagogical Experience Manipulation for Cultural Learning.* Proceedings of the Second Workshop on Culturally Aware Tutoring Systems at the 14th International Conference on Artificial Intelligence in Education, Brighton, UK. Accessed 31 January 2015 from http://people.ict.usc.edu/~core/papers/AIED09-CATS_PedExpManip_WrayLane-Final.pdf

Wresch, W., Arbaugh, J. and Rebstock, M. (2005) International online management education courses: A study of participation patterns, *The Internet and Higher Education* 8(2): 131–144.

Wright, C. (1979) Academics and their aims. English and Scottish approaches to university education in the nineteenth century, *History of Education* 8(2): 91–97.

Yoo, J. and Kim, J. (2014) Can online discussion participation predict group project performance? Investigating the roles of linguistic features and participation patterns, *International Journal of Artificial Intelligence in Education* 24(1): 8–32.

Yuan, B. (2011) Internationalization at home. The path to internationalization in Chinese research universities, *Chinese Education and Society* 44(5): 84–96.

Zajonc, A. (2013) Contemplative pedagogy: A quiet revolution in higher education, *New Directions for Teaching and Learning* 134: 83–94.

Zajonc, A. (2014) Contemplative pedagogy in education: Towards a more reflective academy, in Gunnlaugson, O., Sarath, E., Scott, C. and Bai, H. (Eds.) *Contemplative Learning and Enquiry Across Disciplines.* Albany: State University of New York, 15–30.

Zheng, X. and Berry, J. (1991) Psychological adaptation of Chinese sojourners in Canada, *International Journal of Psychology* 26(4): 451–470.

Zubaida, S. (2002) Middle Eastern experiences of cosmopolitanism, in Vertovec, S. and Cohen, E. (Eds.) *Conceiving Cosmopolitanism. Theory, Context and Practice.* Oxford: Oxford University Press, 32–41.

Index

Abubakar, B. 46
academic citizenship: broadening of, to incorporate international elements 99; notion of 99
active learning 95, 101, 106
active learning pedagogy 95
active thinking 64
ActiveWorlds 120
Adaptive Thinking and Leadership System 122
Adobe Connect 119
Africa, misrepresentation of, in CBS' '60 Minutes' 129
African heritage 20
African migrants in Cape Town 42
African universities 20
Ahmed, M. 17
Ahola, S. 46
A'ishah, A. S. 18
Aksartova, S. 42, 68
Al Azhar, University of, Egypt, claim of, as oldest university 15
Alesina, A. 65
Algarve, University of, Portugal, Erasmus Mundus programme 83
Alibhai, N. 61, 62
Ali-Choudhury, R. 46
allegiances, multiple 11, 38–40, 43, 68, 81
Allen, I. E. 108, 109, 110
Al Qarawiyyin Mosque, Morocco 22, 125; claim of, as oldest university 14–19
Al Quds University, Palestinian Territories, curriculum partnership with Science Po 86
Altbach, P. 48, 125
American University of Sharjah, United Arab Emirates, curriculum partnership with Science Po 86

Anderson, A. 37
Anderson, E. 66, 131
Ang, S. 104
Anthias, G. 34, 38, 39, 47
Antonio, A. 102
Anzar, U. 17, 18
Appiah, K. 2, 31, 32, 35, 40, 47, 67, 68, 73
Araya-Palacios, F. 113
Areden, A. 78
Arendt, H. 93
Arkoudis, S. 101, 102
Asian higher education institutions 53
Asia Pacific Economic Cooperation (APEC) economies 83
assessment: authentic 103, 106; of cross-cultural competence 13, 101–5; learner-centred 103, 106; as part of curriculum design 76; peer 103; performance 103; purpose of 102; self- 103
assessment practice(s): good, characteristics of 13, 101–5; innovative 105; learner-centred 103
Association of American Geographers, Center for Global Geography Education 112, 113
Astin, A. 102
asylum seekers 125; contemporary policies towards 34
Australia, international students in 45, 51
Australian Bureau of Statistics 57, 61
Australian Curriculum 75
Australian society, multicultural nature of 46
Austria, international students in 51
authentic assessment 103, 106
Autio, T. 76

162 Index

Baiio, W. 113
Bainbridge, W. 121
Balaz, M. 45
Bamgbose, A. 51
'banking' education 25, 28
Basedow, J. B. 32, 67
Bauman, Z. 23, 34, 38, 50
Becher, A. 76
Beck, U. 34, 35, 38–42, 47, 61, 67–9, 130, 133
Bégin-Caouette, O. 114
Bell, M. 99
Belliveau, M. 64
belonging, intimate, endemic human need for 39
Belyavina, R. 52
Bender, A. 94
Benhabib, S. 35
Bennett, M. 105
Bennett, R. 46
Berg, M. 42, 117, 118
Berry, J. 62
Berry, W. 9
Bevitt, S. 105
Bianchi, A. 19
Biccum, A. 127
Biggs, J. 92
Bilateral Negotiation Trainer 122
Boateng, A. 88
Bochner, S. 61, 62
Bodemer, D. 116
Boix Mansilla, V. 6
Boko Haram 125
Bolden, R. 100
Boler, M. 94
Boli, J. 23
Bologna, University of, Italy, claim of, as oldest university 15
Bols, A. 102
Bonk, J. 114
Bonwell, C. 95, 100, 101
Boon, V. 31
border dwellers, young people as 1
border thinking 67, 132
Boud, D. 102
Bourdieu, P. 40
Bowser, D. 93
Boyatzis, R. 8
Bracht, O. 48, 49, 98
Brandenburg, U. 98
Bridge, C. 76, 79, 99
Brighouse, H. 35
Brock, G. 35
Brock-Utne, B. 20

Brooks, R. 45, 49, 50, 53
Brustein, W. 9, 79, 99
Buchanan, J. 118
Buck, T. 120
Buddhist philosophy 8, 72
Buder, J. 116
Byrne, D. 45

Cain, T. 20
Cairo, University of, Egypt 86
Calcutt, L. 42
Calhoun, C. 38
Cambridge University, UK 19, 53
Canada, international students in 51
Cape Town, South Africa, African migrants in 42
capitalism, global 24, 45
Carroll, N. 24
Carroll, W. 111
categorical reductionism 38
Catholic Papacy, as instrumental in establishment of European higher education institutions 16
Catholic Relief Services 118
Cavallar, G. 32, 67
Cavallario, P. 109
CBS' '60 Minutes', misrepresentation of Africa in 129
Center for Global Geography Education (CGGE) 112, 113
chain migration 47
Chan, K. 37
Chao, F. 89
Charles, D. 120
Cheah, P. 37, 39, 40
Chen, L. 46
Cheng, C. 7, 16
China, Sung era, establishment of academies in 17
Chinese education, development of 'moral uprightness' for greater good of society as defining factor of 16
Choi, M. 62
Christie, H. 52
Cicero 32
civic activism, as subscale of global civic engagement 104
civic organisations, involvement in, as subscale of global civic engagement 104
Clayton, M. 46
Clegg, S. 77
Clifford, A. 103
cognitive disequilibrium 100

Index   163

Cohen, R. 39, 40, 41, 59, 60
collaborative programmes 89; as highly
   integrated international curricula 82;
   international education accessible
   through 13, 82–5
Collins, M. 88
comfort zone, ability to step outside 63
common good, interest in 67
common possession, right to 33
communication: cross-cultural 117;
   intercultural 104, 113; online
   synchronous 117
communication simulations 122
communication technologies,
   innovations in 107
communist revolution 20
communities of learning 10–11
communities of practice 101;
   cosmopolitan 119
compassion 72, 73, 82, 86, 89, 96, 118;
   meaning of 8
competencies, required for life as a
   global citizen 24
concept maps 116
Confucian model of onto-cosmology of
   self-cultivation 16
Confucian tradition, development of
   cosmopolitan thought in 37
connectivity, web of 3
Constantinou, P. 98
constant unveiling of reality 26
contemplative pedagogy 95, 96, 106
contemplative/ruminative reflection 93
context, roles and actions informed
   by 92
Conway-Gomez, K. 113
cooperation, recognition of value of 92
Coryell, J. 87, 98, 102
cosmopolitan: concept of 7; meaning of
   term 7; use in book 7–8
cosmopolitan aesthetic 41, 68
cosmopolitan approach 7, 22, 34–43,
   67–70, 94, 131; to education 69,
   127, 128; to human consequences
   of globalisation 30; versus
   multiculturalism 38; philosophical
   project of 35, 36; political project
   of 35, 36; political understanding of
   35; social, limitations to 41–2; social
   project of 31, 35, 38, 43
cosmopolitan assessment practice,
   development of 102
cosmopolitan attributes 8, 11, 63, 66,
   105, 106, 113, 115, 118; contribution

of higher education practice to
   12–13, 74–90; development of 13,
   56, 84, 91–3, 99–100, 103, 111, 133;
   opportunity to gain 12, 13, 29, 56, 60,
   61, 74, 75, 84, 90–102, 110, 111, 122,
   123, 126, 128, 131, 133, 134
cosmopolitan canon, as informing
   educational practice 12, 67–71
cosmopolitan canopy(ies) 66, 67, 71, 131
cosmopolitan communities of practice 119
cosmopolitan concept, evolution of 31
cosmopolitan curriculum 92, 106, 107
cosmopolitan disposition 40–1, 67, 68,
   73, 129; notion of 131
cosmopolitan education (*passim*):
   assessment in 101; components of
   67; cosmopolitan approach to 69,
   127, 128; and cultural invasion 26; as
   cultural politics 24; de-parochialisation
   of 94; international, *see* international
   education; international elements of,
   increasing interest in 13; moral, 7;
   as process of inquiry 25; 'problem
   posing' 26
cosmopolitan educators, skills and
   attributes required by 96–101
cosmopolitan elements, critical
   moments for introducing in
   educational process 12
cosmopolitan ethos, essential to
   coexistence 73
cosmopolitan fallacy 41
cosmopolitan habitus 126
cosmopolitan insights 77; benefits of, in
   educational practice 7, 13; informing
   educational practice 67–72
cosmopolitan intent, educational
   interventions with 131
cosmopolitanism: political 37; reflective
   inquiry is an ethical requirement, and
   thus as constitutive element of 93;
   rooted 40
cosmopolitan learning 97, 106, 108, 109,
   112, 118, 122, 123, 131; use of games
   in 120
cosmopolitan opportunities 13, 27–9, 91
cosmopolitan patriotism 40
cosmopolitan pedagogy 92, 93, 96,
   100, 113
cosmopolitan philosophy 30, 97
cosmopolitan potential of online
   learning 111–12
cosmopolitan principles/values 7,
   27, 89, 101, 102; application of, to

Index

higher education 12, 41; application of, to practical challenges in realms of universal norms and global governance 12

cosmopolitan sensibilities, concept of 8, 42, 47, 131

cosmopolitan theory 13, 31, 36, 42, 43, 131; application of, to higher education practice 127

cosmopolitan thinking/thought 3, 7, 13, 27, 29, 30–43, 67, 73, 130, 132; development of, in Persia 37; growth of, through history 12, 31–5; Stoic parentage, Kantian upbringing and postmodern spoiling of 35; three strands of 35–8; value of, for contemporary higher education practice 2, 31

cosmo-political relation 33

cosmo-political system 33

counter-hegemony, definition 24

Cousin, G. 93

CQ 104

critical/analytical reflection 93

criticality 72, 73, 82, 86, 89

critical reflection 27–9, 71, 88, 92, 93, 111

critical thinking 6, 26, 64, 88, 101, 105, 117, 119, 122, 130; about learning process 103

cross-cultural communication 117

cross-cultural competence (3C), assessment of 13, 101–5

Cross-Cultural Rhetoric Project, Stanford University, USA 117

Crystal, D. 50

Cubans in Spain 42

cultural awareness 44

cultural dimensions, identification of five 114

cultural homogeneity, notion of 38

cultural invasion 27; and cosmopolitan education 26; notion of, pertinence of 26

culturalist cosmopolitan perspective 67

culture, notion of, students' understanding of 105

Culver, S. 85

curiosity 6, 67, 72, 104, 105; nurturing 130

Curmi, C. 66, 130

curriculum: definition 75; internationalisation of 77–9, 99 (concept of 79); notion of, redefinition of 74, 75

curriculum design: assessment as part of 76; transnational challenges in 76

curriculum development 75–7; process of 77; study of 75

Cynics 31

Dabbagh, N. 110

Dalgarno, B. 121

Dalit Tamil women in India 42

Danforth, D. 121

Dapous, R. 52

Datta, A. 42

Dawson, J. 62

Deardorff, D. 79, 104

decolonial pedagogy 94, 106

Deem, R. 53

deep learning 117–19

DeJaynes, T. 66, 130

Delanty, G. 7, 31, 32, 35, 37, 38, 40, 42, 68

Delhey, J. 65

De Lissovoy, N. 94, 95

de-parochialisation of education 94

Department of Education and Training 57

Developmental Model of Intercultural Sensitivity 105

Devlin-Scherer, R. 101

Dewey, J. 94

de Wit, H. 125

dialectics of distantiation and participation 93

dialogue, true, conditions for 26

diaspora children 10

Dickson, K. 105

difference: ability to engage with 11, 43, 92; intellectual and emotional engagement with 72, 92

Dinesen, P. 65

Diogenes the Cynic 31

discipline-specific skills, versus generic skills, development of 8

discomfort, pedagogy of 94

dispositions, system of, habitus as 40

distance learning 107–24

diverse groups, moral obligations towards 71, 92

diversity: appreciation of and interest in 40; asset rather than problem 6; cultural 6, 7, 35, 61, 104; engaging with 1

Donald, J. 77

Donnelly-Smith, L. 87, 88

Dray, B. 110

Drew, V. 95

Eagan, K. 98, 109
East European building workers in London 42
education: cosmopolitan (*passim*): assessment in 101; components of 67; cosmopolitan approach to 69, 127, 128; and cultural invasion 26; as cultural politics 24; de-parochialisation of 94; international, *see* international education; international elements of, increasing interest in 13; moral, 7; as process of inquiry 25; 'problem posing' 26; progress towards 27–9
educational cosmopolitanism 70
educational interventions, with cosmopolitan intent 131
educational practice: benefits of cosmopolitan insights in 13; benefits of, to cosmopolitan insights 130; as informed by cosmopolitan canon 12, 67–72; informed by cosmopolitan insights 67–72
educational responses, appropriate, to global contexts 13, 125–7
educators: cosmopolitan, skills and attributes required by 96–101; emerging challenges for 127–30; in higher education institutions, role of 96–101; internationalisation of 99; mobility of, impact of 98; responsibility of, for 200 million higher education students 2; 'service pyramid' for 99
Egron-Polak, E. 78
Egyptian empire 16
Eison, J. 95, 100, 101
Elliott, J. 62
emancipatory change 24, 127
empathy 68, 72, 73, 82, 86, 89, 96, 102, 104, 105, 123; need for 129
employability 9, 44, 52, 53, 65, 76, 83, 97; benefits of mobility for 12, 47–50; graduate 45
Engelmann, T. 116
English, as global language 51
English-language skills 46, 50, 63
Enlightenment 12, 32
Ennew, C. 21
Erasmus programme 48, 49, 50, 83, 98; Erasmus Mundus programme 48, 50, 83, 98; Erasmus+ 83
Eriksson, A. 117
Ertmer, P. 117

ethics of care in teaching 97
Ethiopia, conversion of royal family to Christianity as factor in establishment of higher education institutions 16
ethnocentrism 105
ethnorelativism 105
Eurocentrism 94
Europe: nineteenth-century, expansion of university education in 23; protests in, about US-led invasion of Iraq 42
European Commission 48, 85
European Middle East Virtual University, peace education initiative 118
European Multiple MOOC Aggregator project 109
European Union 48, 49, 77, 86, 109, 125
experiential learning 88, 94, 106, 120, 123; pedagogy of 93; simulated 121
experiential learning model, cyclical 94
exploitation of some groups of people by others, as core component of globalisation 37

Facebook 119
Falchikov, N. 102, 103
Falk, R. 40
Falzon, M. 42, 61
Fanghanel, J. 93, 100, 101
Fardon, R. 38, 39, 133
Farhang, A. 17
Field, J. 64, 133
Fielden, J. 49, 53
Findlay, A. 52
Fine, R. 3, 33, 36, 39
Firer, R. 118
Fischer, F. 116
Fisher, C. 88
flexibility 44, 104, 105, 122
Flickr 119
foreign campuses 81–4; international education accessible at 13, 80–2
Foreign Trade University, Hanoi and Ho Chi Minh City, Viet Nam, and La Trobe University, Australia, collaborative programme with 84
Foreign Trade University, Viet Nam 84
Foucault, M. 22
France, international students in 51
Francois, E. 99, 100
Franzen, A. 64
Freire, P. 12, 24–8, 94, 127
French, H. 19, 48, 85, 129
Frey, B. 103
Frijhoff, W. 12, 14, 19, 22, 126

Index

Fujia, Y. 21
Furnham, A. 61, 62
future leaders, educating 2, 5–8, 65, 82, 125–7, 133–4

gain cosmopolitan attributes 12, 13, 29, 56, 60, 61, 74, 75, 84, 90–3, 95, 97, 99, 100, 102, 110, 111, 122, 123, 126, 128, 131, 133, 134
games 13, 119, 123; use of, in higher education 120
Ganatra, N. 7
Garam, I. 49
generic skills versus discipline-specific skills, development of 8
geography as more advanced discipline in international collaborative online learning 112
Giddens, A. 34
Gill, S. 52
Gingerich, O. 88, 94, 97
Glaeser, E. 65
global attributes, necessary, of graduates 9
global capital, nation states reconfigured to attract 23
global capitalism 24, 45
global challenges, appreciating and finding solutions to 68
global citizen, life as, competencies required for 24
global citizenship 5, 8, 24, 80, 103; definition 6; notion of 104
global civic engagement 6, 104
global competence 6, 79, 104
global competencies 44
global contexts 8, 133; appropriate educational responses to 13, 125–7
global education, role of computers in 111
global governance, application of cosmopolitan principles to 12, 35
Global Higher Education 80
global interconnections, as norm 34
globalisation: challenges and opportunities of 4; changes wrought by 37, 41, 43; core component of, exploitation of some groups of people by others as 37; features of 3; features of, movements of money, goods, ideas, information, power as 3; forces of 3–4, 23; forces of, and higher education institutions 4; forces of, at level of individual and social 3; homogenising force of 128;

homogenising influence of 40; human consequences of, cosmopolitan approach to 30; and virtue 22–4
global knowledge, as subscale of global competence 21, 89, 104
global learning 92; innovations in 74–90
globally interconnected society 70
global mobility of students 4
global significance, issues of 6
Global Solidarity Network Study e-Broad Program 118
global space, operating in, meaning of 97
global ties, widening, deepening and speeding up of 34
global understanding, enhancement of 12
Goldfinch, J. 103
Goleman, D. 8
Google Hangouts 119
Goulah, J. 93
graduate employment, social segmentation in 52
graduates, necessary global attributes of 9
Gramsci, A. 22, 24, 28, 127
Grande, E. 35, 68
Gravois, J. 96
Grayson, P. 60
Green, W. 101
Greenfield, E. 88
Greitzer, F. 120
Grewal, D. 50
Group of Eight Australia 45
Gulz, A. 122
Gundeshapur, pre-Islamic Persia 17
Gunnlaugson, O. 96
Gurin, P. 64
Güriz, K. 45

Haake, M. 122
Habermas, J. 36, 37, 38
habitus 40, 126; cosmopolitan 126; as system of dispositions 40
Haigh, M. 77, 79
Hall, S. 36
Halstead, J. 17, 125
Hammer, M. 105
Hangartner, D. 64
Hannerz, U. 40, 41, 43, 60
Hanoi University, Viet Nam 84; collaborative programmes with Harbin Medical University, China, and La Trobe University, Australia, 84
Hansen, D. 69, 70, 128, 129, 130
Harasim, L. 108

Index 167

Harbin Medical University, China, and Hanoi University, Viet Nam, collaborative programme with 84
Hardaker, G. 18
Harrison, Y. 118
Harvard Business School, USA 8
Harvard University, USA 19
Harvey, D. 32, 36, 67
He, B. 35, 37, 42, 68
Hegel, G. 36
Held, D. 31, 32, 34, 35, 36, 67, 68
Helfand, D. 119
Helsinki Metropolia University of Applied Sciences, Finland 83
Herbst, M. 89
Herold, D. 121
Herring, S. 117
Hesse, F. 116
heterogeneity 58, 66; increasing normality of 6
Hiç Gencer, A. 48
Hierocles 31, 132
higher education (*passim*): decentralisation, commercialisation and expansion of 21; enrollment in 1; history of 15; international, and mobility 12; international aspects of, as market-based 5; role of online modalities in 13; Soviet approach to 20
Higher Education Academy, UK 70
higher education curricula, inclusion of international aspects in 77–80
higher education institutions: development of, learning, utility and virtue as guiding forces of 12, 14, 22, 126; evolution of, learning, utility and virtue as guiding forces of 12; history of 15–18; as ideological arm of state 22; position of, with regard to globalisation 12, 22–4; and social expansion versus social containment 13, 125
higher education practice: aimed at developing cosmopolitan attitudes 12–13, 74–90; application of cosmopolitan theory to 127; and cosmopolitan attributes 12–13; evolution of, over time 11, 15–22
Hill, J. 93
Himmelfarb, G. 39, 47
Hinglish 51
Ho, D. 51, 84
Hodgson, D. 42
Hofstede, G. 114

Hollinger, D. 30, 38, 39, 47
homogeneity: cultural 38; pockets of, 47
homogenizing influence of globalisation 40
Hong Kong Polytechnic University, Hong Kong 121
hope, meaning of 8
Hopper, P. 10, 23, 41, 59
hospitality, universal 33, 132, 133
House of Lords, UK 48
Hudson, R. 78
Hudzik, J. 78
humanity and virtue 24–7
Hurtado, S. 65, 95
Hwang, H. 104, 105
hybridity 35, 39

ICAPS, *see* Intercultural Adjustment Potential Scale
ICONS, *see* International Communication and Negotiation Simulations
identity, impermanence and blurred lines of 71
IDI, *see* Intercultural Development Inventory
India: Dalit Tamil women in 42; steel workers in 42
Indonesian feminists 42
information technology(ies): and exposure to difference 10; innovations in 107
Institut D'études Politiques de Paris (Sciences Po), France 85–90; internationalisation of curriculum 85–90
institutions of higher learning, expansion of in last century 21
interconnectedness: at all levels 3: of humans 94
Intercultural Adjustment Potential Scale (ICAPS) 104, 105
intercultural communication 113; as subscale of global competence 104
intercultural competence 104, 105, 123; definition 6
Intercultural Development Inventory (IDI) 105
intercultural online learning demonstrated 114
intercultural traffic 31
interdependence of humans, awareness of 92
interdependence with others, moral 97

168 *Index*

International Association for the Advancement of Curriculum Studies 75
International Association of Universities 78
International Communication and Negotiation Simulations (ICONS), Center for International Development and Conflict Management, Department of Government and Politics, University of Maryland, USA 120
international curriculum/curricula 75, 77, 78, 91, 93; alternative solutions 80–9; through collaborative programmes 13, 82–5; and foreign campuses 13, 80–2; highly integrated, collaborative programmes as 82; through short-term study abroad 13, 87; through whole of institution approach 13, 85–7
international education 4, 5, 26, 44–7, 56–64, 77, 89, 90, 111, 125; accessible at collaborative programmes 82–5; accessible at foreign campuses 80–2; benefits of 12; concept of 44; experiences of 59–63; at home 56; missed potential of 64; sources of 10; students' hopes for 56–9
international elements of education, increasing interest in 13
international higher education 12, 63; and student mobility 12, 45–8
internationalisation 81, 83–5, 98–100; advanced approaches in 92; of curriculum 77–9, 99; of curriculum, concept of 79; of curriculum, via whole of institution approach 85–7; of educators 99; measurement of 79; of research and teaching activities of educators 98
international league tables 78
international mobility 5, 44, 47, 49, 50, 52, 87; alternatives to 45; benefit for students of 45; impact of 4
International Online Race Conference 118
international perspective, in higher education 4
International State, universal 33
international student mobility 44, 46, 50, 53
international students 4, 9, 45, 46, 51, 57, 58, 62, 77, 78, 81
internet use 10

interpersonal reflexivity 133
invasion, cultural 26, 27
Ireland, international students in 51
Islam 16
Ivy League 19

Jackson, A. 6
Jackson, D. 89
Jackson, J. 88
James, E. 65
James, R. 66
Janssen, J. 116
Johnson, L. 119, 120
Johnson, W. 122
Johnston, R. 47
Jones, E. 92

Kahane, D. 95, 96
Kahn, J. 39
Kant, I. 32, 33, 35, 36, 37, 67, 132
Kaweh, R. 41
Kennedy, P. 42
Keohane, K. 37, 47
Kern, D. 75
Killick, D. 92
Kim, J. 122
Kim, K. 114
Kim, S. 121
King, R. 45, 49, 50
Kinser, K. 80
Kirkpatrick, A. 52
Kivinen, O. 46
Klein, P. 113
Knight, J. 83
Knight, P. 101
knowledge: creation, subjectivity of 71, 92; and skills useful to society, as objective of higher education 14
Kofman, E. 41
Kolb, D. 93, 94
Kreber, C. 96
Kuala Lumpur, Malaysia, University of Nottingham campus in 80, 81
Kuder, M. 83
Kuhling, C. 37, 47
Kumlin, S. 65

Lackey, K. 110
La Ferrara, E. 65
Lamont, M. 42, 68
Lane, H. 122, 123
Lane, J. 80
Langholm, S. 19
language learning 75, 78, 84, 85

language/linguistic skills 49–53, 83, 86, 89, 122; acquisition of, through international education 50–2; English 46, 50, 63

La Trobe University, Australia, collaborative programmes with Foreign Trade University, Hanoi and Ho Chi Minh City, Viet Nam, Hanoi University, Viet Nam, and Singapore Nurses Association 84

Lattuca, L. 101

Law, A. 101

leaders, future, education of 2, 5–8, 65, 82, 125–7, 133–4

learner-centred assessment 106

learning: communities of 10–11; context of 14, 28; cosmopolitan 97, 106, 108, 109, 112, 118, 120, 122, 123, 131; mutual, between students and educators 97; as one of three guiding forces of evolution of higher education institutions 12, 14, 22, 126; online 4, 13, 107–24

learning process, critical thinking about 103

Leask, B. 76, 79, 99

Lee, A. 94, 95, 100, 130

Lee, J. 46

Lee, M. 121

Lee, T. 16, 17

Leeds Metropolitan University, UK 92

Leeds University, UK 19

Leicester, University of, UK, Second World Immersive Future Teaching 121

Levin, B. 117

Lewin, K. 94

Lewis, M. 51

Li, L. 46

Liberman, K. 62

Lim, J. 115

Lin, N. 60, 64, 65

Lincoln Commission 44

Lingard, R. 46, 94, 127

linguistic hegemony, versus extinction of local languages 26

linguistic/language skills 44, 46, 49–53, 83, 86, 89, 122

Linklater, A. 69

Liu, J. 21

Liu, Y. 115

Liverpool University, UK 19

local community, notion of belonging to 132

local languages, extinction of, versus linguistic hegemony 26

London, East European building workers in 42

Lulat, Y. 16

Lutterman-Aguilar, A. 88, 94, 97

Maasai activists in Tanzania 42

McCarthy, C. 76

McCoshan, A. 49, 104, 105

McDaniel, J. 16, 17, 119

Macfarlane, B. 99

McGarr, O. 103

McKee, A. 8

McKenna, A. 20

Mackie, L. 95

McLoughlin, C. 111

McQuiggan, C. 110

Mahidol University, Thailand 83

Maiworm, F. 48

Malaysian women's movement 42

Malcomson, S. 32, 42, 47

Manchester, skilled migrants in 42

Manchester University, UK 19

Marcus Aurelius 32

Marginson, S. 34, 52, 64

Marin, P. 95

Maringe, F. 77, 78

market, based on, international aspects of higher education as 5

Maryland, University of, USA, Center for International Development and Conflict Management, Department of Government and Politics, International Communication and Negotiation Simulations (ICONS) 120

Mason, R. 108

massification, and curriculum decisions 76

Massive Open Online Course (MOOC) 108, 109, 111; European Multiple MOOC Aggregator project 109

Matsumoto, D. 104, 105

Matthews, J. 10

Maxwell, T. 103

Melbourne, University of, Australia 57

Mentkowski, M. 102, 103

meta-narratives 74

Meyer, J. 21, 23, 24

Mezirow, J. 93

Michigan State University, USA, internationalisation as key metric in 99

Mignolo, W. 37, 40, 43, 67, 132, 133

migration, chain 47

170 *Index*

mindfulness 72, 73, 82, 86, 89, 96, 104;
definition 8
Minnesota, University of, USA, short-
term study abroad programme 88
MiriadaX 109
Mitchell, K. 38
mobility: affective elements of 54,
56; benefits of, for employability
and language competence 12;
international 4, 5, 44, 45, 47, 49, 50,
52, 87; global, of students 4
Monash Chinese Island, Chinese
Studies Programme, Monash
University, Australia 121
Monash University, Australia, Chinese
Studies Programme, Monash Chinese
Island 121
MOOC, *see* Massive Open Online
Course
Moogan, Y. 78
Morais, D. 6, 78, 104
moral education, definition 7
moral/ethical reflection 93
moral interdependence, notion of 97
Morgan, A. 95
MPQ, *see* multicultural personality
questionnaire
Mullens, J. 89
multicultural campus 126
multicultural capabilities, need for 80, 89
multiculturalism 47; versus
cosmopolitan approach 38
multicultural personality questionnaire
(MPQ) 105
multiple allegiances 11, 38–40, 43, 68, 81
multiple perspectives: appreciation of
92; awareness and valuing of 119
multiversity 9
mutuality, recognition of value of 92

Narayan, D. 64
nation: notion of 18; persistent power of,
as medium for solidarity 37
National Curriculum, England 75
nationalism 32, 33, 39, 40, 95, 113
National Taiwan Normal University,
Taiwan 121
nation state, concept of 36
Nava, M. 35, 40, 47, 68
Nazi policy of annihilation 34
necessary global attributes, of
graduates 9
Nederveen-Pieterse, J. 31, 34, 57
neoliberal ethic 36

neoliberal ideologies 23
Netherlands, The, internationalisation
of curriculum in higher education
institutions in 77
networks 47, 111; humanity defined by
3; maintenance of 11; scholarly 125
Newton, K. 65
Nichol, D. 114
Nidiffer, J. 20
Ningbo, China, University of
Nottingham campus in 80, 81
Nizamiyya Academy, Baghdad, claim
of, as oldest university 15
Noddings, N. 97
Norton, L. 105
Nottingham, University of, UK 80–2, 84
Nowicka, M. 30, 41, 42
Nulty, D. 103
Nussbaum, M. 31, 32, 39, 67
Nyoni, F. 89

Oakman, D. 57
O'Brien, A. 117
Obst, D. 83
Obst, O. 83
OECD, *see* Organisation for Economic
Co-operation and Development
Ogan, A. 122, 123
Ogden, A. 6, 104
Omenlaniuk, I. 47
online education, five-stage pedagogy
of 121
online interaction, advances in 119–23
online learning 4, 107–24; choice of
technology for 119–23; cosmopolitan
114–19; cosmopolitan potential of
111–12; essential elements of 13;
good educational practices in 110;
initiatives in 110; international
collaborative, discipline of geography
advanced in 112; as mainstream
element of higher education 108;
pedagogical stages in 112; pitfalls of
112–14; value of 111
online modalities 107, 108; role of, in
higher education 13
online pedagogies, evolution of 13, 108–10
online study communities 67
online synchronous communication 117
openness 6, 32, 72, 73, 82, 86, 89, 105,
123, 131, 132; to difference 7, 40, 129;
transnational 67
Open University, UK, online
conferencing system 108

OpenupEd 109
Organisation for Economic Co-operation and Development (OECD) 51
Osman, G. 117
Ossman, S. 39, 47, 68
Oviedo, University of, Spain 83
Oxford University, UK 19, 53

Paige, M. 87
Paige, R. 87
Pampaloni, A. 46
Papastephanou, M. 67, 69, 129
Papatsiba, V. 54
Pappano, L. 108
Paquet, G. 66, 69
Parkes, M. 110
Parry, J. 42, 68
participatory enquiry 70
patriotism, cosmopolitan 40
pedagogical agents 122
pedagogical beliefs, elements of 100
pedagogy: active learning 95; contemplative 95, 96, 106; cosmopolitan 92, 93, 96, 100, 113; decolonial 94, 106; of discomfort 94; enlightened, recognition by, of prior experience and knowledge of students 25; essential elements of 13, 92–6; of experiential learning 93; of transformative learning 93; worldly 93, 106
peer assessment 103
peer reflection 124
Penuel, W. 101
per-ankh 15, 16
performance assessment 103
performativity and curriculum decisions 76
Persia, development of cosmopolitan thought in 37
Persianis, P. 20
Peterson, M. 121
Phillips, T. 43, 66, 73, 131
philosophical project, of cosmopolitan approach 35, 36
philosophy, cosmopolitan 30, 97
Piaget, J. 94
Pinar, W. 76
pitfalls of online learning 112–14
planetary consciousness 80
planetary conviviality 43, 133
political cosmopolitanism 37
political project, of cosmopolitan approach 35, 36

political understanding, of cosmopolitan approach 35
political voice, as subscale of global civic engagement 104
Pollock, S. 39
Popov, V. 114, 115, 116
Post, R. 35, 38
Postiglione, G. 21
power, new forms of 127
Pozniak, K. 118
preconceptions, critical assessment of 92
'problem posing' education 26
progress, doctrine of 32
Prude, M. 111, 121
Pruneri, F. 19
pseudo-cosmopolitan experience 126
Publius Terentius Afer 32
Putnam, R. 47, 54, 60, 95
Puwar, N. 38, 61

quality assurance, and curriculum decisions 76
Quin, R. 99

Radloff, A. 83
Ram, K. 42
Rapport, N. 38
Ratner, R. 24
Ray, W. 113
Raybourn, E. 122
Readings, B. 22
reality, constant unveiling of 26
Reardon, E. 93
Rebick, M. 64
reciprocity 73, 82, 86, 89; meaning of 72
reflection: contemplative/ruminative 93; critical/analytical 93; moral/ethical 93; peer 124; self- 103, 112, 124
reflective inquiry, key forms of 93
reflexivity 64, 123, 133; interpersonal 133
religion, role of, in establishment of higher education 16–18
Richardson, S. 45–7, 51, 56, 61, 62, 81, 83, 84
Richey, S. 66
Riel, M. 111
right to common possession 33
risk taking 12, 54, 63–7
Rizvi, F. 43, 46, 47, 133
Robbins, B. 67
Roberts, J. 20
Robertson, R. 23, 34
Robinson, K. 42
Rodríguez González, C. 48

172 *Index*

Rogers, G. 102
Rohstock, A. 14
role playing 120
rooted cosmopolitanism 40
Rosenthal, D. 65, 66
Rothstein, B. 65
Rousseau, J.-J. 32, 67
Rovisco, M. 30, 42
Rowan, D. 116
Rüegg, W. 16, 17, 18, 19, 21
Rumford, C. 35, 39, 40, 68
Russell, C. 120
Russia, international students in 51

Said, E. 3
Salmon, G. 112, 115, 117, 121
Santarém, Polytechnic Institute of,
  Portugal 83
Sardone, N. 101
Sawir, E. 62
Schofer, E. 21, 24
scholarly networks 125
scholarship, advancing, as characteristic
  of higher education institutions 14
Scholte, J. 23
Sciences Po, *see* Institut D'études
  Politiques de Paris
scientific research 20
Scott, J. 17
Scottish universities 20
Seaman, J. 108, 109, 110, 119
Seattle University, USA 118
Second Life 120, 121
Second World Immersive Future Teaching,
  University of Leicester, UK 121
Seddon, T. 76, 77, 107
self-assessment 103
self-awareness 105; as subscale of global
  competence 104
self-becoming-other 97
self-reflection 103, 112, 124
Semetsky, I. 97
Seneca 32
Serby, T. 121
service learning 71
Shanka, T. 46
Sharjah, American University of, United
  Arab Emirates 86
Sharkey, S. 103
Shepherd, J. 120
Shi, J. 20
short-term study abroad 75, 87–90, 94;
  international curricula via 13, 87–9
Sichone, O. 42

Sidhu, R. 10
Sims, R. 120
simulated experiential learning 121
simulation(s) 13, 119–23;
  communication 122; use of, in higher
  education 120
Sindhis, globally dispersed 42
Singapore Nurses Association,
  collaborative programme with La
  Trobe University, Australia
Singh, M. 47
Singlish 51
situated decision making 123
situatedness-in-displacement, different
  modalities of 68
6 Continents Project 116
Skrbis, S. 35, 40
Skrbis, Z. 42
Slattery, P. 76
Smart, D. 62, 133
Smith, J. 89
Smith, P. 43, 66, 73, 131
Snauwaert, D. 93
social benefits of international education
  52–3, 58, 59
social connections 63–7
social containment 125
social cosmopolitan approach 38, 43;
  limitations to 41–2
social cosmopolitan project 43, 131
social cues, variations in interpretation
  of 115
social expansion; need for 125; versus
  containment, and higher education
  institutions 13
social identity 39
social and ideological containment,
  higher education institutions as
  instrument of 16
social mobility 64
social, moral and religious conduct, as
  objective of further education 15
social networks 47, 65
social project of cosmopolitan approach
  31, 35, 38, 43
social resources, importance of 64
social responsibility 6, 100, 103, 104, 132
social risks 54, 64
social sciences 30, 85
socio-cultural mediation 8
socio-linguistic competence 104
sociology of motion 68
Solem, M. 113
Souto Otero, M. 48

Index 173

Soviet approach to higher education 20
Spain, Cubans in 42
Spain, Islamic 17
Spinelli, G. 82, 83
Spybey, T. 34
Stade, R. 38
Stanford University, USA, Cross-Cultural Rhetoric Project 117
Starke-Meyerring, D. 107
Stepanyan, K. 114
Stephenson, J. 76
Stivens, M. 42
Stoics/Stoic philosophy 31, 35, 38
Stoner, K. 87
Strathdee, R. 45
Strydom, P. 66
student mobility 5, 44–54, 78, 80, 81, 91, 126, 130; global 4; international 44, 46, 50, 53; and international higher education 12, 45–7
students, international 4, 9, 45, 46, 51, 57, 58, 62, 77, 78, 81
study abroad, short-term 13, 75, 87–90, 94
Switzerland, international students in 51
synchronous communication, online 117
Sypnowich, C. 41
Szerszynski, B. 7
Sznaider, N. 68

Tactical Language and Culture Training System 122
Tajfel, H. 62
Talbani, A. 16, 18, 125
Tallon, R. 94
Tang, C. 92
Tanzania, Maasai activists in 42
Tapanes, M. 115
Taras, V. 114
taxation, as motivating factor in establishment of higher education institutions 16
technology, choice of, for online learning 119–23
Tegos, S. 122
Teichler, U. 48
Tekin, U. 48
Thelin, J. 19
Thompson, A. 88
3-D virtual environment(s), education in 120–1
time, changed conception of 18
Tinti-Kane, H. 119
Todd, S. 129
Torres, C. 24, 28, 127

Toven-Lindsey, B. 108, 111
Tran, L. 97
transformative learning, pedagogy of 93
transnational challenges in curriculum design 76
transnational openness 67
transnational social fabric 39
Treml, M. 105
Trice, A. 62
Trowler, P. 76
Try, S. 64
Tsekleves, E. 120
Tsinghua University, China 20; visiting international educators in 98
Tumblr 119
twenty-first century, cognitive and intercultural complexity of 130
Twitter 119

UNESCO, *see* United Nations Educational, Scientific and Cultural Organization
United Kingdom, international students in 51
United Nations Educational, Scientific and Cultural Organization (UNESCO) 23, 109
United States: colleges in, service learning and community activities 71; international students in 51
universal hospitality 33, 132, 133
universalism 12, 38
universal norms, application of cosmopolitan principles to 12, 37
universities (*passim*): development of, elements of 22; development of contemporary models of 18–22; early, development of 15–18; as producers of skilled workforce 20; University of Cairo in Egypt, curriculum partnership with Science Po 86; university education, expansion of, in nineteenth century Europe 23
University of Nottingham: campus in Kuala Lumpur, Malaysia 80; campus in Ningbo, China 80, 81
Urry, J. 7
utility, as one of three guiding forces of evolution of higher education institutions 12, 14, 22, 126
Uzuner, S. 114

Valente, A. 122
value creative dialogue, concept of 93

174 *Index*

van der Land, S. 121
van der Wende, M. 48, 52, 77
van der Zee, K. I. 105
van Oudenhoven, J. P. 105
Vardi, I. 99
Varghese, N. 45
Vat Vixun, Laos 16, 17
VeLure Roholt, R. 88
Vertovec, S. 39, 40, 41, 59, 60
virtual communities 111
Virtual Environment Cultural Training
  for Operational Readiness 122
virtual learning environments 122
virtue: and globalisation 22–4; and
  humanity 24–7; notion of 22; as one
  of three guiding forces of evolution of
  higher education institutions 12, 14, 22,
  126; role of in higher education 22–7

Waks, L. 69
Walker, P. 94
Wallace, R. 111
Walsh, J. 19, 20
Wang, J. 105
Wang, M. 115
Wang, X. 21
Warhurst, R. 101
Warwick, P. 78
Waters, J. 45, 52, 53
Waters, M. 23, 34
Watkins, C. 95
Webb, R. 120

Webber, K. 103
Weenink, D. 45
'Weltbürger'/world citizen 32
Werbner, P. 42
whole of institution approach,
  internationalisation of curriculum via
  13, 85–7
Wiggins, B. 123
Wiggins, G. 103
Williams, A. 45
Wilson, M. 107
Woodward, I. 40, 41, 42, 43
Woolcock, M. 64
Woolf, M. 79, 87
world, changed conception of 18
worldly pedagogy 93, 106
Wray, R. 122, 123
Wresch, W. 114
Wright, C. 20

XuetangX, China 109

Yarmouk University, Jordan, curriculum
  partnership with Science Po 86
Yoo, J. 122
Yorke, M. 76
Yuan, B. 98

Zajonc, A. 96
Zeno of Citium 31
Zheng, X. 62
Zubaida, S. 37